The Trials of Charles the First, and of Some of the Regicides: With Biographies of Bradshaw, Ireton, Harrison, and Others, and with Notes

Charles I, Great Britain. High Court Of Justice For The Trying And Judging Of Charles Stuart, King Of England

Engraved by W. Wildman.

Charles R

THE TRIALS

OF

CHARLES THE FIRST,

AND OF

SOME OF THE REGICIDES:

With Biographies

OF

BRADSHAW, IRETON, HARRISON, AND OTHERS.

AND WITH NOTES.

THE SEVENTH EDITION.

LONDON: WILLIAM TEGG.

1861.

Ergo, regibus occisis, subversa jacebat
Pristina majestas soliorum, et sceptra superba:
Et capitis summi praeclarum insigne cruentum
Sub pedibus vulgi magnum lugebat honorem:
Nam cupide conculcatur nimis ante metutum.
Res itaque ad summam faecem turbasque redibat,
Imperium sibi cum, ac summatum quisque petebat.

LUCRETIUS, lib. v.

Then prostrate lay, — the rightful monarch slain —
The throne's proud majesty and ancient reign:
The diadem that crown'd th' anointed head
Crush'd by the vulgar foot dark blood-drops shed.
Law's just restraint, once fear'd, was vilely spurn'd,
And the state's fabric into dust return'd,
When each at will grasp'd at imperial power,
And strove to reign the despot of an hour.

LUCRETIUS, book 5. (W. S.)

The axe that strikes the King lays Order low —
In every limb old Reverence feels the blow;
Law, Faith, Love, Honour, Grace are trampled down
In the same bloody quagmire with the Crown.
The awe of ages poison'd into hate,
Fierce leaps the rabble hoof on all that's great —
Till vulgar rage, expert Ambition's tool,
Dies out — and some cold scoundrel grasps the rule.

LUCRETIUS, book 5. (J. G. L.)

CONTENTS.

.

.

DIRECTIONS FOR THE PLATES.

Portrait of Charles the First - - - *to face the Title.*

Trial of the King, from an engraving of the period,

Page 21

Cotemporary Explanation of the Print, showing the Trial of King Charles the First.

A THE KING sitting in a large elbow-chair, covered with crimson velvet, with gold fringe and nails, and a velvet cushion, in a distinct apartment, directly over against the Lord President; between the space allotted for the Counsel of the Commonwealth, standing on the right hand of the King, and the like, vacant, space leading from the head of the stairs to the King's apartment aforesaid.

In the partition allotted for the King was also placed a small table covered with a Turkey carpet, and a standish and paper set thereon, if his Majesty should have occasion for it.

B The Lord President BRADSHAW sitting in an elbow-chair, advanced upon the first rising of the Court, having a large desk fixed before him, covered with a velvet pall, and a large velvet cushion thereupon.

C JOHN LISLE
D WILLIAM SAY } sitting on the { right / left } hand of the Lord President.

These two being appointed to be his Lordship's assistants.

The said Lord President and his said assistants, being all three of the long robe, sate in their gowns; the rest of the Commissioners in their usual habits, as gentlemen and souldiers.

E ANDREW BROUGHTON,
F JOHN PHELPS, } the two Clerks appointed to attend the Court, being seated at the feet of the said Lord President, under the covert of his desk.

G The table placed before the said clerks, whereon sometimes lay the Commonwealth's mace and sword of state or justice; sometimes, I say, for at other times, the said sword was advanced in the head of the guards with partizans standing in the Court, on the right hand of the King, as he sate, and the said mace was sometimes handed by their Serjeant at arms, on the out-side of the bar, nigh the King on his left hand.

H   The scale of benches (which were covered with scarlet bays, and the foot-steps matted) reaching up from the floor of the Court within five or six feet of the very glassing of the south-west window of Westminster Hall, whereon sate the rest of the Commissioners.

I   The atchievement of the Commonwealth of England, in direct view of the King.

K OLIVER CROMWELL } sitting on the { right side { of the escutcheon or shield, as the
L HENRY MARTIN   left side { supporters of the Commonwealth.

M The galleries and scaffolds on either side the Court, thronged with spectators.

N The floor of the Court matted, and kept clear and open (as here represented) by the guards on either side, no person being permitted to abide between the King, the Counsel, and the Court, but the known Officers and Messengers appointed to attend the Court.

O A passage (lined with souldiers on both sides), leading from the Court of Wards into the High Court of Justice, and through which the Commissioners coming from the Painted Chamber made their entry into the said Court.

P The place where the moving-guard with partizans (who, together with the Serjeant at arms, and a person carrying the Sword of state or justice, always came along with the Commissioners from the Exchequer Chamber into the Court,) stood, sitting the Court.

Q The place where the moving-guards with partizans (which always attended the King, from Sir Robert Cotton's House up into the said Court, and back thither again) stood, sitting the Court.

R The passage leading from the stair head, to the distinct apartment appointed for the King, as aforesaid.

S T U The partition where the Counsel of the Commonwealth, viz. Cooke, Dorislaus, and Aske, stood alone on the right hand of the King, as he was sitting.

V The stairs by which the King ascended up into the Court out of Westminster-Hall.

W The passage leading into Westminster-Hall, from Sir Robert Cotton's house, where his Majesty was kept under strong guards, in readiness when the Court should from time to time order him to be brought up.

X A large free passage leading from Westminster-Hall gate, straight through the said Hall, within twelve or fourteen feet of the bottom of this Court.

Y   Another such like passage (going cross the upper end of the last mentioned passage) reaching and extending itself from one side of the said Hall to the other.

Both these passages were strongly rayled to keep the multitude (who, when the Court was set, was freely permitted to fill the Hall, between the rayls and the wall,) from breaking in upon the souldiers, who were planted all along within the rayls, to observe and awe the multitude, and secure the Court.

Z   The thronging multitudes between the rayls and the Hall walls

The officers walking up and down in the free passages (between the souldiers standing within the rayls) ready to give the necessary orders and commands upon all occasions.

Execution of Charles, from an old Dutch print,   *Page* 107

THE

TRIAL

OF

CHARLES THE FIRST.

INTRODUCTION. — The events that led from the extraordinary seizure of Charles I. by Cornet Joyce and the army at Holdenby House, in Northamptonshire, to his imprisonment in the Isle of Wight, his prosecution, and his death, are familiar to most persons, either in the delightful narratives of Clarendon and Hume, the more detailed memorials of Rushworth, Whitlock, and Ludlow, or the late works of Godwin[1] and D'Israeli. As long as the power of the parliament formed, in some degree, a balance to that of Cromwell, the officers, and the army, the cause of the King, though he was in strict custody of the latter, appeared slightly to gain ground. He was treated with respect even by the agitators of the army[2], courted

[1] Godwin's History of the Commonwealth of England. D'Israeli's Commentaries on the Life and Reign of Charles I.

[2] "All the officers of the army kissed his hand, and all kneeled, except Fairfax and Cromwell." — Clarendon State Papers, vol. ii. Append.

by the parliamentary leaders, negotiated with by Cromwell, Ireton, and Fairfax; and he was frequently heard to say, with some imprudence and with his usual sanguineness, " You cannot do without me; you cannot settle the nation without my assistance." [1]   But when the parliament gradually yielded to all the encroachments of the army, and were subdued by the troops in July, 1647, (when Manchester and Lenthal, the speakers of the two Houses, and deputations of the members met Cromwell and the army at Hounslow,) the hopes of the loyal and the cause of the King declined.   His confident rejection of the propositions now made to him by the army exasperated that body, at the very time when the parliament had become too weak to be looked to for any support.   His abode at Hampton Court (whither he had been removed from Caversham, and where he lived at first with comfort and dignity [2],) became now every day more irksome, and even dangerous.   His guards were doubled, restric-

[1] When the General Fairfax heard of Joyce's seizure of the King (which Joyce confessed was done by secret orders of Cromwell), he sent Colonel Whalley with two regiments of horse to remove the force, and to apologise to the King for the outrage; but Charles was then advanced several miles towards Cambridge, with the army.   Fairfax waited on him next day at Sir John Cutts's, near Cambridge, and persuaded him to return to Holderby; but the King refused, having been deluded into the belief that Joyce and the soldiers and agitators were really his friends.   He told Fairfax at parting, " Sir, I have as good an interest with the army as you." — " By which," says Fairfax, " I plainly saw the broken reed he leaned upon." — See Fairfax's Memoirs, by himself.

[2] See Baron Maseres's Tracts. in two vols.

tions placed on his intercourse with his friends, and intimations perpetually sent to him (whether by Cromwell or by the royalists) of atrocious designs against his person.[1]   Under these circumstances, Charles took the hasty and ill-contrived, but perhaps necessary, step of making his escape to Tichfield, and thence to the Isle of Wight[2], where he was made prisoner by

[1] There can be little doubt that Charles, in flying to the Isle of Wight, was only pursuing, unwittingly, the course which the machinations of Cromwell drove him upon. Andrew Marvell, writing of his friend Cromwell, says,—

> " And Hampton shows what part
>   He had of wiser art,
> Where twining subtle fears with hope,
> He wove a net of such a scope,
>   That Charles himself might chase
>   To Carisbrook's narrow case."
>   Ode on Cromwell's Return from Ireland.

There is no doubt that Cromwell informed Colonel Whalley, the officer commanding at Hampton, that the agitators designed to seize his person, and that Cromwell advised him to remove as soon as possible.   Ten days before his departure, Charles received an anonymous letter, signed E. R., giving the same information, and stating that " Mr. Dell and Mr. Peters, two of the preachers of the army, would willingly bear company in the design ; for they had often said to the agitators that ' your Majesty is but as a dead dog.' "— Parliamentary Hist. vol. xvi. 328.

[2] The details of this flight have given rise to much speculation, and are differently represented by Clarendon, Ludlow, Sir John Berkley, and Dugdale.   The matter seems now to be cleared up by Lord Ashburnham's recent publication of the full narrative of Ashburnham, the King's favourite groom of the bedchamber, who, along with Berkley, accompanied him.   From this it appears that, in consequence of apprehensions of danger to his life

Hammond the governor, (the friend of Cromwell and son-in-law of Hampden, who had been

---

from the soldiers and agitators of the army, the King determined to leave Hampton Court, and that Ashburnham (who, from a short conversation with Hammond not long before, had reason to think him well affected towards the King,) suggested that he should go to Sir John Oglander's house, in the island, and remain concealed till he could learn whether the governor would protect him. On arriving within twenty miles of the coast, Charles resolved to go himself with Colonel Legge to the Earl of Southampton's, at Tichfield; and desired Ashburnham and Berkley to proceed to the island and learn what conduct the King could expect from Hammond, and then to bring their report to Tichfield. Ashburnham, though unwilling to leave the King, went accordingly, with Berkley, to Newport; and on meeting the governor, Berkley, according to Ashburnham's account (which appears confirmed by Hammond's letter to the House), very unskilfully and abruptly announced that the King had left Whitehall for fear of assassination, and was in the neighbourhood. Hammond gave a vague answer, in substance that he would act as must be expected from a man of honour in his position. After dinner, it was at first agreed that Berkley should remain in the castle, while Ashburnham went to the King to announce Hammond's answer; but afterwards the extraordinary measure was adopted, (with the full concurrence, if not on the suggestion, of Ashburnham,) that Hammond should accompany them at once to the King; and, accordingly, Berkley and Ashburnham, the governor, and a captain, went directly to Tichfield. Ashburnham alone went up stairs to the King, and astonished him by announcing the governor's presence. The King exclaimed, " Oh, Jack! you have undone me; for I am, by this means, made fast from stirring." Ashburnham wept bitterly, and, in his despair, proposed to the King that he should make away with the governor and the captain. Charles dissented, and said, " It is too late to think of any thing but going through the way you have forced upon me, and so

lately appointed to the governorship,) and confined in Carisbrook Castle. The parliament being
at his feet, and the King thus quietly imprisoned,
Cromwell directed his energies against those violent seditions in the regiments, which he had before fomented for his own ambitious ends,—and
which were, indeed, the necessary consequence
of the institution of *agitators*[1], and the sort of

---

leave the issue to God;" and he accordingly went with
Hammond to Carisbrook. Ashburnham accounts for his
conduct by saying it was the best way to meet the difficulty
occasioned by Berkley's indiscretion; since the governor,
after Berkley's disclosure, would have sent spies to follow
him, and find where the King was. Charles acquitted
Ashburnham of all treachery, as did Berkley and Clarendon. — See John Ashburnham's Narrative, published by
the late Earl of Ashburnham. Sir John Berkley's Memoirs. Lord Ashburnham has reprinted these Memoirs in
an appendix to his work.

[1] Mr. Godwin says, "their office being to *aid* the regular
council of war, or to *agitate* such questions as the interest
of the army required to have considered." It seems probable that the first was the object which their name was intended to imply, and that their proceedings procured them
the significant appellation of *agitators.* Ludlow, Ashburnham, Berkley, and Hobbes, in his Behemoth, spell the word
"adjutator;" but writers in general use the other spelling,
which is used in most pamphlets of the day. At first, two
persons were chosen by the *private* soldiers (for they now refused to be called *common* soldiers) of each troop or company,
to form a sort of representative or lower assembly; while the
superior officers formed a general council of themselves.
But this body being found too numerous, afterwards acted as
electors; and chose two or more representatives, either soldiers or subalterns, for each regiment, forming a " *council
of agitators.*" Berry, who had been a gardener, and was
captain in Fairfax's regiment of horse, a confidential ally
of Cromwell, was president of this council soon after its

mimic parliament which had been introduced with Cromwell's connivance into the army. The trial of three ringleaders on the field, and the summary execution of one at the rendezvous at Ware, having partially and apparently restored discipline, Cromwell, under the counsels of Ireton his son-in-law, assembled a council of officers at Windsor, to deliberate on the settlement of the nation, and the future disposal of the King's person. "In this conference," says Hume, following Clarendon, "which commenced with devout prayers poured forth by Cromwell himself and other inspired persons (for the officers of this army received inspiration with their commission), was first opened the daring, cruel, and unheard-of counsel of bringing the King to justice, and of punishing by a judicial sentence their sovereign for his pretended tyranny and mal-administration."[1] While the King lived, whether in prison or at large, Cromwell well knew he must be the rallying point for the efforts of those large bodies of his subjects who were sincerely attached to the monarchy and to his person, and of all those other numerous classes who were now disgusted with the oppressive domination and immense pecuniary

---

commencement; and its proceedings were secretly encouraged by Cromwell, Ireton, and Skippon, who early made Fairfax their tool or their dupe. — See Rushworth, vol. vi. 485. Baxter's Life, p. 98. Godwin's Commonwealth, vol. ii. 296.

[1] Hume is confirmed, as to this point, by Sir John Berkley, and by Allen, the adjutant-general of the army. — See the authorities cited by Mr. Hallam, Constitutional History, vol. ii. 303.

levies of the army and the parliament. [1]   " To murder him privately," says Hume, " was exposed to the imputation of injustice and cruelty, aggravated by the baseness of such a crime. Some unexpected procedure must, therefore, be attempted, which would astonish the world by its novelty, would bear the semblance of justice, and would cover its barbarity by the audaciousness of the enterprise."   Towards the execution of this sanguinary project events were rapidly tending.   The refusal of Charles to accede to the four preliminary proposals (virtually extinguishing all effective royal authority), sent by the parliament to him at Carisbrook, was followed by his close confinement without friends or attendants in the castle, and by the vote of the Commons passed under the open threats of Cromwell and the army, declaring that no more addresses would be sent to the King, nor messages received from him, and that all intercourse with him without leave of the parliament should be treason.   The Duke of Hamilton's invasion from Scotland, and

[1] " About the month of August, 1646, at Henley on Thames, a woman, having taken notice of the unwonted taxation imposed on her and others by this parliament, expressed (yet in civil terms) some dislike thereof; which being made known to a committee there, she was by them ordered to have her tongue fastened by a nail to the body of a tree by the highway side on a market day, which was accordingly done; and a paper in great letters, setting forth the heinousness of the fact, fixed to her back to make her the more notorious."   From a paper endorsed by Lord Clarendon, " Skippon's Relation of some particular Extravagances of the Parliament."— See Appendix to Clarendon's State Papers, vol. ii.

the risings of the royalists and the presbyterians
in Essex, Kent, Surrey, and Wales, gave, indeed,
a slight check to the triumphant proceedings of
the army: for while Cromwell and the troops were
engaged in suppressing these opponents of military usurpation, the moderate presbyterian or
constitutional party regained a brief ascendency
in parliament. Hollis and the eleven excluded
members returned, the vote of non-addresses was
repealed, and five peers and ten commoners
were sent commissioners to Newport to treat
with the king. In the two months' negotiations
which followed, Charles, unassisted, carried on a
contest of argument on arduous political and religious topics with these fifteen of the ablest
senators of the day; and the commissioners were
not more struck with the ravages which persecu-
tion and suffering had wrought in his appearance
(his hair had become entirely grey), than with
the clearness of intellect, the readiness of elocution, and the dignity of deportment which he
displayed at these important conferences.[1] " The

[1] The King wrote to the Prince Charles from the Isle
of Wight several very able and detailed accounts of the
state of the negotiation, which letters are preserved in
vol. ii. of Lord Clarendon's State Papers. Sir Philip Warwick, who attended him at Newport, says, " Every night
when the King was alone, about 8 o'clock, except when
he was writing his own papers, he commanded me to come
to him, and he looked over the notes of that day's treaty,
and the reasons upon which it moved, and so dictated the
heads of a despatch which from time to time he made concerning the treaty unto his Majesty, then prince; and this
Mr. Oudert, whose hand his Majesty used in those de-
spatches, transcribed." — Memoirs, 325.

King is much changed," said the Earl of Salisbury to Sir Philip Warwick; " he is extremely improved of late." — " No," replied Sir Philip; " he was always so, but you are now at last sensible of it." Had the parliament in this treaty been content with any moderate and reasonable concessions from the King, it is possible that a cordial union between the crown and the legislature might have been effected in time to resist the tyranny of Cromwell and the army, and to avert that utter destruction of the constitution which afterwards followed. But Charles, after consenting to strip himself of almost all his regal power and prerogative, was pressed to abandon his friends and supporters to attainder and exile, to sacrifice the liberty of his own private worship, and the privilege of the Queen's exemption from the penalties against the mass. These demands he peremptorily refused; — as to others he hesitated and reasoned; and the treaty was thus fatally spun out till the army had overcome their various enemies, and wanted nothing to complete their triumph but the entire subjugation of the two Houses and the destruction of the monarch and the monarchy. Charles was seized by the army, and placed in close confinement in Hurst Castle, an unwholesome blockhouse on a narrow, cold, shingly promontory projecting for three miles from the coast of Hampshire, opposite the Isle of Wight. The generals presented a remonstrance to parliament complaining of the treaty, and demanding the King's punishment for the blood spilt during the war; and totally despising the votes of the Houses which disclaimed

the imprisonment of the King, and commanded
the troops not to approach London, they marched
to the metropolis, and established their quarters
in Whitehall, Palace Yard, St. James's, Covent
Garden, and the Mews.   A few days afterwards
they seized the treasuries of many of the London Companies, and took 20,000*l.*, from the
Weavers' Company alone, for satisfying their arrears of pay; Fairfax notifying the seizure by a
letter to the lord mayor.   The parliament, in
the face of the army, still desperately attempted
to close their treaty with the King; and on the
5th of December, after three days' debate, in
which Prynne made his most celebrated speech
in favour of the King, the Commons voted, by a
large majority, that the King's concessions were
a foundation for the Houses to proceed upon for
the settlement of the kingdom.   The leaders of
the army now immediately resolved to overpower the refractory commons by that physical
force which they had at command; and the next
morning early Colonel Pride and Lord Grey, provided with a list of obnoxious members, agreed
on by the officers at Whitehall, surrounded the
house with two regiments, seized forty-one of
the presbyterian or moderate members in the
lobby as they were entering the House, and excluded 160 others from entrance, — an act of
unheard-of violence, well known by the name of
Colonel Pride's purge.[1]   The excluded members
were for some hours confined in the Court of Wards,
and in the coffee-house called Hell under the
Exchequer, and afterwards kept for several days

[1] See *post*, in the Memoir of Ireton.

at inns in the town. The House being thus reduced to about eighty, chiefly of the most vehement independents and republicans, reversed the vote of the 5th December; declared the King's concessions unsatisfactory; renewed the vote of non-addresses; and committed to prison the leaders of the moderate and presbyterian party, who had for a time headed and excited the opposition of the parliament to the crown, but who were now swept from influence by the fanatical officers, expounding colonels, and more accomplished republican demagogues, who enjoyed the support of the soldiers. The House did, indeed, resolve to send for the excluded members, — " rather," as Ludlow says, " upon account of decency than from any desire they had that their message should be obeyed;" and when the serjeant-at-arms returned and acquainted them that the excluded members were detained by the army, the House quietly proceeded in the business before them.[1] The

[1] Ludlow says, that Cromwell the night after the interruption of the House arrived from Scotland, and lay at Whitehall; where, and at other places, he declared he had not been acquainted with this design: yet, since it was done, he was glad of it, and would endeavour to maintain it. Clarendon says Fairfax, the general, knew nothing of it; which Fairfax in his Memoirs confirms: but Ludlow says, Ireton communicated the intention to Fairfax. The plan seems to have been agreed on by Ludlow, Ireton, and four other officers and members of the House, the day before it was executed. See Ludlow's Memoirs. Ireton, when he and Cromwell were in treaty with Charles, and making protestations of fidelity, said to the King, that " they would purge, and never cease purging the Houses, till they had made them of such a temper as would do his Majesty's business." Pride rose, it is said, from a drayman to be a brewer, and then a colonel, and was knighted by

leaders of the army had no desire to dip their hands in the blood of the King, either by an assassination or a trial, without dividing the odium and responsibility with the parliament, or at least with the Commons. Their memorable purification of the House removed all the obstacles which existed to its concurrence. In order to give a semblance of regularity and principle to their plan, it was necessary to make a law for the prosecution and punishment of the King, for which nothing either in the common or statute law of England gave a shadow of authority. The purified Commons accordingly voted, " that by the fundamental law of the land it is treason for the King of England for the time being to levy war against the parliament and kingdom;" and sent the resolution to the Lords for their concurrence. The Lords, *without a dissentient voice, rejected this vote*, and adjourned for ten days, with a view, if possible, to retard the violent and revolutionary career of the Commons. The Commons then passed a vote, specious in appearance, but fallacious in principle, and most perilous in its practical application, " that the people are the origin of all just power;" and grounded on it a de-

---

Cromwell (according to Ludlow with a fagot stick), and made a lord of his house of peers, in which Lord Warwick refused to sit with him and with Hewson, another regicide, who had been a cobbler. Pride was nicknamed "Cromwell's dray-horse," and, according to Noble, received a grant of the manor and estate of Holmby, where he cut down the woods. Cromwell once said to Ludlow, when they were in the House, and molested by the presbyterian party, " These fellows will never be quiet till they are pulled out by the ears." — See D'Israeli's Commentaries on the Life and Reign of Charles, vol. v. 242.

claration, " that the House of Commons, being chosen by and representing the people, are the supreme power in the nation,—that *whatsoever is enacted or declared for law by the Commons in parliament hath the force of a law, and the people are concluded thereby, though the consent of the King and the Peers be not had thereto.*" On the same day the Commons passed an ordinance for erecting a High Court of Justice for trying the King, and proceeding to sentence against him ; appointing 135 persons commissioners for this purpose, of whom any twenty were empowered to act —a measure which was strongly urged on the House by petitions presented from the Common Council of London, the borough of Southwark, and some counties in England. The list of commissioners included Fairfax, Cromwell, Ireton, Waller, Skippon, Harrison, Whalley, Pride, Ewer, Tomlinson— in all, three generals and thirty-four colonels of the army; the Lords Mounson, Grey of Grooby, and Lisle ; the principal members of the reduced House of Commons; Wilson, Fowks, Pennington, and Andrews, aldermen of the city of London ; Bradshaw, Thorpe, and Nicholas, serjeants at law; twenty-two persons who are designated either as knights or baronets; various citizens of London, and some few country gentlemen, " whose zeal," as Clarendon says, " had been taken notice of for the cause, and who were like to take such a preferment as a testimony of the parliament's confidence in them." Whitlock, Sir Thomas Widdrington, Wilson, and other members even of the reduced House, declined any share in so monstrous a proceeding. The former, however, accepted afterwards the office of one of the commissioners of the new great seal (which Widdrington refused), and in that capacity reluctantly drew the act " for *taking away the House of Lords*," though he had expressly dissented from the vote to that effect. The twelve judges, ten of whom had been created by the parliament, were at first named in the commission ; but, as they unanimously declared it contrary to every principle of English law that the King should be tried by his subjects, their names were erased ; and six of them shortly afterwards declined to retain their judicial offices under the usurping commonwealth.

The King was in the mean time conveyed, under the escort of Harrison and a body of dragoons, from Hurst Castle to Windsor. Harrison treated him during the journey with a mixture of rigour and respect ; kept himself uncovered ; was very laconic in his speech ; but in some degree consulted his wishes, and even permitted him to rest and dine at Bagshot with his loyal friends, Lord and Lady Newburgh [1], who had corresponded with the King constantly in cipher, and who had written to press his visiting them on his road, with a view to attempt his escape. It was proposed that the King should object to the horse he had ridden, and that Lord Newburgh should offer to put him on a very fleet horse which he possessed, by which he might seize an opportunity of riding away from his escort and gain

[1] Clarendon is confirmed as to this visit by the evidence of Lord Newburgh on the trial of Harrison. — See State Trials, vol. v.

certain stations in Windsor Forest, where relays
of horses should be placed for him. On arriving
at Lord Newburgh's, the King was secretly told
that the horse in question was accidentally lamed
a few days before; but that another would be
supplied him. The King, however, abandoned
the project, which the strictness of Harrison, and
the vigilance of his guards, must have defeated
had it been attempted; and he arrived that night
at Windsor Castle. Here he enjoyed a hurried
interview with the Duke of Hamilton, his faithful
and zealous friend and supporter, who was confined at Windsor on a capital charge for his exertions in the King's cause, and whose blood was
soon afterwards shed by the murderers of his
master. Hamilton fell on his knees before
Charles, exclaiming—" *My dear master!* "—" I
have been so, indeed, to you," replied Charles,
embracing him; when his guards immediately
hurried him away; and he was shortly afterwards
conveyed by Harrison to St. James's.

On the 9th of January, 1648–9, pursuant to
order of the commissioners and of the rump of the
House of Commons, proclamation was solemnly
made by Dendy, serjeant-at-arms, in Westminster
Hall, (he riding into the middle of the hall with
the mace on his shoulder, when the Court of
Chancery was sitting at a general seal,) and also
at the Old Exchange and Cheapside, announcing
the trial. Drums were beating and trumpets
sounding. The streets were thronged with spectators; but no violence or injury occurred. John
Bradshaw, serjeant-at-law, was (contrary to his
earnest desire, and his objections to the title

given him,) named Lord President of the court;
Mr. Aske, Dr. Dorislaus[1], Mr. Steel (attorney),
and Mr. Cook (solicitor), were appointed counsel
for the kingdom of England, to prepare and prosecute the charge against the King; in which
business eight of the commissioners were expressly associated with them.   Sir Hardress
Waller and Colonel Harrison were ordered to desire the Lord General to appoint sufficient guards
for the occasion; and Colonel Tichbourne and
others were charged to make preparations that
the trial might be *performed in a solemn manner*.

The serjeant-at-arms was ordered to search

[1] Dorislaus was afterwards sent by the usurping government as their agent to the states of Holland, where he
was barbarously assassinated at the Hague, as he sat at
supper, by six Scotchmen in the train of the Marquis of
Montrose.   His body was brought to England and buried
in Westminster Abbey; and was one of those (Cromwell's,
Pym's, and Blake's were others) which were taken up by
the dean and chapter under the King's warrant after the
restoration, and interred in the churchyard.   The counsel
for " the kingdom " were, according to Clarendon, very
obscure men, scarce known or heard of in their profession.
Cook was rewarded by the usurper with the appointment
of Chief Justice in Ireland.   He appears to have been a
man of some talent and reading, but a violent fanatic.
He had travelled in Italy, and lived with Milton's friend,
Diodati, at Geneva.   He was tried and executed with others
of the regicides in 1660; and his last letters to and convers-
ations with his wife and his friends present a strange mixture
of pedantry and exulting religious enthusiasm.   One of his
letters to a friend after his condemnation commences thus:
— " Dear brother, beloved in the Lord, ' *condemnatus sum
ad mortem;* ' and this is my cordial farewell to you and all
saints from my Jeremiah's prison: to-morrow, I shall be in
eternal glory in the bosom of Christ, where my father Abraham is, and a guard of angels will convey my soul thither."
— See State Trials, vol. v. 1271.

and secure the vaults under the Painted Chamber, with such assistance of soldiery as should be needful. Separate committees were named to consider of the manner and order of the trial, of the place where it was to be held, of the manner of bringing the King to the court, and of lodging him during the trial, and of securing the safe sitting of the court. Hilary term being near at hand, the court resolved that it was fit a fortnight of it should be adjourned, and Mr. Lisle was desired to move the House accordingly.[1] Sir Robert Cotton's house in Palace Yard, on the bank of the Thames, adjoining Westminster Hall, was appointed for the King's lodging, to which the King was conveyed by water, and where his Majesty slept after the first night of the trial in

[1] The Commons passed an ordinance for the purpose. But when this was brought to the Commissioners of the Great Seal, with an order to frame writs accordingly, they objected, because the Lords had not concurred in the act ; and they deemed the authority of the Commons alone insufficient. When *the Commons heard this, they refused, by a large majority, to send to the Lords for their concurrence.* The Lords, however, in a few days, of their own motion, passed an ordinance to the effect of that of the Commons; but the Commons having before voted " that the Commons were the supreme power, and that the committees which were before of the Lords and Commons might thenceforward act, though the Lords join not," they would *not own the Lords as formerly by agreeing to their ordinance.* The commissioners still objecting to issue the writs, the Commons ordered that the Commons' commissioners should issue them, though the Lords' commissioners should not join, which Sir Thomas Widdrington and Mr. Whitlock at last agreed to do. — Rushworth, vol. vii. Whitlock's Memorials. This matter occasioned a debate of a whole day.

the chamber next the study; the great chamber adjoining the bedchamber being used as his dining-room. A *corps de garde* for 200 foot soldiers was constructed by the water-side in Sir Robert Cotton's garden. Thirty officers attended the King as his guard, two of the number sleeping in his bed-chamber; while ten companies of foot guarded Sir Robert Cotton's house. Bradshaw was lodged at Sir Abraham Williams's house in New Palace Yard; and Sir Henry Mildmay and others were charged with providing all necessaries for him, as well as for the King, during the trial.

The place appointed for the trial was the site of the old Courts of King's Bench and Chancery, at the upper or south end of Westminster Hall, the partition which divided them being taken down. The hall was divided by two strong bars placed across it about forty feet to the north of the court. The great Gothic portal of the hall was open to the people, who witnessed the proceeding in vast crowds. A rail ran from the court down the length of the hall to the western side of the great door, for separating the people from the soldiers; the latter being stationed in great force, armed with partisans or halberts, within the rail on its western side, by the old Courts of Common Pleas and Exchequer Chamber; while the public thronging in at the great door formed a dense crowd in the large space left open on the eastern or Thames side of the rail. Strong guards were stationed upon the leads, and at the windows looking on the hall. All the narrow avenues to the hall were either stopped up with masonry, or strongly guarded;

and it was expressly ordered, "that all back doors from the house called *Hell* [1] (a coffee-house under the old Exchequer Chamber) be stopped up during the King's trial." For ten days previous to the opening of the trial, the commissioners (sometimes to the number of fifty-eight, sometimes a much smaller number,) met in private in the Painted Chamber, where they received the reports of the committees appointed to arrange the proceedings, conferred with the counsel ordered to prepare the charge, and directed the arrangements and preparations for the proceeding. On the very morning of the trial, their private conference was broken up by the serjeant-at-arms from the Commons, (whose numbers were, as it has been seen, now reduced to about eighty,) demanding the immediate attendance in the House of all its members who were of the court. Ten or twelve of the commissioners absenting themselves from these private meetings, it was necessary to issue warrants, and compel their attendance by a serjeant-at-arms. The commissioners ordered that none of the court should speak openly during the trial but the Lord President and the counsel; and that in case of any difficulty arising to any one, he should desire the President that the court might retire and advise —a precaution that appeared in the result by no means needless, and to be shrewdly devised for

---

[1] There was also another tavern called *Heaven*, on the site of the present Committee Rooms of the House of Commons, at which Pepys, in his Memoirs, speaks of dining, and which Butler calls —

"False Heav'n at the end of the Hall." — Hudibras.

avoiding any public dissensions in the court.
The method of proceeding as to sending for and
bringing in the prisoner, or commanding him,
away, acquainting him with the cause of bringing
him in, and demanding his answers, reprehending
and admonishing him, in case his language or
carriage towards the court should be in their
judgment insolent or contemptuous, was expressly left to the discretion of Bradshaw, to
whom John Lisle and William Say were appointed assistants, and ordered to sit next to him
in the court. The court decided not to insist on
the King's pulling off his hat for that day; and if
he desired time to answer, the Lord President
was to grant it.

During these preparations for the audacious
act which was about to take place, the minds of
the vulgar were lost in vague astonishment, while
those of the sagacious and reflecting were, in
some instances, filled with silent indignation and
horror, and in all with gloomy forebodings for
their own and their country's safety. Whitlock,
who was behind the scenes in all the transactions
of these times, leaves some curious details of
their character and spirit. A week before the
trial commenced, he writes, he " visited Chief
Justice Rolle, a wise and learned man. He
seemed much to scruple the casting off of the
Lords' House, and was much troubled at it;
yet he greatly encouraged me to attend the
House of Commons, notwithstanding the present
force upon them, which could not dispense with
their attendance and performance of their duty,
who had no force upon them in particular."

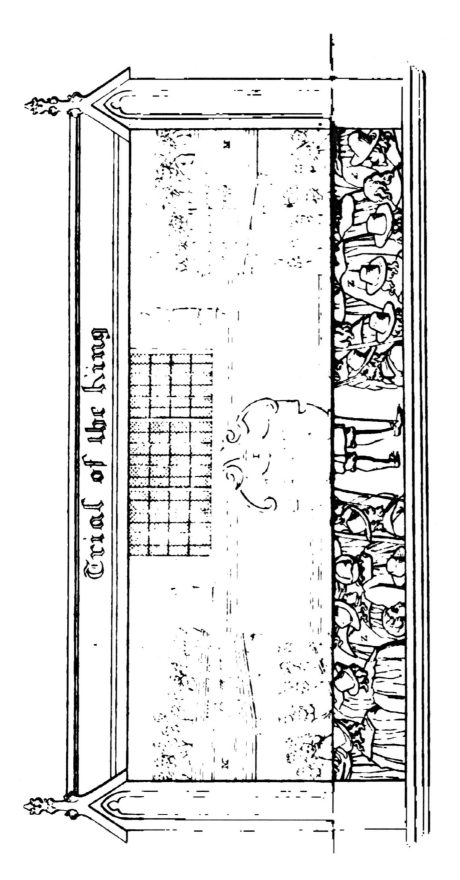

Trial of the King

London, Published by William Tegg & Co. Cheapside.

Next day he says, " The commissioners for trial of the King being to sit in the afternoon (a preliminary sitting), the House adjourned earlier;"—and then proceeds with an honest ingenuousness :— " We heard demurrers forenoon and afternoon. The counsel were more peremptory and unsatisfied than ordinary, and *used us like declining officers."* And two days after he says, " The times were indeed full of dread and danger, and of trouble and change, which caused many a perplexed thought in sober men, who yet put their trust in God, and resolved to depend on Him, and to go on in the way wherein He had set them, whilst they were permitted." [1]

The Trial.—On the 20th of January, 1649, the Lord President Bradshaw, his assistants, and the commissioners, having adjourned from the Painted Chamber, proceeded to the Hall to open the court. The royal sword of state (which had been taken for the purpose from the custody of Sir Henry Mildmay [2], the former keeper of the

---

[1] Memorials.

[2] Rushworth says, there were large debates in the Painted Chamber, whether the commissioners should have both a sword and mace with the arms of the King, and it was agreed to have both. Clarendon says, " The two men who were alone known to the King (of all the Commissioners) before the troubles, were Sir Henry Mildmay, the Master of the King's Jewel House, one who had been bred up in the court, being younger brother of a good family in Essex, and who had been prosecuted with so great favours and bounties by King James and by his Majesty, that he was raised by them to a great estate, and preferred to that office in his house, which is the best under those which entitle the officers to be of the Privy Council." Clarendon's sketch of the characters of these

Jewel House to the King,) was borne by one
Humphreys before Bradshaw, who was also preceded by a mace, and attended by the ushers
and officers of the court, and a guard of twenty-
one gentlemen carrying partisans.   Bradshaw
in a scarlet robe, and covered by his " broad-
brimmed hat," placed himself in a crimson
velvet chair in the centre of the court, with
a desk and velvet cushion before him ; Say and
Lisle on each side of him; and the two clerks
of the court sitting below him at a table, covered with a rich Turkey carpet, on which was
laid the sword of state and the mace.   The rest
of the court, with their hats on, and, according
to Rushworth, " in their best habits," took their

---

two renegade regicides is highly instructive and curious.
Of Mildmay he says, " No man was *more obsequious than
he to the court whilst it flourished; — a great flatterer of
all persons in authority*, and a spy in all places for them.
From the beginning of the parliament he concurred with
those who were most violent against the court, and most
like to prevail against it; and being thereupon branded
with ingratitude, as that brand commonly makes men most
impudent, he continued his desperate pace with them`till
he became one of the murtherers of his master.   The
other was Sir John Danvers, the younger brother and heir
of the Earl of Danby, who was a gentleman of the Privy
Chamber to the King; and being neglected by his brother,
and having by a vain *expense in his way of living contracted
a vast debt which he knew not how to pay*, and being a proud,
formal, weak man, between being seduced and a seducer,
became so far involved in their counsels, that he suffered
himself to be applied to their worst offices, taking it to be
a high honour to sit on the same bench with Cromwell,
who employed and contemned him at once; nor did that
party of miscreants look upon any two men in the kingdom
with that scorn and detestation, as they did upon Danvers
and Mildmay.' — Book xi. p. 197.

seats on side benches, hung with scarlet; and the guard of partians divided themselves on each side of the court.

The commissioners present were, —

John Bradshaw, Serjeant at Law, Lord President,

Oliver Cromwell,
Henry Ireton,
Sir Hardress Waller,
Valentine Wauton,
Thomas Lord Grey of Grooby,
William Lord Mounson,
Sir John Danvers,
Sir Thomas Mauleverer, Bart.,
Sir John Bourchier, Knight,
Isaac Pennington, Alderman of London,
Henry Marten,
William Purefoy,
John Barkstead,
John Blackiston,
Gilbert Millington,
Sir William Constable, Bart.,
Edmond Ludlow,
John Hutchinson,
Sir Michael Livesey, Bart.,
Robert Tichbourne,
Owen Roe,
Robert Lilbourne,
Adrian Scroope,
Thomas Horton,
Thomas Hammond,
John Lisle,
Nicholas Love,
Vincent Potter,
Augustine Garland,
Richard Deane,
John Okey,
John Huson,
William Goffe,

Thomas Harrison,
Edward Whalley,
Thomas Pride,
Isaac Ewer,
Cornelius Holland,
John Carew,
John Jones,
Thomas Lister,
Peregrine Pelham,
Francis Allen,
Thomas Challoner,
John Moore,
William Say,
John Alured,
Francis Lassels,
Henry Smith,
James Challoner,
Humphry Edwards,
Gregory Clement,
John Fry,
Sir Gregory Norton, Bart.,
Edmund Harvey,
John Venn,
Thomas Scot,
William Cawley,
Anthony Stapeley,
John Downs,
John Dixwell,
Simeon Meyne,
James Temple,
Peter Temple,
Daniel Blagrave,
John Brown.

The court being thus sat, and silence enjoined, the great gate of the hall was thrown open, when the vast area was presently filled by a crowd eager to witness the astonishing spectacle of a monarch tried by his revolted subjects. Silence being again proclaimed, the act of the Commons for erecting the court was read aloud by one of the clerks. The commissioners were thereupon called; and each commissioner rose as he answered to his name. Bradshaw's name was first called, and next that of Fairfax, the Lord General, to which no answer was made. The name was repeated by the clerk, on which a voice in the crowd was heard to say, " He has more wit than to be here," which occasioned some disorder in the court, and loud enquiries for the name of the audacious speaker; but silence was restored, and the clerk, passing Fairfax's name, without any notice being taken of his absence, proceeded.

When all the commissioners present had answered to their names, the court commanded the serjeant-at-arms to send for the prisoner; and in a quarter of an hour Colonel Tomlinson, who had the King in charge, conducted him into court. He was attended by Colonel Hacker, and thirty-two officers, holding partisans, and by his own servants, and advanced up the side of the Hall next the Thames from the house of Sir Robert Cotton. The serjeant-at-arms, with his mace, received the King in the Hall, and conducted him to the bar, where a crimson-velvet chair was placed for him facing the court. After a stern and steadfast gaze on the court, and on the people in the galleries on each side of him, the King placed himself in the chair, not at all moving his hat, showing neither the least emotion nor the slightest respect to the tribunal before him. Presently he rose up, and turned about, looking down the vast hall : first on the guards which were ranged on its left or western side, and then on the eager waving multitude of his own subjects which filled the space on the right. The guard attending him divided on each side of the court, and the King's servants who followed him to the bar stood on the left of their master.

The King being again seated, Bradshaw addressed him, telling him that the Commons of England being sensible of the calamities brought on the nation, and of the innocent blood which had been shed in it, which was fixed on him as the principal author, had resolved to make inquisition for this blood; and, according to the debt they owed to God, to justice, the kingdom, and themselves, and according to the fundamental power and trust reposed in them by the people, had resolved to bring him to trial and judgment. They had constituted the court before which he was brought; he would hear the charge read; and the court would proceed according to justice. Cook, the solicitor for the commonwealth, (Steel the attorney having two days before excused himself on the ground of being sick, and in bed,) then rose to speak; but the King wishing to be heard, softly laid his staff two or three times on Cook's shoulder, and bade him hold. Bradshaw interposed, and ordered Cook to proceed, when Cook (according to the order of the commissioners delivered to the counsel before the trial) exhibited on behalf of the people of England a charge of high treason, and other higher crimes, against Charles Stuart, King of England, and pray-ed that the charge might be received and read. He then delivered in the charge in writing to the court, when Bradshaw ordered the clerk to read it. The King interrupted the reading, and desired to speak; but Bradshaw ordered the clerk to read, and told the King if he had any thing to say after the reading the court would hear him.

THE CHARGE. — The "charge," which could not from its very nature possess either the form or substance of any proceeding known to the law of England, seems yet to have been framed with a desire of giving it some faint resemblance to a known and established judicial procedure; viz. an indictment for the offence of treason, in "levying war" against the sovereign: the "parliament and the people" being in the charge the alleged objects of the war levied, instead of the King of the realm; and the "people of England" being the prosecutors, instead of "the King." It stated, that Charles Stuart being admitted King of England, and trusted with a limited power to govern according to the laws, and by his trust and oath being obliged to use his power for the good of his people, and for the preservation of their liberties; yet, out of wicked design to uphold in himself unlimited and tyrannical power, and to overthrow the rights and liberties of his people, and to take away the foundations thereof, for the acccomplishment of his designs treacherously and wickedly *levied war* against the parliament and the people therein represented, particularly on the 30th of June, 1642, at Beverley, in Yorkshire; and on the 4th of August at the town of Nottingham; and on the 23d of October in the same year at Edge Hill and Keynton Field, in the county of Warwick; and on the 30th of November in the same year at Brentford in Middlesex; and on the 30th of August, 1643, at Caversham Bridge, near Reading, in the county of Berks; and on the 31st of July, 1644, at Cropredy Bridge, in Oxon; and on the 8th of June, 1645, at the town of Leicester; and on the 14th of the same month at Naseby Field, in the county of Northampton; at which times and places, and in 1646, he Charles Stuart caused thousands of the free people of the nation to be slain, and by divisions within the land, invasions from foreign parts, and other means carried on the said war by land and sea, and particularly for that purpose gave commission to his son, the prince, and others. By which unnatural wars much innocent blood of the free people of this nation had been spilt, families undone, the public treasury wasted and exhausted, trade decayed, and parts of the land spoiled even to desolation; and for further prosecution of his designs, the said Charles Stuart continued his commissions to the prince and other rebels, and to the Earl of Ormond and the Irish rebels. All which wicked designs and wars were carried on for the advancement of a personal interest of will and power, and a pretended prerogative to himself and his family, against the liberty and peace of the nation, by and for whom he was intrusted as aforesaid. And the said

John Cook, by protestation reserving, on behalf
of the people of England, the liberty of exhibit-
ing any other charge; and also of replying to the
answers which the said Charles Stuart should
make to the premises, did, for the said treasons
and crimes, impeach the said Charles Stuart as
a tyrant, traitor, murderer, and a public and im-
placable enemy to the commonwealth of England,
and prayed that he might be put to answer the
premises, and that such proceedings should be
had as were agreeable to justice.

During the reading of the charge, the King sat
entirely unmoved in his chair, looking sometimes
to the court and sometimes to the galleries. Occasionally he rose up and turned about to behold
the guards and spectators, and then sat down
again, looking very sternly, but with a majestic
and composed countenance, unruffled by the
slightest emotion, till the clerk came to the
words *Charles Stuart as a tyrant, traitor, murderer,* &c.; at which the King laughed, as he sat,
in the face of the Court. The silver head of his
staff happened to fall off, at which he appeared
surprised: Herbert, who stood near him, offered
to pick it up, but Charles, seeing he could
not reach it, stooped for it himself. When the
words were read stating the charge to be exhibited " on behalf of the people of England,"
a voice, in a loud tone, called out, " No, nor the
half of the people — it is false — where are they
or their consents?—Oliver Cromwell is a traitor!"
This occasioned a confusion in the court; Colonel Axtell even commanded the soldiers to fire
into the box from which the voice proceeded.

But it was soon discovered that these words, as well as the former exclamation on calling Fairfax's name, were uttered by Lady Fairfax, the General's wife, who was immediately compelled by the guard to withdraw.[1]

[1] Clarendon says, "She was of a very noble extraction, one of the daughters and heirs of Horace Lord Vere of Tilbury, who having been bred in Holland had not that reverence for the church of England as she ought to have had, and so had unhappily concurred in her husband's entering into rebellion, never imagining what misery it would bring upon the kingdom, and now abhorred the work in hand as much as any body could do; and did all she could to hinder her husband from acting any part in it. Nor did he ever sit in that bloody court, though he was thought overwitted by Cromwell, and made a property to bring that to pass which could very hardly have been otherwise effected." Book xi. p. 196. That Lady Fairfax, sitting with Mrs. Nelson, the sister of Sir Purbeck Temple, was the person making these exclamations, was proved by Sir Purbeck and other witnesses on the trial of Colonel Axtell. See State Trials, vol. v. Fairfax, who was a man of consummate military skill, and of a generous and feeling nature, of whom his son-in-law, Villiers, Duke of Buckingham, writes,

> "He had the fierceness of the manliest mind,
> And all the meekness, too, of woman-kind,"

attended the first meeting of the commissioners in the Painted Chamber on the 8th of January, but was never afterwards present at the court. Mr. Godwin labours to show that his wife's influence overcame his own real principles. But in his own Memoirs, p. 125., he says, " From the time that the council of officers declared their usurped authority at Triplow Heath, I never gave my free consent to any thing they did." And of the trial he says, " My afflicted and troubled mind for it, and my earnest endeavours to prevent it, will, I hope, sufficiently attest my dislike and abhorrence of the fact. *And what will they not do*

'These expressions of sympathy for the King, and of indignation against the proceeding, were, according to Whitlock, not confined to this spirited lady, but were frequently exhibited by the spectators in the gallery.

The charge being read,

Bradshaw began : — Sir, You have now heard your charge read; the court expects your answer.

The King. I would know by what power I am called hither ; I was not long ago in the Isle of Wight; how I came there, is a longer story than is fit at this time for me to speak of; but there I entered into a treaty with both Houses of Parliament, with as much public faith as it is possible to be had of any people in the world. I treated there with a number of honourable lords and gentlemen, and treated honestly and up-rightly. I cannot say but they did very nobly with me. We were upon a conclusion of the treaty. Now I would know by what authority, I mean lawful (there are many unlawful authorities in the world, thieves and robbers by the highways) — but I would know by what authority I was brought from thence, and carried from place to place ; and when I know by what lawful authority, I shall answer. Remember I am your

---

with the shrubs, having cut down the cedar ?" And yet Fairfax signed the declaration of the army calling for the punishment of the King, ordered his removal to Hurst Castle, and marched with the troops to London. Every where, but in battle, his conduct appears to have been vacillating ; — influenced by his own diffident and amiable feelings, and, perhaps by the counsels of his wife.

King, your lawful King, and what sins you bring upon your heads, and the judgment of God upon this land; think well upon it, — I say, think well upon it, before you go further from one sin to a greater. Let me know by what lawful authority I am seated here, and I shall not be unwilling to answer. In the mean time, I have a trust committed to me by God, by old and lawful descent, — I will not betray it, to answer to a new unlawful authority: therefore resolve me that, and you shall hear more of me.

Bradshaw. If you had been pleased to have observed what was hinted to you by the court, at your first coming hither, you would have known by what authority; which authority requires you, in the name of the people of England, of which you are elected King, to answer.

The King. No, Sir, I deny that.

Bradshaw. If you acknowledge not the authority of the court, they must proceed.

The King. I do tell them so: England was *never* an elective kingdom, but an hereditary kingdom for near these thousand years; therefore let me know by what authority I am called hither: I do stand more for the liberty of my people than any here that come to be my pretended judges; let me know by what lawful authority I am seated here, and I will answer it, otherwise I will not answer it.

Bradshaw. Sir, how well you have managed your trust is known: your way of answer is to interrogate the court, which beseems not you in this condition. You have been told of it twice or thrice.

The King. Here is a gentleman, Lieu-

tenant Colonel Cobbet; ask him, if he did not
bring me from the Isle of Wight by force. I
do not come here as submitting to the court: I
will stand as much for the privilege of the House
of Commons, rightly understood, as any man. I
see no House of Lords here, that may constitute
a parliament; and the King too should have been.
Is this the bringing of the King to his parliament?
Is this the bringing an end to the treaty in the
public faith of the world? Let me see a legal
authority warranted by the word of God, the
Scriptures, or warranted by the constitutions of
the kingdom, and I will answer.

Bradshaw. Sir, you have propounded a
question, and have been answered. Seeing you
will not answer, the court will consider how to
proceed: in the mean time, those that brought
you hither, are to take charge of you back again.
The court desires to know, whether this be all
the answer you will give, or no.

The King. Sir, I desire that you would give
me, and all the world, satisfaction in this. Let me
tell you, it is not a slight thing you are about.
I am sworn to keep the peace, by that duty
I owe to God and my country, and I will do it to
the last breath of my body; and therefore you
shall do well to satisfy first God, and then the
country, by what authority you do it: if you do
it by an usurped authority, you cannot answer
it. There is a God in heaven, that will call you,
and all that give you power, to account. Satisfy
me, and I will answer; otherwise I betray my
trust, and the liberties of the people: for I do
avow, that it is as great a sin to withstand lawful

authority, as it is to submit to a tyrannical or any otherways unlawful authority; and therefore satisfy God and me, and all the world in that, and you shall receive my answer. I am not afraid of that bill.

Bradshaw. The court expects you should give them a final answer; their purpose is to adjourn to Monday next: if you do not satisfy yourself, we are satisfied with our authority; it is upon God's authority and the kingdom's.

The King. For answer, let me tell you, you have shown no lawful authority to satisfy any reasonable man.

Bradshaw. That is in your apprehension; we are satisfied that are your judges.

The King. It is not my apprehension, nor yours, that ought to decide it.

Bradshaw. The court hath heard you, and you are to be disposed of as they have commanded.

So commanding the guard to take him away, his Majesty only replied, " Well, Sir !" And at his going down, pointing with his staff towards the sword, he said, " I do not fear that." As he went down the stairs, the people in the hall cried out, " God save the King !" notwithstanding some were set there by the republicans and soldiers to lead the clamour for " justice." [1]

The course pursued by the King, in steadily denying the jurisdiction of the court, is said to have been advised by the celebrated Matthew Hale, then a serjeant-at-law. It saved Charles from being insulted by a laboured, pedantic, sophistical,

[1] Nalson.

and canting speech, which Cook was prepared to deliver, in case the King had pleaded, and which he afterwards printed for the benefit of the world. This speech, like the charge, assumes throughout that the mere fact of the King's being in arms against the parliamentary forces established the newly created treason of levying war against the parliament and the people, and showed Charles, beyond dispute, chargeable with all the blood spilt and the suffering endured in the contest. It does not even touch the only real question between the King and the parliament—what were the origin and causes of the war, and which of the parties to it was fairly to be regarded as the aggressor. To give a summary of a tissue of flagrant sophistry, exaggerated assertion, contumelious abuse, and mystical declamation, is no easy or profitable task. Cook lays down the proposition, that the kings of England are intrusted with a limited power to govern according to law, and cites Fortescue for that unquestionable principle; and then, in order to show that Charles had from the first a design to subvert the laws and rule despotically, he rakes up the absurd story made a charge against Archbishop Laud on his trial, that he had at the coronation omitted in the oath the words, " which the people shall choose;"—" which certainly," says this fair advocate, " he *durst not have done* without the King's special command." It appears from Laud's defence, State Trials, vol. iv. p. 465., that the oath used at the coronation of Charles was in fact the same as that used at the coronation of James, if not of Queen Elizabeth. But supposing that the

Archbishop had altered it, what relevancy had this to the charge against Charles, of levying war on his people? Cook then chooses to assume, without a shadow of foundation, that Charles in his defence, had he not been interrupted by his judges, intended to have justified his acts by quoting from the first book of Samuel, chap. viii., the description of the absolute king which the Lord ordained for the discontented Israelites who clamoured for a king; and then he elaborately argues, that this is not to be deemed the model of a good king approved by God; nor even to be taken as a proof that the Almighty approved of kings at all: " for," says the regicide solicitor, " he gave them a king in his wrath; therein dealing with them as the wise physician with the distempered and impatient patient, who desiring to drink wine, tells him the danger of inflammation; yet wine he will have, and the physician considering a little wine will do but little hurt, rather than his patient by fretting should take greater hurt, prescribes a little white wine — wherein the physician doth not approve his drinking of wine, but of two evils chooseth the least. The Jews would have a king for majesty and splendour, like the heathens. God permits this, he approves it not."

The solicitor, then, in order " to open and prove the King's wicked design wherewith he stands charged," asserts that Charles had granted the judges' patents during pleasure instead of during good behaviour; had sold judges' places for 5000*l.* or 10,000*l.*, and then ordered the judges to deliver opinions in his favour: — atrociously insinuates, without venturing to charge, that Buckingham had murdered James I. with Charles's connivance. " How the King first came to the crown, God and his own conscience best know ;" and then, after declaiming at large on this insinuation as if it were a fact proved, impudently and hypocritically concludes, " but I leave it as a riddle which at the day of judgment will be expounded and unriddled, &c. &c. Had he studied Scripture half so much as Ben Jonson or Shakspeare, he might have learned that when Amaziah was settled in the kingdom, he suddenly did justice upon those servants which had killed his father Joab. (2 Kings, xii. 20., and xiv. 1. 5.)[1]   Nor," says the counsel

[1] That Charles *connived* at Buckingham's conduct in *poisoning* King James (if Buckingham had done so) was a wanton invention of republican malignity. Even the exasperated Commons, who impeached Buckingham at the commencement of Charles's reign, never dreamt of charging him with the *murder of the King by poison*. They charged him with " transcendent presumption in giving the King physic ; " which they say is " an offence and misdemeanour of so high a nature as may justly be called, and is by the said Commons deemed, to be an act of transcendent presumption, and of dangerous consequence," and which is only introduced as the 13th article of impeachment after others of extortion, procuring honours for his kindred, &c. &c. That Buckingham's conduct was presumptuous and indiscreet cannot be denied ; and it was certainly not wise in Charles to put an end to the investigation by dissolving the parliament. But to declaim on it as " concealment of a murder," and as showing Charles " without natural affection for his father," was an absurd and monstrous proposition worthy of this fanatical solicitor " for the people of England." — See the proceedings on Buckingham's impeachment, State Trials, vol. ii.

for the people, " does the common objection that
the judges and evil counsellors, and not the
King, ought to be responsible for such mal-ad-
ministrations, injustice, and oppression, bear the
weight of a feather in the balance of right reason.
For, first, who made such wicked and corrupt
judges? Were they not his own creatures?
And ought not every man to be accountable for
the work of his own hands?"

Cook then proceeds to "*prove*," as he asserts.
" that the King set up his standard of war for
the advancement and upholding of his personal
interest, power, and pretended prerogative against
the public interest, of common right, peace,
and safety." His proofs are truly extraordinary. They consist of little more than a statement of the claims asserted by the King to
all the most unquestionable prerogatives of the
kings of England, viz. to have the power and
disposal of the militia by land and sea; the
power to convoke, prorogue, and to dissolve parliaments; to have a negative voice as to the passing of laws; to enjoy the power of conferring
honours and creating peers; to create the judges
of the land; to pardon criminals, or, as Cook can-
didly states it, " to pardon murderers, whom the
Lord says shall not be pardoned;" to fix the
value of money by proclamation. All these prerogatives, exercised immemorially and without
dispute by the King's predecessors, this lawyer
declares to be " no legal prerogatives, but usurpa-
tions, encroachments, and invasions on the people's
rights;" and cites the assertion of them by Charles
as triumphant proofs of his illegal and wicked

motives in levying the war against the parliament.
Such wild absurdities and monstrous assertions
did fanaticism and sedition at that time engender
in the minds of rational and even educated beings.
The learned solicitor's alliterations and plays
upon words are the most innocent parts of his
speech. He says, " Anglia hath been made an
Akeldama, and her younger sister, *Ireland*, a *land
of ire* and misery."

The solicitor then encounters the somewhat
perplexing question, " But by what law is the
King condemned ?" to which he gives this highly
precise and satisfactory answer, " By the fundamental law of this kingdom — by the general
law of all nations — and the unanimous consent
of all rational men in the world, written in every
man's heart with the pen of a diamond in capital
letters, and a character so legible, that he that
runs may read."—" This law of nature," says he,
" is the law of God, written in the fleshly tables of
men's hearts."—" This law of nature is an *in-
dubitable legislative authority* of itself, that hath a
suspensive power over all human laws." — " If the
pilot of a ship be drunk and running on a rock, if
the passengers cannot otherwise prevent it, they
may throw him into the sea to cool him," says
the ingenious solicitor. " Is it not senseless for
the vessel to ask the potter by what law he calls
him to account ?"—" For him not only to set up
a standard of war in defiance of his *dread sovereign
the people*, (for so they truly were in nature,
though *names have befooled us*,) but to persist so
many years in such cruel persecutions, who with
the word of his mouth might have made a peace,

—if ever there were so superlative a treason let the Indians judge, and whosoever shall break and violate such a trust and confidence, *anathema maranatha* be unto them."

The maxim that the King can do no wrong, which is now rationally understood as only implying the settled doctrine of ministerial responsibility, is absolutely denied by the republican lawyer. "I do aver it with confidence, that there is no such case to be found in the law, that if the king rob, or murder," (as if Charles had done aught approaching to either,) "or commit such horrid extravagances, that it is no wrong;" and then he cites a case which is directly against his assertion: "indeed the case is put in Henry VII., by a chief judge, that if the king kill a man it is *no felony* to make him suffer death."—— "But," says Cook, with a flagrant *petitio principii*, "there is *no doubt* but the parliament *might* try the King, or appoint others to judge him for it."—— "But," says he afterwards, "I am sure there is no case in law, that if the King levy war against the parliament and people, that it is *not* treason;" entirely forgetting that he had taken upon himself the burden of showing affirmatively, that the King's act *was treason.* To show that the act might lawfully be punished, although no law existed rendering it a crime, he says, "Before any statute against witchcraft, many witches have been hanged in England, because it is death by God's law. If any Italian mountebank should come over hither, and give any man poison that should lie in his body above a year and a day, and then kill him, as it is reported

D 4

that they can give a man poison that shall con-
sume the body in three years, will any make
scruple or question to hang up such a rascal?"

He then elaborately enters into the vague
calumny against the King, of betraying the Protestants of Rochelle to the French; of which he
says, "he *heard so much* in Geneva, and by the
protestant ministers in France, that he *could believe no less* than that the King was guilty of it."
Loose and indefinite as the procedure was, it
would have been difficult for Cook to make out
that evidence, the most conclusive, of the King's
connivance with Buckingham in betraying French
protestant subjects into the hands of their catholic sovereign, could have any bearing whatever
on the charge upon which Charles was now
accused. It was obviously one among the number of inflammatory and unfounded topics of declamation which "the people's" counsel dragged
together to please the military audience, and, if
possible, to exasperate the hate of his judges
against their fallen monarch. The peroration of
this wretched fanatic, in which he speaks, "first,
concerning the prisoner, then concerning himself,"
exceeds, in hypocritical insolence, all his former
extravagances. "I am troubled in my spirit in
regard to his eternal condition, for fear that he
should depart this life without love and recon-
ciliation to all those saints whom he hath scorned
under the notion of Presbyterians, Anabaptists, Independents, and Sectaries. It cannot be
denied that he hath spent all his days in im-
measurable pride—that during his whóle reign
he hath deported himself as a god, been de-.

pended upon and adored as a god; that he hath challenged and assumed an omnipotent power, an earthly omnipotence, that with the breath of his mouth hath dissolved parliaments: his *non placet* hath made all the counsels of that supreme court to become abortives. — *Non curo* hath been his motto, who instead of being honoured as good kings ought to be, and no more, hath been idolised and adored as our good God only ought to be." (If this were so, was it treason in Charles that he was idolised by his people, or by a portion of them?) — " A man that hath shot all his arrows against the upright in the land, hated Christ in his members, swallowed down unrighteousness as the ox drinks water, esteemed the needy as his footstool, crushed honest, public-spirited men, and grieved when he could not afflict the honest more than he did, counted it the best art and policy to suppress the righteous, and to give way to his courtiers, so to gripe, grind, oppress, and over-reach the free people of the land, that he might do what he list. But all sins to an infinite mercy are equally pardonable; therefore, my prayer for the poor wretch shall be, that God would give him repentance to life, that he may believe in that Christ whom he hath imprisoned, persecuted, and murdered in his saints," &c. &c.

The illustrious Samuel Butler, in a pamphlet entitled " The Plagiary Exposed; or an Old Answer to a newly revived Calumny against the Memory of King Charles I., being a Reply to the Book entitled ' King Charles's Case,' formerly written by John Cook, of Gray's Inn, Barrister [1] "

---

[1] Printed in Lord Somers's Tracts.

exposed the sophistries and misrepresentations of this speech with admirable acumen and spirit.

On Sunday, the 21st January, the commissioners held a fast in company at Whitehall, and heard much praying and preaching.[1]   On Monday, the 22d, they met again privately in the Painted Chamber, when an excuse was sent from Mr. John Corbet for not further attending the court. They deliberated on the demeanour of the King on the former day, and resolved that he should not be suffered to question their jurisdiction; and that, in case he fell again into that discourse,

[1] The celebrated Hugh Peters, "the pulpit buffoon," as Dugdale calls him, one of the most active assistants of Cromwell, Ireton, and Harrison, and a vehement preacher against the King and the throne, was appointed to preach before the commissioners at St. Margaret's church on this day.   His text was from the last psalm but one : — " Bind your kings with chains, and your nobles with links of iron."   The purport of his vehement discourse was proved by several witnesses on his trial in 1660.   " Here is," says he, " a great discourse and talk in the world : ' What! will ye cut off the King's head? the head of a protestant prince and king?'   Turn to your Bibles, and you shall find it there, ' Whosoever sheds man's blood, by man shall his blood be shed.'   And I see neither King Charles, nor Prince Charles, nor Prince Rupert, nor Prince Maurice, nor any of that rabble excepted out of it."   He afterwards exclaimed, " *Blessed be God!* the House, the Lower House, is purged; and *the House of Lords themselves, they will down suddenly.*"   He perpetually styled the King Barabbas; and after making a long prayer, he said, " I have prayed and preached these twenty years, and now I may say with old Simeon, ' Lord, now lettest thou thy servant depart in peace, for mine eyes have seen thy salvation.' " — See Peters's Trial, State Trials, vol. v.

Bradshaw should let him know that he must be satisfied with this answer to the questions he had propounded, " That the Commons of England assembled in parliament have constituted this court, whose power shall not be permitted to be disputed by him, and that they were resolved he should answer the charge."

The court then in the afternoon adjourned into the hall, when seventy of the commissioners were present.[1]   The hall door being opened, and

[1] Seventy-one was the largest number of commissioners ever present at the trial.   Sixty-seven were present on the day when the sentence was pronounced.   Forty-eight only appeared at the next sitting, when the King's execution was ordered; and fifty-nine signed the warrant for his decapitation.   Some few of the commissioners, such as Algernon Sidney, Sir Thomas Wroth, Herbert Morley, John Fagg, attended the preliminary meetings in the Painted Chamber, but never sat as judges, or attended the court after the trial commenced.   From forty to fifty of the commissioners appear never to have taken any part in the proceedings, notwithstanding the summonses ordered by the court, and the exertions of the serjeant-at-arms. Among these were Sir Thomas Honeywood, Mr. Mildmay, Philip Lord Lisle, General Skippon, Col. Desborough the brother-in-law of Cromwell, Sir William Alanson, Sir William Masham, Sir John Barrington, Sir William Brereton, Sir Peter Wentworth, K. B., Mr. Godfrey Bosvile, Mr. John Lambert, Sir Arthur Haselrig, Mr. Robert Dukenfield, Sir William Armyn, Serjeant Thorp, Mr. Richard Darley, Mr. James Nelthrop, Sir William Roberts, Mr. Fowks, alderman of London, Mr. Roger Gratwick, Mr. George Fenwick, Serjeant Nicholas, John Lenthal (the well known Speaker of the Commons), Col. Rowland Wilson, alderman of London. Lord Leicester in his journal, p. 54., says, " My two sons, Philip (Lord Lisle) and Algernon (Sidney), came unexpectedly to Penshurst, Monday the 22d (January), and

the crowd having instantly filled the hall, three
proclamations were made, and then the serjeant-
at-arms brought in the royal prisoner with the accustomed ceremonies. Cook then rose: — "May
it please you, my Lord President,—I did at the
last court exhibit a charge of high treason and
other crimes against the prisoner at the bar,
whereof I do accuse him in the name of the
people of England. Instead of answering, he
did dispute the authority of this high court. I
move, on behalf of the kingdom of England, that
the prisoner may be directed to make a positive
answer by way of confession or negation; and that,
if he refuse to do so, the charge be taken *pro
confesso*, and the court may proceed according
to justice."

Bradshaw. Sir, you may remember, at the
last court you heard a charge read against you,
containing a charge of high treason and other high
crimes against this realm of England: you heard,
likewise, that it was prayed, in the behalf of the
people, that you should give an answer to that
charge. You were then pleased to make some

---

stayed till Monday the 29th; so as neither of them was at
the condemnation of the King." Algernon Sidney says of
himself, " I was at Penshurst when the act for the King's
trial passed; and coming up to town I heard that my
name was put in. I presently went to the Painted
Chamber, where those who were nominated for judges
were assembled. A debate was raised, and I positively
opposed the proceeding. Cromwell used these formal
words, ' *I tell you, we will cut off his head with the crown
on it.*' I replied, ' You may take your own course, — I
cannot stop you; but I will keep myself clean from having
any hand in this business.' " — Blencowe, p. 237.

scruples concerning the authority of this court, and knew not by what authority you are brought hither: you were answered that it was by authority of the Commons of England, assembled in parliament, that did think fit to call you to account for those high and capital misdemeanors wherewith you were then charged. Since that, the court hath taken into consideration what you then said; they are fully satisfied with their own authority, and they hold it fit you should stand satisfied with it too. They do expect you should either confess or deny the charge: if you deny, it is offered, in the behalf of the kingdom, to be made good against you; their authority they do avow to the whole world, that the whole kingdom are to rest satisfied in, and you are to rest satisfied with it.

The King. When I was here last, it is very true I made that question; and if it were only my own particular case, I would have satisfied myself with the protestation I made the last time I was here against the legality of this court, and that a king cannot be tried by any jurisdiction on earth: but it is not my case alone, it is the freedom and the liberty of the people of England; and do you pretend what you will, I stand more for their liberties. For if power without law may make laws, may alter the fundamental laws of the kingdom, I do not know what subject he is in England that can be sure of his life, or any thing that he calls his own: therefore when that I came here, I did expect particular reasons to know by what law, what authority, you did proceed against me here. And therefore I am

a little to seek what to say to you in this particular, because the affirmative is to be proved, the
negative often is very hard to do: but since I
cannot persuade you to do it, I shall tell you my
reasons as short as I can.

My reasons why in conscience and the duty I
owe to God first, and my people next, for the
preservation of their lives, liberties, and estates, I
conceive I cannot answer this, till I be satisfied
of the legality of it, are these:— All proceedings
against any man whatsoever ——

Bradshaw. Sir, I must interrupt you, which
I would not do, but that what you do is not agreeable to the proceedings of any court of justice:
you are about to enter into argument, and dispute
concerning the authority of this court, before
whom you appear as a prisoner, and are charged
as an high delinquent; if you take upon you to
dispute the authority of the court, we may not
do it, nor will any court give way unto it: you
are to submit unto it; you are to give a punctual
and direct answer, whether you will answer your
charge or no, and what your answer is.

The King. Sir, by your favour, I do not know
the forms of law; I do know law and reason,
though I am no lawyer professed,— but I know as
much law as any gentleman in England, and
therefore (under favour) I do plead for the liberties of the people of England more than you do:
and therefore if I should impose a belief upon
any man, without reasons given for it, it were
unreasonable; but I must tell you, that by that
reason that I have, as thus informed, I cannot
yield unto it.

Bradshaw. — Sir, I must interrupt you : you speak of law and reason ; it is fit there should be law and reason, and there is both against you. Sir, the vote of the Commons of England assembled in parliament, it is the reason of the kingdom, and they are these too that have given that law, according to which you should have ruled and reigned. Sir, you are not to dispute our authority, you are told it again by the court.

The King. I do not know how a king can be a delinquent ; but by any law that ever I heard of, all men, (delinquents, or what you will,) let me tell you, may put in demurrers against any proceeding as legal : I do demand that, and demand to be heard with my reasons ; if you deny that, you deny reason.

Bradshaw. Sir, you are concluded, you may not demur to the jurisdiction of the court ; if you do, I must let you know, that they over-rule your demurrer ; they sit here by the authority of the Commons of England, and all your predecessors and you are responsible to them.

The King. I deny that ; show me one precedent.

Bradshaw. Sir, you ought not to interrupt while the court is speaking to you. If you offer it by way of demurrer to the jurisdiction of the court, they have considered of their jurisdiction ; they do affirm their own jurisdiction.

The King. I say, Sir, by your favour, that the Commons of England was never a court of judicature : I would know how they came to be so.

Bradshaw. Sir, you are not to be permitted to go on in that speech and these discourses.

Then the clerk of the court, by order of Bradshaw, read, —

" Charles Stuart, King of England, you have been accused on the behalf of the people of England of high treason, and other high crimes; the court have determined that you ought to answer the same."

The King.   I will answer the same, so soon as I know by what authority you do this.

Bradshaw.   If this be all that you will say, then, you that brought the prisoner hither, take charge of him back again.

The King.   I do require that I may give in my reasons why I do not answer, and that you give me time for that.

Bradshaw.   Sir, it is not for prisoners to require.

The King.   Prisoners! Sir, I am not an ordinary prisoner!

Bradshaw.   The court hath considered, and have already affirmed their jurisdiction; if you will not answer, we will give order to record your default.

The King.   You have never heard my reasons yet.

Bradshaw.   Sir, your reasons are not to be heard against the highest jurisdiction.

The King.   Show me that jurisdiction where reason is not to be heard.

Bradshaw.   Sir, we show it you here, — the Commons of England; and the next time you are brought you will know more of the pleasure of the court; and, it may be, their final determination.

The King. Show me where ever the house of commons was a court of judicature of that kind.

Bradshaw. Serjeant, take away the prisoner.

The King. Well, Sir, remember that the King is not suffered to give in his reasons for the liberty and freedom of all his subjects.

Bradshaw. Sir, you are not to have liberty to use this language : how great a friend you have been to the laws and liberties of the people, let all England and the world judge.

The King. Sir, under favour, it was the liberty, freedom, and laws of the subject, that ever I took — for them I defended myself with arms ; I never took up arms against the people, but for the laws.

Bradshaw. The command of the court must be obeyed; no answer will be given to the charge.

The King. Well, Sir!

Then Bradshaw ordered the default to be recorded, and the contempt of the court; and that no answer would be given to the charge.

The King was guarded forth to Sir Robert Cotton's house with the accustomed ceremonies.

The court adjourned to the Painted Chamber on Tuesday at twelve o'clock, and from thence they notified their intention to adjourn to Westminster Hall, at which time all persons concerned were to give their attendance.

On this day the Scotch commissioners, who were in London for the purpose of treating with the King and the parliament, (the Earl of Lothian, Sir John Chiesly, and William Glendinning,) and who were

E

dissatisfied with the concessions of the King at Newport, especially as to matters of religion, sent to the Speaker of the House of Commons their unanimous and solemn protest against all proceedings for bringing Charles to trial. It concluded thus : — " To the end it may be manifest to the world, how much they abominate and detest so horrid a design against his Majesty's person, we do, in the name of the parliament and kingdom of Scotland, hereby declare their dissent from the said proceedings, and the taking away of his Majesty's life, and protest, that, as they are altogether free from the same, so they may be free from all the evils, miseries, confusions, and calamities that may follow thereon to these distracted kingdoms." This protest was referred to a committee to prepare an answer.

On Tuesday, the 23d of January, the court, consisting of sixty-three commissioners, met again in the Painted Chamber in private ; and after deliberating on the proceedings of the day before, and the demeanour of the King, they resolved to try once more whether he would acknowledge their authority. They accordingly ordered Bradshaw to acquaint him that, if he continued contumacious, he must expect no further time ; that the court required his positive and final answer to the charge. If he submitted to answer, and desired a copy of it, Bradshaw was to grant it, and require him to answer by one o'clock in the next afternoon. The court then adjourned, with the usual ceremonies, into Westminster Hall. The King was brought in from Sir Robert Cotton's with the accustomed guard. After *oyez* had

been twice proclaimed, Cook rose :—" My Lord
President, this is now the third time that, by
the great grace and favour of this high court,
this prisoner hath been brought to the bar before any issue is joined in the cause. I exhibited
a charge against him of the highest treason ever
wrought on the theatre of England. My Lord,
he did dispute the authority of the court. Your
Lordship gave him a day to consider and put in
his answer yesterday, but he was then pleased
to demur to the jurisdiction of the court, which
the court did over-rule. — I now move for speedy
judgment against the prisoner. I might press
your Lordship, that when a prisoner is contumacious, according to the law of the land, it shall
be taken *pro confesso* against him. But, my Lord,
the House of Commons, the supreme authority
and jurisdiction of the kingdom, have declared
that it is notorious the charge is true, as it is,
in truth, as clear as crystal, and as the sun that
shines at noon-day; which, however, if the court
are not satisfied in, I have, on the people of
England's behalf, several witnesses to produce,
and therefore I pray (and yet it is not so much
I, as the innocent blood that hath been shed, the
cry whereof is very great for justice and judgment,) that speedy judgment be pronounced
against the prisoner.

Bradshaw went on in the same strain; —
concluding, " You are to give your positive and
final answer in plain English, whether you be
guilty or not guilty of these treasons laid to your
charge."

The King, after a little pause, said, — " When

I was here yesterday, I did desire to speak for the liberties of the people of England : I was interrupted. I desire to know yet, whether I may speak freely or not."

Bradshaw. Sir, you have had the resolution of the court upon the like question the last day, and you were told, that, having such a charge of so high a nature against you, your work was, that you ought to acknowledge the jurisdiction of the court. When you have once answered, you shall be heard at large. Make the best defence you can. But, Sir, I must let you know from the court, that you are not to be permitted to issue out into any other discourses, till such time as you have given a positive answer concerning the matter charged upon you.

The King. For the charge, I value it not a rush; it is the liberty of the people of England that I stand for. For me to acknowledge a new court that I never heard of before, I that am your king, that should be an example to all the people of England for to uphold justice, to maintain the old laws: indeed I know not how to do it. You spoke very well the first day that I came here (on Saturday), of the obligations that I had laid upon me by God, to the maintenance of the liberties of my people: the same obligation you spake of, I do acknowledge to God that I owe to him and to my people, to defend as much as in me lies the ancient laws of the kingdom. Therefore, until that I may know that this is not against the fundamental laws of the kingdom, by your favour I can put in no particular answer. If you will give me time, I will show you my reasons why I cannot do it, and this ——

Here being interrupted, Charles said, — " By your favour, you ought not to interrupt me. How I came here I know not; there is no law for it to make your king your prisoner. I was in a treaty upon the public faith of the kingdom, that was the known — with the two houses of parliament that was the acknowledged, representative of the kingdom; and when I had almost made an end of the treaty, then I was hurried away, and brought hither; and therefore ——"

Bradshaw. Sir, you must know the pleasure of the court.

The King. By your favour, Sir.

Bradshaw. Nay, Sir, by your favour, you may not be permitted to fall into those discourses; you appear as a delinquent; you have not acknowledged the authority of the court; once more they command you to give your positive answer. — Clerk, do your duty.

The King. Duty, Sir!

The clerk reads: —

" Charles Stuart, King of England, you are accused in the behalf of the Commons of England, of divers high crimes and treasons; which charge hath been read unto you: the court now requires you to give your positive and final answer, by way of confession or denial of the charge."

The King. Sir, I say again to you, so that I might give satisfaction to the people of England of the clearness of my proceeding, not by way of answer, not in this way, but to satisfy them that I have done nothing against that trust that hath been committed to me, I would do it: but to acknowledge a new court, against their privileges, to alter the fundamental laws of the kingdom, Sir, you must excuse me.

Bradshaw. Sir, this is the third time that you have publicly disowned this court, and put an affront upon it: how far you have preserved the privileges of the people, your actions have spoke it; but truly, Sir, men's intentions ought to be known by their actions: you have written your meaning in bloody characters throughout the whole kingdom. But, Sir, you understand the pleasure of the court. — Clerk, record the default. — And, gentlemen, you that took charge of the prisoner, take him back again.

The King. I will only say this one word more to you: if it were only my own particular I would not say any more, nor interrupt you.

Bradshaw. Sir, you have heard the pleasure of the court, and you are (notwithstanding you will not understand it) to find that you are before a court of justice.

The King was then conducted away by the guard, and the court, with the ordinary proclamations, adjourned to the Painted Chamber, the cryer calling out, " *God bless the kingdom of England !* "

The court re-assembled on Wednesday the 24th, and resolved to examine certain witnesses against the King in the Painted Chamber. They were accordingly sworn, and sixteen of the commissioners, of whom eleven bore the designation of colonels, were appointed a committee to take the examinations. The court then adjourned till the next day, at nine in the morning, in the Painted Chamber.

The next morning the commissioners having met accordingly in private, it was ordered, that the Dean's house in Westminster Abbey should be provided and furnished for the lodging of Bradshaw, and his guards and attendants. The court being informed that Major Fox of the President's guard was arrested (probably for debt), and confined in Ludgate, it was ordered, that the keeper should forthwith bring him before the court, and also attend himself in person. One Mr. Holder, a prisoner in Whitehall, being brought before the court by the Marshal-general of the army, to give evidence against the King, objected, that his answers would tend to accuse himself, whereupon the commissioners thought fit to wave his examination, and remanded him back to Whitehall.[1] Various witnesses were then examined *privately in the Painted Chamber* against the King, whose depositions were chiefly as follows : — The evidence was directed to the single point of the military movements personally directed and carried on by the King against the parliamentary forces, and the bloodshed thereby occasioned.

January 25. 1649.

William Cuthbert, of Patrington, in Holderness (in the county of York), gent., aged 42 years, saith, that, living at Hull-bridge, near Beverley, in July, 1642, he did then hear that forces

---

[1] This person was the agent to the Prince of Wales then in Holland, and shortly after the King's execution made his escape from Whitehall by the Thames.

were raised, about 3000 foot, for the King's
guard under Sir Robert Strickland: and that
about the 2d of July, 1642, he saw a troop of
horse come to Beverley, being the Lord's day,
about four or five o'clock in the afternoon, called
the Prince's troop; Mr. James Nelthorp being
then major of the said town: and that he did see
that afternoon the said troop march from Beverley
into Holderness, where they received ammunition brought up by the river Humber: and that
the same night, there came about 300 foot
soldiers (said to be Sir Robert Strickland's regiment), under the command of Lieutenant-colonel
Duncombe, and called the King's Guard, unto
this deponent's house, called Hull-bridge, near
Beverley, about midnight, and broke open, and
possessed themselves of the said house; and that
the Earl of Newport, the Earl of Carnarvon, and
divers others, came that night thither to the said
forces: and that the same night Sir Thomas
Gower, then high sheriff of the said county, came
thither, and left a warrant for staying all provisions from going to Hull to Sir John Hotham;
which warrant was then delivered to this deponent, being constable, by Lieutenant-colonel Duncombe: that he was by the said forces put out
of his house, and did with his family go to Beverley; and that after that, viz. the Thursday
following, he did see the King come to Beverley,
to the Lady Gee's house, where he did often see
the King with Prince Charles and the Duke of
York: and that the trained bands were then
raised in Holderness; who were raised (as
was reported) by the King's command: and
that the night after the said forces had possessed

themselves of deponent's house, Colonel Legard's
house was plundered by them, being upon a
Monday; which aforesaid entry of this deponent's
house was the first [1] act of hostility that was committed in those parts: and this deponent saith,
that the warrant he now produceth is the ori-
ginal warrant aforesaid spoken of, and is as followeth: —

" It is his Majesty's command, that you do not
" suffer any victuals or provision, of what sort
" soever, to be carried into the town of Hull,
" without his Majesty's special licence first ob-
" tained. And of this you are not to fail at your
" peril. Tho. Gower, Vi. Co. Dated at Beverley,
" 3 Julij, 1642. To all head constables and con-
" stables in the East Riding of the county of York,
" and to all other his Majesty's loyal subjects."

John Bennet, of Harwood, in the county of
York, glover, saith, that he being a soldier under
the King's command, the first day that the King's
standard was set up at Nottingham, which was
about the middle of summer last was six years,
he did work at Nottingham; and that he did see
the King within the castle, within two or three
days after the standard was so set up; and that
the standard did fly the same day that the King
was in the castle: and that he, and the regiment
of which he then was, had their colours then given
them; and Sir William Penyman, the colonel of
the regiment, was present with his said regiment
at that time: and that there was then there the

---

[1] " Sir John Hotham's keeping Hull as a garrison
against the King, which was before this, was, it seems, no
act of hostility, in this perjured villain's account." — Note
by Nalson, in his report of the trial.

Earl of Lindsey's regiment, who had then their
colours given them, and that the Earl of Lindsey
was then also proclaimed there the King's general:
and that it was proclaimed at the head of every
regiment, that the said forces should fight against
all that came to oppose the King, or any of his
followers ; and in particular against the Earl of
Essex, the Lord Brooke, and divers others : and
that the said Earl of Essex, the Lord Brooke, and
others, were then proclaimed traitors ; and that
the same proclamations were printed and dispersed by the officers throughout every regiment.
And this deponent further saith, that the said
standard was advanced upon the highest tower
of Nottingham Castle ; and that he did see the
King often in Nottingham for the space of one
month ; and that the drums for raising volunteers
to fight under the King's command were then
beaten all the said county over, and divers other
forces were raised there : and that he did take
up arms under the King's command as aforesaid,
for fear of being plundered ; Sir William Penyman giving out that it were a good deed to fire
the said town, because they would not go forth
in the King's service : and that this deponent's
father did thereupon command him to take up
arms as aforesaid, and that divers others did then
also take up arms for the King, for fear of being
plundered. And this deponent further saith, that
in or about the month of October, 1642; he did
see the King at Edge Hill in Warwickshire;
where he, sitting on horseback while his army
was drawn up before him, did speak to the colonel
of every regiment that passed by him, that he

would have them speak to their soldiers to encourage them to stand it, and to fight against the Lord of Essex, the Lord Brooke, Sir William Waller, and Sir William Balfour[1]: and he did see many slain at the fight at Edge Hill, and that afterwards he did see a list brought in unto Oxford, of the men slain in that fight; by which it was reported, that there were slain 6559 men: and afterwards, in or about the month of November, 1642, he did see the King in the head of his army at Hounslow Heath, in Middlesex, Prince Rupert then standing by him; and did then hear the King encourage several regiments of Welshmen in the field, which had run away at Edge Hill, saying unto them, "that he did hope they would regain their honour at Brentford, which they had lost at Edge Hill."

Robert Lacy, of the town and county of Nottingham, painter, deposeth, that he, this deponent, in summer time, in the year 1642, by order from my Lord Beaumont, did paint the standard pole which was set up on the top of the old tower of Nottingham Castle: and he further saith, that he saw the King in the town of Nottingham divers times while the standard was up there, and the flag flying; and the King did lie at the house of my Lord of Clare in Nottingham town.

Samuel Morgan, of Wellington, in the county

---

[1] Nalson, who has left a report of the trial, observes, How is it possible this fellow could swear the King spoke this to every colonel, seeing it was as they passed by? And when his colonel was passed by, he could hear no more.

of Salop, felt-maker, deposeth, that he, this deponent, upon a Sunday morning, in Keynton Field, saw the King upon the top of Edge Hill, in the head of the army, some two hours before the fight, which happened after Michaelmas on a Sunday, the year 1642: and he saw many men killed on both sides in the same time and place and in the year 1644 he saw the King in his army near Cropredy Bridge, where he saw the King light off his horse, and draw up the body of his army in person himself.

James Williams, of Ross, in Herefordshire, shoemaker, deposeth, that he, about October, 1642, saw the King in Keynton Field, below the hill in the field, with his sword drawn in his hand; at which time and place there was a great fight, and many killed on both sides: and he further deposeth, that he saw the King at Brentford on a Sunday, in the forenoon, in November the year aforesaid, while the King's army was in the said town, and round about it.

Samuel Lawson, of Nottingham, maltster, aged 30 years or thereabouts, saith, that about August, 1642, he saw the King's standard brought forth of Nottingham Castle, borne upon divers gentlemen's shoulders, who (as the report was) were noblemen; and he saw the same by them carried to the hill close adjoining to the castle, with a herald before it, and there the said standard was erected with great shoutings, acclamations, and sound of drums and trumpets; and that when the said standard was so erected, there was a proclamation made; and that he saw the King present at the erecting thereof: and the said town was then full of the King's soldiers, of which some quartered in this deponent's house; and that when the King with his said forces went from the said town, the inhabitants of the said town were forced to pay a great sum of money to the King's army, being threatened that, in case they should refuse to pay it, the said town should be plundered.

Arthur Young, citizen and barber-chirurgeon, of London, being aged 29 years or thereabouts, saith, that he was present at the fight at Edge Hill, between the King's army and the parliament's, in October, 1642, and did see the King's standard advanced, and flying in his army in the said fight. And that he did then take the King's said standard in that battle from the King's forces, which was afterwards taken from him by one Middleton, who was afterwards made a colonel.

John Thomas, of Llangollen, in the county of Denbigh, husbandman, aged 25 years, saith, that he saw the King at Brentford, in Middlesex, on a Saturday night at twelve of the clock, soon after Edge Hill fight, attended with horse and foot soldiers, the King being then on horseback, with his sword by his side; and this deponent then heard the King say to the said soldiers, as he was riding through the said town, " Gentlemen, you lost your honour at Edge Hill, I hope you will regain it again here," or words to that effect: and this deponent further saith, that there were some skirmishes between the King's army and the parliament's army, at the same time, both before and after the King spake the said words; and that many men were slain on both sides.

William Jones, of Uske, in the county of Monmouth, husbandman, aged 22 years, saith, that he, this deponent, did see the King within two miles of Naseby Field, the King then coming fromwards Harborough, marching in the head or his army, towards Naseby Field, where the fight was; and that he did then see the King ride up to the regiment which was Colonel St. George's, and did hear the King ask the regiment, "Whether they were willing to fight for him?" To which the soldiers made an acclamation, crying, "All! all!" And this deponent saw the King in Leicester with his forces, the same day that the King's forces had taken it from the parliament's forces; and he saw the King in his army that besieged Gloucester, at the time of the said siege.

Humphry Browne, of Whitsondine, in the county of Rutland, husbandman, aged 22 years or thereabouts, saith, that at such time as the town of Leicester was taken by the King's forces, being in or about June, 1645, Newark Fort in Leicester aforesaid was surrendered to the King's forces, upon composition that neither clothes nor money should be taken away from any of the soldiers of that fort, which had so surrendered, nor any violence offered to them; and that, as soon as the said fort was upon such composition surrendered, the King's soldiers, contrary to the articles, fell upon the soldiers, stripped, cut, and wounded many of them: whereupon one of the King's officers rebuking some of those that did so abuse the said parliament's soldiers, this deponent did hear the King reply, "I do not care if they cut

them three times more, for they are mine enemies," or words to that effect; and that the King
was then on horseback, in bright armour, in the
said town of Leicester.

Gyles Gryce, of Wellington, in Shropshire,
gentleman, sworn and examined, deposeth, that
he saw the King in the head of his army at Cropredy Bridge, with his sword drawn in his hand,
that day when the fight was against Sir William
Waller, on a Friday, in the year 1644, about the
month of July. And he saw the King in the same
summer in Cornwall, in the head of his army, about
Lestwithiel, at such time as the Earl of Essex was
there with his army. And he also saw the King
in the head of his army at the second fight near
Newbury; and in the front of the army in Naseby
Field, having back and breast on. And he saw
the King at the head of the army, at what time
the town of Leicester was stormed; and he saw a
great many men killed on both sides at Leicester,
and many houses plundered.

John Vinson of Damorham, in the county of
Wilts, gentleman, saith, that he did see the King
at the first Newbury fight, about the month of
September, 1643, in the head of his army, where
this deponent did see many slain on both sides.
He did see the King at the second battle at
Newbury, about the month of November, 1644,
where the King was at the head of his army, in
complete armour, with his sword drawn; and did
then see the King lead up Colonel Thomas Howard's regiment of horse, and did hear him make
a speech to the soldiers, to this effect,—" That the
said regiment should stand to him that day, for

that his *crown lay upon the point of the sword;*
and if he lost that day, he lost his honour and
his crown for ever." And that this deponent did
see many slain on both sides at that battle. This
deponent further saith, that he did see the King in
the battle at Naseby Field, in Northamptonshire,
in June, 1645, completely armed with back,
breast, and helmet, and he had his sword drawn,
where the King himself, after his party was routed,
did rally up the horse, and caused them to stand;
and he did see many slain on both sides.

Michael Potts, of Sharpereton, in the county
of Northumberland, vintner, deposeth, that he
saw the King in the head of the army in the fields
about a mile and a half from Newbury town, upon
the heath, the day before the fight was; it being
about harvest-tide, in the year 1643. And that
he saw the King on the day after, when the fight
was, standing near a great piece of ordnance in
the fields. And that he saw the King in the
second Newbury fight in the head of his army,
being after or about Michaelmas, 1644. And
that he saw a great many men slain at both the
said battles. And that he saw the King in the
head of his army, near Cropredy Bridge, in the
year 1644. And he further saith, that he saw
the King in the head of his army, in Cornwall,
near Lestwithiel, while the Earl of Essex lay
there with his forces, about the middle of harvest,
1644.

George Cornwall, of Aston, in the county of
Hereford, ferryman, aged 50 years, saith, that
he did see the King near Cropredy Bridge,
about the time of mowing of corn, 1644, in the

van of the army there; and that he drew up his army upon a hill, and faced the parliament's army; and that there was thereupon a skirmish between the King's and the parliament's army, where he saw divers persons slain on both sides.

Henry Gooche, of Gray's Inn, in the county of Middlesex, gentleman, saith, that, upon or about the 30th day of September last, he was in the Isle of Wight, and had access unto and discourse with the King, by the means of the Lord Marquis of Hertford and Commissary Morgan: where this deponent told the King, that his Majesty had many friends; and that, since his Majesty was pleased to justify the parliament's first taking up arms, the most of the presbyterian party, both soldiers and others, would stick close to him. To which the King answered, that he would have all his old friends know, that though for the present he was contented to give the parliament leave to call their own war what they pleased, yet that he neither did at that time, nor ever should, decline the justice of his own cause. And this deponent told the King, that his business was much retarded, and that neither Colonel Thomas, nor any other, could proceed to action, through want of commission. The King answered, that he being upon a treaty, would not dishonour himself; but that if he, this deponent, would take the pains to go over to the prince, his son (who had full authority from him), he, the said deponent, or any for him, should receive whatsoever commissions should be desired; and to that purpose he would appoint the Marquis of Hertford to write to his son in his name: and was pleased to express much

F

joy and affection, that his good subjects would engage themselves for his restoration.

Robert Williams, of the parish of St. Martin's, in the county of Cornwall, husbandman, aged 23 years, saith, that he, this deponent, did see the King marching in the head of his army, about September, 1644, a mile from Lestwithiel, in Cornwall, in armour, with a short coat over it, unbuttoned. And he saw him after that in St. Austell Downs, drawing up his army. And he did after that see the King in the head of his army near Foy; and that the Earl of Essex and his army did then lie within one mile and a half of the King's army.

Richard Price, of London, scrivener, was produced as a witness to the charge against the King; who, being sworn, saith, that upon occasion of some tampering by the King's agents with the Independents in and about London, to draw them from the parliament's cause to the King's party, and this being discovered by some of those so tampered with, unto sundry members of the committee of safety, who directed a carrying on of a seeming compliance with the King; he, deponent, did travel to Oxford in January, 1643, having a safe-conduct under the King's hand and seal, which he, this deponent, knoweth to be so; for that the King did own it when he was told that this deponent was the man that came to Oxon with that safe-conduct. And this deponent also saith, that, after sundry meetings between him and the Earl of Bristol, about the drawing of the Independents unto the King's cause against the parliament, the substance of the discourse at which meetings, the said earl told this deponent, was communicated to the King; he, this deponent, was by the said earl brought to the King to confer further about that business; where the King declared, that he was very sensible that the Independents had been the most active men in the kingdom for the parliament against him; and thereupon persuaded this deponent to use all means to expedite their turning to him and his cause. And, for their better encouragement, the King promised on the word of a king, that if they, the Independents, would turn to him, and be active for him against the parliament, as they had been active for them against him, then he would grant them whatsoever freedom they would desire. And the King did then refer this deponent unto the Earl of Bristol, for the further prosecuting of the said business. And the said earl thereupon (this deponent being withdrawn from the King) did declare unto this deponent, and willed him to impart the same unto the Independents for their better encouragement, that the King's affairs prospered well in Ireland; that the Irish subjects had given the rebels (meaning the parliament's forces) a great defeat; that the King had sent the Lord Byron with a small party towards Cheshire, and that he was greatly multiplied, and had a considerable army, and was then before Namptwich, and would be strengthened with more soldiers out of Ireland, which were come and expected daily. And when this deponent was to depart out of Oxford, four safe-conducts, with blanks in them for the inserting of what names this deponent pleased, were delivered

F 2

to him, under the King's hand and seal. And one Ogle was sent out of Oxon with this deponent, to treat about the delivering up of Ailesbury to the King, it being then a garrison for the parliament; and at the same time Oxford was a garrison for the King.

The King remaining firm in his rational and dignified denial of the authority of his judges, and the Court having gone through the mockery of the proof of treason exhibited in the above depositions, they now determined on proceeding direct to the object of their whole machinations — the destruction of their prisoner's life. The intercession of his ancient allies, the states of Holland, the entreaties of Charles's queen, and the offer, by Prince Charles, of any conditions to save his father's life, availed nothing either with the degraded parliament or with the ferocious council of the army. Pau, the pensioner of Holland, who was sent ambassador to the parliament with letters, could neither get leave to see the King, nor obtain an audience of the parliament, till the black tragedy was concluded. Henrietta Maria's letter to the speaker of the house contained, says Clarendon, " a very passionate lamentation of the sad condition the King, her husband, was in, desiring that they would grant her a pass to come over to him ; offering to use all the credit she had with him that he might give them satisfaction. However, if they would not give her leave to perform any of those offices towards the public, she prayed that she might be permitted to perform the duty she owed him, and to be near him in the uttermost extremity." This letter was *laid aside, and not read.*[1] The prince, knowing that the parliament was utterly powerless, and prostrate at the feet of the troops, addressed an earnest letter to Fairfax and the council of war, calling on them to choose " whether they would raise lasting monuments to themselves of loyalty and piety, by restoring their sovereign to his just rights, and their country to peace and happiness; or to make themselves the authors of endless misery to the kingdom, by contributing or consenting to an act which all Christians, into how different opinions soever divided, must abhor, as the most inconsistent with the elements of any religion, and destructive to the security and being of any kind of government." This letter was, with much ado, delivered

[1] There is little doubt that Charles owed his death in great measure to the Queen, who had by urgent advice prevented his escaping to the Continent from the Isle of Wight when it was in his power. Whether this was the advice of affection, or whether (as Warburton and Burnet thought, and as Bishop Kennet seems half to suspect) it was given in order to prevent the interruption of her familiar intercourse with Jermyn, is a matter of doubt. — Burnet is positive that the Queen was mother of a child by Jermyn. — On the passage where Clarendon describes the Queen on hearing of her husband's death as suffering " as great a passion of sorrow as she was able to sustain," Warburton makes the remark, " *Ironice.*" — Mademoiselle de Montpensier, describing her visit of condolence to the Queen at the Louvre, says, " Je ne la trouvai pas si sensiblement touchée qu'elle aurait dû l'être par l'amitié que le Roi son mari avait pour elle."— See Ashburnham's Narrative, vol. ii. p. 158.

into the hands of Fairfax, read in the council of war, and laid aside.[1]

At a private sitting, in the Painted Chamber, on the 25th of January, the Court voted a preparatory resolution, " That the Court will proceed to sentence of condemnation against Charles Stuart, King of England; that the condemnation of the King shall be for a tyrant, traitor, and murderer, and likewise for being a public enemy to the commonwealth of England: that this condemnation shall extend to death." A question appears to have been agitated as to the deprivation and deposition of the King, in order to his execution; but it was postponed till a future time, and the commissioners, Scot, Marten, Harrison, Say, Lisle, Ireton, and Love, or any three of them, were ordered to prepare the draft of a final sentence, with a blank for the manner of death. All the members of the Court in or near London were summoned to attend its sitting on the following day.

On the 26th of January the Court met in private, and finally agreed on the sentence, and ordered it to be engrossed. They directed the King to be brought the following day to Westminster Hall, to hear the sentence passed upon him.

On the 27th of January, the commissioners assembled in the morning in the Painted Chamber, when Bradshaw was ordered to manage the

[1] Clarendon, vol. iii. p. 243. This letter was accompanied by a *carte blanche* under the seal and signature of the Prince Charles; in which any conditions might be inserted, provided his father's life were spared.

discourse between himself and the King, according to his discretion, with the advice of his two assistants. In case the King should change his conduct, and submit to the Court's jurisdiction, the commissioners determined to withdraw and advise; which course they also resolved to adopt in case the King should offer any thing else worth the Court's consideration. If the King should not submit to answer, and no occasion should arise for the Court's withdrawing, Bradshaw was to order the sentence to be read; having heard what the King desired to say before the sentence, but not after it. The Court then deliberated on the question, whether Bradshaw should address any speech to the King before the sentence, according to the practice observed in the case of other condemned malefactors. It was left to him to use his discretion, and urge such matter as seemed suitable to the occasion.

The Court then adjourned into Westminster Hall, in the afternoon, with the accustomed ceremonies; the King entered the court in his usual manner, with his hat on, when some of the soldiers (who were instigated by Axtell and other officers) began to cry aloud for " Justice! Justice! Execution!" Silence was at length enforced by the guards. The King, seeing Bradshaw in his scarlet robes and full costume, and hearing the shouts of the soldiers, readily perceived that sentence was about to be pronounced on him; he therefore addressed the Court with earnestness.

The King. I desire a word to be heard a little, and I hope I shall give no occasion of interruption.

Bradshaw. You may answer in your time; hear the Court first.

The King. If it please you, Sir, I desire to be heard, and I shall not give any occasion of interruption, and it is only in a word. A sudden judgment ——

Bradshaw. Sir, you shall be heard in due time; but you are to hear the Court first.

The King. Sir, I desire — it will be in order to what I believe the Court will say; Sir, an hasty judgment is not so soon recalled.

Bradshaw. Sir, you shall be heard before the judgment be given; and in the mean time you may forbear.

The King. Well, Sir, shall I be heard before the judgment be given?

Bradshaw. Gentlemen, it is well known to you that the prisoner at the bar hath been several times brought before this Court to make answer to a charge of treason, and other high crimes exhibited against him in the name of the people of England [here a lady interposed, saying aloud, " Not half the people ;" but she was silenced with threats [1]]; to which charge being required to answer, he hath been so far from obeying the commands of the Court, as he began to take upon him to offer reasoning and debate unto the authority of the Court, and of that highest Court that constituted them to try and judge him : but being over-ruled in that, he was still pleased to continue contumacious, and to refuse to submit or answer. Hereupon the Court, that they might not be wanting to themselves, to the trust reposed

[1] See the trial of Daniel Axtell, Oct. 15. 1660. — State Trials, vol. v.

in them, nor that any man's wilfulness prevent justice, have considered of the charge — they have considered of the contumacy, and of that confession which in law doth arise upon that contumacy : — they have likewise considered of the notoriety[1] of the fact charged upon this prisoner ; and upon the whole matter they are resolved, and are agreed upon a sentence to be pronounced against this prisoner. But in respect he doth desire to be heard, before the sentence be read and pronounced, the Court hath resolved that they will hear him. Yet, Sir, thus much I must tell you beforehand, that if that which you have to say be to offer any debate concerning the jurisdiction, you are not to be heard in it; you have offered it formerly, and you struck at the root, that is, the power and supreme authority of the Commons of England, which this Court will not admit a debate of. But, Sir, if you have any thing to say in defence of yourself concerning the matter charged, the Court hath given me in command to tell you they will hear you.

The King. Since I see that you will not hear any thing of debate concerning that which, I confess, I thought most material for the peace of the kingdom, and for the liberty of the subject, I shall wave it ; I shall speak nothing to it ; but only I must tell you, that this many a day all things have been taken away from me, but that I call more dear to me than my life, which is my conscience and my honour : and if I had a respect

---

[1] Bradshaw, who was a lawyer, does not venture to allude to the *evidence*. He considered even the vague and absurd ground of " notoriety " as a safer basis to proceed upon than the mockery of evidence which is above stated.

to my life more than the peace of the kingdom and the liberty of the subject, certainly I should have made a particular defence for myself; for by that at leastwise I might have delayed an ugly sentence, which I believe will pass upon me. Therefore, certainly, Sir, as a man that hath some understanding, some knowledge of the world, if that my true zeal to my country had not overborne the care that I have for my own preservation, I should have gone another way to work than that I have done. Now, Sir, I conceive that an hasty sentence once passed, may sooner be repented of than recalled; and truly, the self-same desire that I have for the peace of the kingdom, and the liberty of the subject, more than my own particular ends, makes me now at last desire, before sentence be given, that I may be heard in the Painted Chamber before the Lords and Commons. This delay cannot be prejudicial to you, whatsoever I say; if that I say no reason, those that hear me must be judges: if it be reason, and really for the welfare of the kingdom, and the liberty of the subject, I am sure it is very well worth the hearing; therefore I do conjure you, as you love that that you pretend,—I hope it is real,—the liberty of the subject, the peace of the kingdom, that you will grant me this hearing before any sentence be past. I only desire this, that you will take this into your consideration, it may be you have not heard of it beforehand; if you will, I'll retire, and you may think of it: but if I cannot get this liberty, I do protest, that these fair shows of liberty and peace are pure shows, and that you will not hear your King.

Bradshaw.   Sir, you have now spoken.

The King.   Yes, Sir.

Bradshaw.   And this that you have said is a further declining of the jurisdiction of this Court, which was the thing wherein you were limited before.

The King.   Pray excuse me, Sir, for my interruption, because you mistake me ; it is not a declining of it, you do judge me before you hear me speak.

Bradshaw.   I understand you well, Sir ; but nevertheless that which you have offered seems to be contrary to that saying of yours ; for the Court are ready to give a sentence ; it is not, as you say, that they will not hear their King ; for they have been ready to hear you, they have patiently waited your pleasure for three courts together, to hear what you would say to the people's charge against you, to which you have not vouchsafed to give any answer at all.   Sir, this tends to a further delay.   Truly, Sir, such delays as these neither may the kingdom nor justice well bear : you have had three several days to have offered in this kind what you would have pleased.   This Court is founded upon that authority of the Commons of England, in whom rests the supreme jurisdiction ; that which you now tender, is to have another jurisdiction, and a co-ordinate jurisdiction.

This entreaty of the King to be heard in the Painted Chamber was supposed to relate to a proposal, which he desired to make, for abdicating the crown in favour of his eldest son.   Bradshaw was proceeding in his usual harsh and verbose strain to refuse the King's demand.   But the re-

quest, which was urged "with the greatest earnestness, and yet in no unseemly passion," had gone
to the heart and the conscience of one among the
regicides on the bench, John Downes. He was
sitting between William Cawley and Colonel Valentine Wauton, the brother-in-law of Cromwell.
He became agitated as Bradshaw was refusing the
King's petition, and said repeatedly to his neigh-
bours, " Have we hearts of stone ? are we men ? "
Cromwell, who sat on the bench below, hearing
his words, looked sternly at him, and asked him
what he meant to do, that he could not be quiet.
Downes rose, and said in a trembling voice, "My
Lord, I am not satisfied to give my consent to this
sentence, but have reasons to offer to you against
it ; and I desire the Court may adjourn to hear
me." The President was surprised, — the members gazed on Downes, — and the Court adjourned
in some disorder.

The King. Shall I withdraw ?

Bradshaw. Sir, you shall know the pleasure
of the Court presently.

The Court then withdrew into the inner Court
of Wards, where Cromwell immediately called
on Downes to give an account why he had
occasioned this trouble and disturbance in the
Court. Downes urged that it was just and humane to hear the King's proposition ; that they
would never be justified if they passed sentence
on the King without hearing him fully ; and that
no judge at an assize would do so against even a
common person. According to Downes's own
account, " Cromwell did answer with a great deal
of storm." He said, " Sure the gentleman did
not know that they had to do with the hardest-

hearted man upon earth ; and that it was not fit
the Court should be hindered from their duty by
one peevish man." The members of the Court,
after some debate, resolved to proceed, without
regarding the King's request. Downes went into
the Speaker's chamber, as he says, " to ease his
heart with tears;" and the regicides returned
into the hall.[1] Which done, Bradshaw commanded — " Serjeant-at-arms, send for your prisoner." The King, who had passed the time of
his absence in a conference for more than half an
hour with Bishop Juxon, returned to his seat in
the Hall.

Bradshaw. Sir, you were pleased to make
a motion here to the Court, to offer a desire
of yours, touching the propounding of somewhat to the Lords and Commons in the Painted
Chamber, for the peace of the kingdom. Sir,
you did, in effect, receive an answer before the
Court adjourned; truly, Sir, their withdrawing
and adjournment was *pro formâ tantum;* for
it did not seem to them that there was any difficulty in the thing : they have considered of what
you have moved, and have considered of their own

---

[1] Whitlock says, that many of the commissioners were
for hearing the King, but the majority voted that his proposal tended to delay. Colonel Harvey and several other
commissioners thereupon withdrew from the Court, and
never again attended it. Downes was a citizen of London, of low birth, and timid disposition. Notwithstanding
the tenderness of conscience which he displayed in the above
scene, he had not firmness to continue his resistance to the
proceedings, and he signed the warrant for the King's death.
His life was spared, when he was found guilty, with the other
regicides ; and he died in prison See the Trial of the
Regicides, State Trials, vol. v.

authority.   Sir, the return I have to you from the
Court is this : That they have been too much delayed by you already, and this that you now offer
hath occasioned some little further delay ; and
they are judges appointed by the highest authority; and judges are no more to delay than they
are to deny justice : they are good words in the
great old charter of England : — "Nulli negabi-
mus, nulli vendemus, nulli differemus justitiam." *
There must be no delay ; but the truth is, Sir, and
so every man here observes it, that you have much
delayed them in your contempt and default, for
which they might long since have proceeded to
judgment against you ; and, notwithstanding what
you have offered, they are resolved to proceed
to punishment and to judgment, and that is their
unanimous resolution.

The King.   Sir, I know it is in vain for me to
dispute ; I am no sceptic for to deny the power
that you have ; I know that you have power
enough.   But, Sir, I think it would have been
for the kingdom's peace, if you would have taken
the pains to have shown the lawfulness of your
power.   For this delay that I have desired, it is a
delay very important for the peace of the kingdom : for it is not my person that I look at
alone, it is the kingdom's welfare, and the
kingdom's peace.   It is an old sentence, That
we should think on long before we resolve
of great matters.   Therefore, Sir, I do put at
your doors all the inconveniency of a hasty
sentence.   I have been here now, I think, this

* Did Bradshaw forget that the Great Charter declared
that no man should be judged except by his peers, or according to the laws of the land ?

week; this day eight days was the day I came here first, — but a little delay of a day or two farther may give peace; whereas a hasty judgment may bring on that trouble and perpetual inconveniency to the kingdom, that the child that is unborn may repent it; and therefore again, out of the duty I owe to God and to my country, I do desire that I may be heard by the Lords and Commons in the Painted Chamber, or any other chamber that you will appoint me.

Bradshaw. Sir, you have been already answered to what you even now moved, being the same you moved before; and the Court now requires to know whether you have any more to say for yourself than you have said, before they proceed to sentence.

The King. I say this, Sir, that if you hear me, if you will give me but this delay, I doubt not but I shall give some satisfaction to you all here, and to my people after that; and therefore I do require you, as you will answer it at the dreadful day of judgment, that you consider it once again.

Bradshaw. Sir, I have received direction from the Court.

The King. Well, Sir.

Bradshaw. If this must be re-enforced, your answer must be the same; and they will proceed to sentence, if you have nothing more to say.

The King. Sir, I have nothing more to say! but I shall desire that this may be entered what I have said.

Bradshaw. The Court then, Sir, hath something to say unto you; which, although I know it will be very unacceptable, yet notwithstanding

they are willing, and are resolved to discharge
their duty.

Sir, you speak very well of a precious thing
which you call peace ; and it had been much to be
wished that God had put it into your heart that
you had as effectually and really endeavoured and
studied the peace of the kingdom, as now in words
you seem to pretend : but, as you were told the
other day, actions must expound intentions ; yet
actions have been clean contrary. And truly,
Sir, you have held yourself, and let fall such
language, as if you had been no way subject to the
law, or that the law had not been your superior.
Sir, the Court is very sensible of it, and I hope so
are all the understanding people of England, that
the law is your superior ; that you ought to have
ruled according to the law. Sir, I know very
well your pretence that you have done so ; but,
Sir, the difference hath been who shall be the ex-
positors of this law : Sir, whether you and your
party, out of courts of justice, shall expound law,
or the courts of justice, who are the expounders :
nay, the sovereign and the high court of justice,
the parliament of England, that are not only the
highest expounders, but the sole makers of the
law. Sir, for you to set yourself, and those that
adhere unto you, against the highest court of
justice, that is not law. Sir, as the law is your
superior, so truly, Sir, there is something that is
superior to the law, and that is indeed the parent
or author of the law, *the people of England:*
for, Sir, as they are those that at the first did
choose to themselves this form of government,
even for justice sake, so, Sir, they gave laws to

their governors, according to which they should govern; and if those laws should have proved prejudicial to the public, they had a power in them to alter as they should see cause. Sir, it is very true that some of your side have said, " Rex non habet parem in regno." This Court will say the same, while King, that you have not your peer in some sense, for you are *major singulis;* but they will aver again that you are *minor universis.* And the same author tells you, that " non debet esse major eo in regno suo in exhibitione juris, minimus autem esse debet in judicio suscipiendo." [1]

This we know to be law, " Rex habet superiorem, Deum et legem, etiam et curiam ;" so says the same author. And truly, Sir, he makes bold to go a little further; " Debent ei ponere frœnum : " they ought to bridle him. " Justitiæ fruendi causa reges constituti sunt." This we learn: the end of having kings, or any other governors, it is for the enjoying of justice; that is the end. Now, Sir, if so be the king will go contrary to that end of his government, Sir, he must understand that he is but an officer in trust, and he ought to discharge that trust; and they are to take order for the punishment of such an offending governor.

This is not law of yesterday, Sir, but it is law of old. And we know very well the authors and the authorities that do tell us what the law was in that point upon the election of kings, upon the oath that they took unto their people: and if they did not observe it, there were those things called parliaments; the parliaments were they

[1] Bract. de Leg. lib. i. c. 8.

that were to adjudge (the very words of the author) the plaints and wrongs done of the king and the queen, or their children ; such wrongs especially, when the people could have nowhere else any remedy. Sir, that hath been the people of England's case : they could not have their remedy elsewhere but in parliament. Sir, parliaments were ordained for that purpose, to redress the grievances of the people. Sir, by the old laws of England, I speak these things the rather to you, because you were pleased to let fall the other day, you thought you had as much knowledge in the law as most gentlemen in England. It is very well, Sir. And truly, Sir, it is very fit for the gentlemen of England to understand that law under which they must live, and by which they must be governed. And then, Sir, the Scripture says, " They that know their master's will, and do it not :" what follows ? The law is your master, the acts of parliament.

The parliaments were to be kept anciently, we find in our old author, twice in the year, that the subject upon any occasion might have a ready redress for his grievance. Afterwards, by several acts of parliament in the days of your predecessor Edward III., they should have been once a year. Sir, what the intermission of parliaments hath been in your time, it is very well known, and the sad consequences of it : and what in the interim instead of these parliaments hath been by you by an high and arbitrary hand introduced upon the people, that likewise hath been too well known and felt. But when God, by his providence, had so far brought it about, that you could no longer decline the calling of a parliament, Sir, yet it will appear what your ends were against the ancient and your native kingdom of Scotland: the parliament of England not serving your ends against them, you were pleased to dissolve it. Another great necessity occasioned the calling of this parliament: and what your designs, and plots, and endeavours all along have been, for the crushing and confounding of this parliament, hath been very notorious to the whole kingdom. And truly, Sir, in that you did strike at all; that had been a sure way to have brought about that that this charge lays upon you, your intention to subvert the fundamental laws of the land: for the great bulwark of the liberties of the people is the parliament of England; and to subvert and root up that, which your aim hath been to do, certainly at one blow you had confounded the liberties and the property of England.

Truly, Sir, it makes me to call to mind—I cannot forbear to express it; for, Sir, we must deal plainly with you —it makes me call to mind that we read of a great Roman emperor, (by the way, let us call him a great Roman tyrant,) that Caligula, that wished that the people of Rome had had but one neck, that at one blow he might cut it off. And your proceedings have been somewhat like to this: for the body of the people of England hath been (and where else) represented but in the parliament; and could you but have confounded that, you had at one blow cut off the neck of England. But God hath pleased for to confound your designs, and to break your forces, and to bring your person into custody, that you might be responsible to justice.

Sir, we know very well that it is a question much on your side pressed, by what precedent we shall proceed? Truly, Sir, for precedents, I shall not upon these occasions institute any long discourse; but it is no new thing to cite precedents almost of all nations, where the people (when power hath been in their hands) have made bold to call their kings to account; and where the change of government hath been upon occasion of the tyranny and misgovernment of those that have been placed over them, I will not spend time to mention either France, or Spain, or the empire, or other countries; volumes may be written of it. But truly, Sir, that of the kingdom of Aragon, I shall think some of us have thought upon it, where they have the justice of Aragon [1], that is, a man *tanquam in medio positus*, betwixt the King of Spain and the people of the country; that if wrong be done by the king, he that is King of Aragon, the justice hath power to reform the wrong; and he is acknowledged to be the king's superior, and is the grand preserver of their privileges, and hath prosecuted kings upon their miscarriages.

Sir, what the tribunes of Rome were heretofore, and what the ephori were to the Lacedæ-

[1] Without noticing the absurdity of justifying the dethronement and slaughter of an English King by a precedent from Spain, Bradshaw's instance is singularly inapplicable. The authority of the Justice of Aragon was a part of the Spanish constitution, whereas the English constitution had provided no judicial power having jurisdiction over the King.

monian state, we know that is the parliament of
England to the English state: and though Rome
seemed to lose its liberty when once the em-
perors were; yet you shall find some famous acts
of justice even done by the senate of Rome; that
great tyrant of his time, Nero, condemned and
judged by the senate. But truly, Sir, to you I
should not need to mention these foreign examples. If you look but over Tweed, we find
enough in your native kingdom of Scotland. If
we look to your first king, Fergus, that your
stories make mention of, he was an elective king;
he died, and left two sons, both in their minority;
the kingdom made choice of their uncle, his brother, to govern in the minority. Afterwards the
elder brother, giving small hopes to the people
that he would rule or govern well, seeking to sup-
plant that good uncle of his that governed them
justly, they set the elder aside, and took to the
younger. Sir, if I should come to what your
stories make mention of, you know very well you
are the hundred and ninth King of Scotland; for
not to mention so many kings as that kingdom
according to their power and privilege, have made
bold to deal withal, some to banish, and some to
imprison, and some to put to death, it would be
too long; and as one of your own authors says,
it would be too long to recite the manifold examples that your own stories make mention of.
Reges, &c. (say they) we do create; we created
kings at first: *leges*, &c. we imposed laws upon
them. And we will be bold to say, that no kingdom hath yielded more plentiful experience than
that your native kingdom of Scotland hath done

concerning the deposition and the punishment of their transgressing kings, &c.

It is not far to go for an example : near you your grandmother set aside, and your father, an infant, crowned. And the state did it here in England : here hath not been a·want of some examples. They have made bold (the parliament and the people of England) to call their kings to account : there are frequent examples of it in the Saxons' time, the time before the Conquest. Since the Conquest there want not some precedents neither. King Edward II., King Richard II. were dealt with so by the parliament, as they were deposed and deprived.[1] And truly, Sir, who-

[1] There is far more pedantry than discretion in all Bradshaw's references to history for precedents. What must have been the president's estimation of the proceedings against Charles, when he could seek to justify them by the violent expulsion of Edward the Second, by his adulterous wife, her paramour and his own son, for no crime but weakness of character? As to the deposition of Richard, if that was to be cited as analogous, at least the President and his party should have acted according to it — they should simply have deposed the King, as Richard was deposed, by an act of both Houses, have preserved the constitution, and vested the Crown in the next successor. And they should have done this by a direct and manful charge against the King, of those violations of the constitution, and stretches of the prerogative, which were complained of, instead of jesuitically and inhumanly putting him on his trial for *treason* and *murder*, on account of blood shed in open and equal warfare. The depositions of Edward and Richard at least could afford no precedent for the destruction of the constitution, the abolition of the monarchy and the peerage, nor for the slaughter of the King — unless, indeed, Bradshaw intended (which can hardly be supposed,) to liken himself and

ever shall look into their stories, they shall not find the articles that are charged upon them to come near to that height and capitalness of crimes that are laid to your charge — nothing near.

Sir, you were pleased to say, the other day, wherein they dissent; and I did not contradict it. But take altogether, Sir: if you were as the charge speaks, and no otherwise, admitted King of England: but for that you were pleased then to allege, how that for almost a thousand years these things have been, stories will tell you, if you go no higher than the time of the Conquest; if you do come down since the Conquest, you are the twenty-fourth king from William called the Conqueror; you shall find one half of them to come merely from the state, and not merely upon the point of descent. It were easy to be instanced to you; but time must not be lost that way. And, Sir, your oath, the manner of your coronation, doth show plainly, that although it is true, by the law the next person in blood is designed; yet if there were just cause to refuse him, the people of England might do it. For there is a contract and a bargain made between the king and his people, and your oath is taken; and certainly, Sir, the bond is reciprocal; for as you are the liege lord, so they liege subjects. *Ligeantia est duplex.* The one tie, the one bond, is the bond of protection that is due from the sovereign; the other is the bond of subjection that is due from the subject.

---

his accomplices to Matravers and Piers Exton, and to justify the bloody scene before Whitehall by the atrocities of Berkeley Castle and of Pontefract.

Sir, if this bond be once broken[1], farewell sove-
reignty ! *Subjectio trahit*, &c.

These things may not be denied, Sir; and I
pray God it may work upon your heart, that you
may be sensible of your miscarriages. For
whether you have been, as by your office you
ought to be, a protector of England, or the destroyer of England, let all England judge, or all
the world that hath looked upon it.[2] Sir, though
you have it by inheritance in the way that is
spoken of, yet your office was an office of trust,
and, indeed, an office of the highest trust lodged
in any single person: for as you were the grand
administrator of justice, and others were as your
delegates to see it done throughout your realms;
if your greatest office were to do justice, and
preserve your people from wrong, and instead of
doing that, you will be the great wrong-doer
yourself; if, instead of being a conservator of the
peace, you will be the grand disturber of the
peace; surely, this is contrary to your office,
contrary to your trust. Now, Sir, if it be an
office of inheritance, as you speak of your title
by descent, let all men know that great offices
are seizable and forfeitable, as if you had it but
for a year, and for your life. Therefore, Sir, it
will concern you to take into your serious consideration your great miscarriages in this kind.

---

[1] Whether Charles or the republican faction broke this
bond was the real question between him and the nation. Into
this question Bradshaw dared not enter.

[2] This republican lawyer, whenever he descends from
his pedantic generalities to any allusion to the King's *acts*,
conveniently treats *notoriety* as equivalent to proof.

Truly, Sir, I shall not particularise the many miscarriages of your reign. It had been happy for the kingdom, and happy for you too, if it had not been so much known, and so much felt, as the story of your miscarriages must needs be, and hath been already.

Sir, that which we are now upon, by the command of the highest court, hath been and is to try and judge you for these great offences of yours. Sir, the charge hath called you *tyrant*, a *traitor*, a *murderer*, and a *public enemy* to the commonwealth of England. Sir, it had been well if that any of all these terms might rightly and justly have been spared.

The King. Ha!

Bradshaw. Truly, Sir, we have been told, " Rex est dum benè regit, tyrannus qui populum opprimit :" and if so be, that be the definition of a *tyrant*, then see how you come short of it in your actions, whether the highest *tyrant*, by that way of arbitrary government, and that you have sought for to introduce, and that you were putting upon the people,—whether that was not as high an act of *tyranny* as any of your predecessors were guilty of, nay, many degrees beyond it.

Sir, the term *traitor* cannot be spared. We shall easily agree it must denote and suppose a breach of trust; and it must suppose it to be done to a superior. And, therefore, Sir, as the people of England might have incurred that respecting you, if they had been truly guilty of it, as to the definition of law; so, on the other side, when you did break your trust to the kingdom,

you did break your trust to your superior: for
the kingdom is that for which you were trusted.
And, therefore, Sir, for this breach of trust when
you are called to account, you are called to account by your superiors. " Minimus ad majorem
in judicium vocat." And, Sir, the people 'of
England cannot be so far wanting to themselves,
(God having dealt so miraculously and gloriously
for them); but that, having power in their hands,
and their great enemy, they must proceed to do
justice to themselves and to you: for, Sir, the
Court could heartily desire, that you would lay
your hand upon your heart, and consider what
you have done amiss, that you would endeavour
to make your peace with God. Truly, Sir, these
are your high crimes, tyranny and treason.

There is a third thing, too, if those had not
been, and that is *murder*, which is laid to your
charge. All the *bloody murders* which have been
committed since this time that the division was
betwixt you and your people, must be laid to
your charge, which have been acted or committed in these late wars.[1]   Sir, it is an heinous
and crying sin; and truly, Sir, if any man will
ask us what punishment is due to a murderer,
let God's law, let man's law, speak.   Sir, I will

[1] This is a compendious mode of evading, by a confident assertion, the real difficulty which lay on the King's
judges — that of showing him to be in any legal, or even
any moral, sense responsible for the blood shed in the war.
Bradshaw having assumed this point, boldly cites the
scriptural denunciations against " *murder*," not choosing
to see that these canons of God's law and man's law forcibly
and directly applied to the act in which he and his accomplices were engaged.

presume that you are so well read in Scripture, as to know what God himself hath said concerning the shedding of man's blood: Gen. ix., Numb. xxxv., will tell you what the punishment is, and which this Court, in behalf of the whole kingdom, are sensible of, of that innocent blood that has been shed, whereby, indeed, the land stands still defiled with that blood; and, as the text hath it, it can no way be cleansed but with the shedding of the blood of him that shed this blood. Sir, we know no dispensation from this blood in that commandment, " Thou shalt do no murder :" we do not know but that it extends to kings as well as to the meanest peasants: the command is universal. Sir, God's law forbids it; man's law forbids it; nor do we know that there is any manner of exception, not even in man's laws, for the punishment of murder in you. It is true, that in the case of kings every private hand was not to put forth itself to this work. But, Sir, the people represented having power in their hands, had there been but one wilful act of murder by you committed, had power to have convened you, and to have punished you for it.

But then, Sir, the weight that lies upon you n all those respects that have been spoken, by reason of your tyranny, treason, breach of trust, and the murders that have been committed; surely, Sir, it must drive you into a sad consideration concerning your eternal condition. As I said at first, I know it cannot be pleasing to you to hear any such things as these are mentioned unto you from this Court, for so we do call ourselves, and justify ourselves to be a Court, and

a high court of justice, authorised by the
highest and solemnest court of the kingdom;
and although you do yet endeavour to discourt
us, yet we do take knowledge of ourselves to be
such a Court as can administer justice to you;
and we are bound, Sir, in duty to do it.   Sir, all
I shall say before the reading of your sentence,
it is but this: the Court does heartily desire
that you will seriously think of those evils that
you stand guilty of.   Sir, you said well to us the
other day, you wished us to have God before
our eyes.   Truly, Sir, I hope all of us have so:
that God who we know is a King of kings, and
Lord of lords; that God with whom there is no
respect of persons; that God who is the avenger
of innocent blood; we have that God before us,
— that God who does bestow a curse upon them
that withhold their hands from shedding of blood,
which is in the case of guilty malefactors, and
that do deserve death: that God we have before
our eyes.   And were it not that the conscience
of our duty hath called us unto this place, and
this employment, Sir, you should have had no
appearance of a Court here.   But, Sir, we must
prefer the discharge of our duty unto God, and
unto the kingdom, before any other respect
whatsoever. And although at this time many of
us, if not all of us, are severely threatened by
some of your party, what they intend to do,
Sir, we will say, and we will declare it, as those
children in the fiery furnace, that would not
worship the golden image that Nebuchadnezzar
had set up, " that their God was able to deliver
them from that danger that they were near unto:"

but yet if he would not do it, yet they would not fall down and worship the image. We shall thus apply it; that though we should not be delivered from those bloody hands and hearts that conspire the overthrow of the kingdom, though we should perish in the work, yet by God's grace, and by God's strength, we will go on with it. And this is all our resolutions. Sir, I say for yourself, we do heartily wish and desire that God would be pleased to give you a sense of your sins, that you would see wherein you have done amiss, that you may cry unto him, that God would deliver you from blood-guiltiness. A good king was once guilty of that particular thing, and was clear otherwise, saving in the matter of Uriah. Truly, Sir, the story tells us that he was a repentant king; and it signifies enough that he had died for it, but that God was pleased to accept of him, and to give him his pardon, " Thou shalt not die, but the child shall die: thou hast given cause to the enemies of God to blaspheme."

The King. I would desire only one word before you give sentence; I desire that you would hear me concerning those great imputations that you have laid to my charge.

Bradshaw. Sir, you must give me now leave to go on; for I am not far from your sentence, and your time is now past.

The King. But I shall desire you will hear me a few words to you: for truly, whatever sentence you will put upon me in respect of those heavy imputations, that I see by your speech you have put upon me; Sir, it is very true, that ——

Bradshaw. Sir, I must put you in mind.

Truly, Sir, I would not willingly, at this time especially, interrupt you in any thing you have to say, that is proper for us to admit of; but, Sir, you have not owned us as a Court, and *you look upon us as a sort of people met together;* and we *know what language we receive from your party.*[1]

The King. I know nothing of that.

Bradshaw. You disavow us as a Court; and therefore for you to address yourself to us, not acknowledging us as a Court to judge of what you say, it is not to be permitted. And the truth is, all along, from the first time you were pleased to disavow and disown us, the Court needed not to have heard you one word: for unless they be acknowledged a Court, and engaged, it is not proper for you to speak. Sir, we have given you too much liberty already, and admitted of too much delay, and we may not admit of any further. Were it proper for us to do it, we should hear you freely; and we should not have declined to hear you at large, what you could have said or proved on your behalf, whether for totally excusing, or for in part excusing those great and heinous charges that in whole or in part are laid upon you. But, Sir, I shall trouble you no longer; your sins are of so large a dimension, that if you do but seriously think of them, they may improve in you a sad and serious repentance; and that the Court doth heartily wish that

---

[1] To men who must have been conscious of the utter want of lawful authority for their acts, the King's determined denial of their jurisdiction must not only have occasioned much difficulty in their proceedings, but must have inflicted an unpardonable wound on their pride, and a sting on their consciences.

you may be so penitent for what you have done
amiss, that God may have mercy, at least-wise,
upon your better part: truly, Sir, for the other,
it is our part and duties to do that which the
law prescribes. We are here not *jus dare*, but
jus dicere. We cannot be unmindful of what the
Scripture tells us, " For to acquit the guilty is of
equal abomination as to condemn the innocent:"
we may not acquit the guilty. What sentence
the law affirms to a traitor, tyrant, a murderer,
and a public enemy to the country, that sentence
you are now to hear read unto you; and that is
the sentence of the Court.

Make an O-yes, and command silence while
the sentence is read.—Which done,

The clerk read the sentence. It recited
the act of the Commons establishing the Court,
and the charge exhibited before it against the
King; his Majesty's refusal to answer, or to admit
the Court's jurisdiction; that the Court had therefore given judgment against him for his contumacy, but, for further and clearer satisfaction,
had examined witnesses on oath touching the
charge; and it alleged that, on mature deliberation of the premises, and consideration had of
the notoriety of the matters of fact charged on
the prisoner, the Court was in conscience satisfied
that the said Charles Stuart was guilty of levying
war against the parliament and people, and by
the general course of his government, counsels,
and practices before and since the parliament
began (which had been and are notorious and
public), the Court was fully satisfied in their consciences that he was guilty of the wicked designs

and endeavours in the charge set forth ; and that
he had been, and was, the occasioner, author,
and continuer of the said unnatural, cruel, and
bloody wars, and therein guilty of high treason,
and of the murders, rapines, burnings, spoils, de-
solations, damages, and mischiefs to this nation
acted and committed in the said war, and occasioned thereby. " For all which treasons and
crimes this Court doth adjudge that he, the said
Charles Stuart, as a tyrant, traitor, murderer,
and public enemy to the good people of this nation, shall be put to death, by severing his head
from his body."

Bradshaw then said, — " The sentence now read
and published is the act, sentence, judgment, and
resolution of the whole Court ;" to which all the
commissioners expressed their assent by standing
up, as had been before arranged in the Painted
Chamber. The King, who during the reading of
the sentence had smiled, and more than once lifted
his eyes to heaven, then said, " Will you hear
me a word, Sir ?"

Bradshaw.   Sir, you are not to be heard after
the sentence.

The King.   No, Sir ?

Bradshaw. No, Sir, by your favour. Guards,
withdraw your prisoner.

The King.   I may speak after the sentence,
by your favour, Sir. I may speak after the sentence, *ever*. By your favour——

Bradshaw.   Hold !

The King.   The sentence, Sir. I say, Sir, I
do——

Bradshaw.   Hold !

The King. I am not suffered to speak. *Expect what justice the people will have!*" [1]

As the King uttered these words, he was removed from the Court by the guard. In passing down into the Hall he was compelled to endure the insults and scoffs of a few of the soldiers. Some cast the smoke of their tobacco into his face (an odour peculiarly disgusting to him at all times); others threw their pipes in his way; and one inhuman wretch had the brutality to spit in his Majesty's face [2], of which he took no notice, but calmly wiped his face with his handkerchief. As he passed along, hearing the rabble and the soldiery crying out "Justice! Justice! Execution!" (to which they were instigated by Colonel Axtell and other officers [3],) he mildly said to Herbert, his attendant, "Poor souls! for a piece of money they would do the same for their commanders." He was first conducted as usual to Sir Robert Cotton's, but was immediately removed from thence in a sedan chair, with a strong guard, by the Privy Gardens, to Whitehall, where he remained till the night before his execution, when

[1] Ludlow, one of the most determined of the regicides, apologises for silencing the King after the sentence by a legal fiction absurdly misapplied. " The King would have spoken something before he was withdrawn : but, being *accounted dead in law* immediately after sentence pronounced, it was not permitted."—Memoirs, p. 121.

[2] See Trials of the Regicides, State Trials, vol. v.

[3] Augustine Garland, one of the commissioners (an Essex man, elected member of parliament in 1648,) who signed the King's sentence, and who was tried and hanged in 1660 for this treason, was charged with committing this brutal indignity; but he solemnly denied it; and the evidence is not very conclusive.

he slept at St. James's. Sir Thomas Herbert, who was with Charles, says the files of soldiers through which he passed were silent; but the stalls, shops, and windows were filled with people, many of whom shed tears, and many with an audible voice prayed for the King. One soldier, unlike his companions, called to the King, " God bless you, Sir !" for which sin his officer struck him repeatedly with his cane. On which the King observed, " Methinks the punishment exceeds the offence."

On the evening of the day on which he received sentence (Saturday, the 27th of January,) the King sent a message to the commissioners, desiring that his children might be brought to him, and that Dr. Juxon, Bishop of London, might attend to read and pray with him, and to administer the holy sacrament to him; which requests were, with some little hesitation, granted. On Sunday, the 28th, he was attended by a guard from Whitehall to St. James's, where the Bishop of London preached before him on these words (Romans, ii. 16.): " In the day when God shall judge the secrets of all men by Jesus Christ, according to my gospel." After the service the King received the sacrament; and he spent the rest of the day in private devotion, and in conferences with the bishop, declining to admit any visiters, even the Prince Elector, the Duke of Richmond, the Marquis of Hertford, and others, who came to pay their last duties to their monarch. The King said, " My time is short and precious; I hope they will not take it ill that none have access to me but my children. The best office they can now do me is to pray for me." The next day Charles underwent the cruel pang of separating from his two children (who alone were in England), Henry Duke of Gloucester, who was about seven years of age, and the Princess‑ Elizabeth, who was about thirteen.[1] Their interview with him was long, tender, and afflicting ; and evinced not more the warmth and depth of the King's domestic affections, than that

[1] The Duke of York, then about fifteen years of age, had escaped from St. James's a few months before, at the recommendation of Charles, and by the assistance of Colonel Bamfield. The Duke, in descending into the garden, knocked against a door in the palace, and feared an alarm ; "but no alarm being taken, he ventures down and out of the door by the Tilt Yard end, where Colonel Bamfield attended *with a periwig and black patches,* which the Duke having put on, they hie to Spring Gardens, *as gallants come to hear the nightingale,* and, being passed through that, enter into a coach." At Greenwich, whither they proceeded on board a vessel, the Colonel was unluckily recognised by a bargemaster ; and he was espied tying on the Duke's garter, which, as the Prince had before "shifted into gentlewoman's clothes," was considered extraordinary ; and they with difficulty, by threats and promises, persuaded the captain to proceed with them. Rainsborough's squadron, which lay in the Downs, occasioned them some alarm ; but they arrived safe at Middleburgh, where the Prince slept, "and gave much wonder to the hostess that à young gentlewoman would not let the maids help her to bed ; but be served by a pretended brother in the same chamber in another bed." On arriving at Maesland Sluys, the Prince of Orange came on board to his brother-in-law ; and on landing, "the Princess Royal came to the street-door to embrace her brother, the affectionateness of which meeting," says an eye-witness, "I cannot express." — See a Letter to Mr. Secretary Nicholas in the Appendix to Clarendon's State Papers, vol. ii.

perpetual and conscientious regard to the principles belonging to his station, and that fervent
piety, which ever animated his conduct.   He
bade the Lady Elizabeth tell her mother that his
thoughts had never strayed from her, and that
his love should be the same to the last; and
begged her to remember to tell her brother
James, whenever she should see him, " that it
was his father's last desire that after his death he
should no longer look on his brother Charles
merely as his elder brother, but should be obedient to him as his sovereign; and that they
should both love one another, and forgive their
father's enemies.— But," said the King to her,
" Sweetheart, you will forget this?"—"No,"
said she; " I will never forget it as long as
I live."   He prayed her not to grieve for him,
for he should die a glorious death; it being for
the laws and liberties of the land, and for maintaining the true Protestant religion.   He charged
her to forgive those people, but never to trust
them; for they had been most false to him, and
to those that gave them power, and he feared
also to their own souls.   He then urged her to
read " Bishop Andrews's Sermons," " Hooker's
Ecclesiastical Polity," and " Archbishop Laud's
Book against Fisher," which would strengthen
her faith, and confirm her in a pious attachment
to the Church of England, and an aversion from
popery; and in remembrance of him he gave her
two seals set with diamonds.   Then taking the
Duke of Gloucester on his knee, the King said
to him, " Sweetheart, now they will cut off thy
father's head" (upon which words the child looked

very earnestly and steadfastly at him). " Mark, child, what I say, they will cut off my head, and perhaps make thee a king : but mark me, you must not be a king so long as your brothers, Charles and James, do live ; for they will cut off your brothers' heads when they can catch them, and cut off thy head at last too ; and therefore I charge you do not be made a king by them :" at which the child said earnestly, " I will be torn in pieces first ;" which ready reply from so young an infant, filled the King's eyes with tears of admiration and pleasure. At parting, the King commanded them both to be obedient to their mother, and bade the Lady Elizabeth send his blessing to the rest of her brothers and sisters, with his commendations to all his friends.

The commissioners, to the number of forty-eight, met on the same day, (Monday, the 29th January,) in the Painted Chamber, when they pronounced an order that the King should be beheaded on the following day, in the open street before Whitehall, and drew up and engrossed the warrant for his execution, which many of them immediately signed. The warrant, was as follows : —

" At the High Court of Justice for the trying and judging of Charles Stuart, King of England, January 29. 1648.

" Whereas Charles Stuart, King of England, is, and standeth convicted, attainted, and condemned of high treason, and other high crimes ; and sentence upon Saturday last was pronounced against him, by this Court, to be put to death, by the severing of his head from his body, of which sentence execution yet remaineth to be done: these are, therefore, to will and require you to see the said sentence executed, in the open street before Whitehall, upon the morrow, being the thirtieth day of this instant month of January, between the hours of ten in the morning and five in the afternoon of the same day, with full effect: and for so doing, this shall be your sufficient warrant. And these are to require all officers, soldiers, and others, the good people of this nation of England, to be assisting unto you in this service.

" Given under our hands and seals." [1]

Then follow the signatures of fifty-nine commissioners, including Bradshaw, Lord Grey, Cromwell, Sir John Danvers, Ireton, Pride, Harrison, Waller, Say, Scroope, Ludlow, Marten, Ingoldsby, Ewers, Thos. Challoner, Scot, Carew, Corbet, &c.

The commissioners also made an order that the officers of the ordnance within the Tower of London should deliver to Edward Dendy, Esq., the serjeant-at-arms, the bright axe for the exe-

---

[1] The fact mentioned by Hume and Ludlow, that Oliver Cromwell and Henry Marten blacked each other's faces with a pen as they were signing the warrant in the Painted Chamber, was proved on oath by an eye-witness called Ewer, at the trial of Marten, in 1660. — See State Trials, vol. v. 1200. Marten, in his defence, said the fact did not imply malice. For the story as to Cromwell forcing Colonel Ingoldsby to sign the warrant, see *post*, in the memoir of Ingoldsby.

cuting of malefactors. They ordered five eminent ministers, Calamy, Vines, Caryll, Dell, and Goodwin, to be sent to the King for his spiritual assistance. Charles, who had chosen the Bishop for that office, declined to receive them, but begged them to offer their prayers to God for him. They also gave orders that the King's scaffold should be covered with black.

On the morning of his death, Charles, according to the relation of his faithful attendant, Sir Thos. Herbert, awoke about two hours before daybreak, after a sound sleep of four hours. He called to Herbert, who lay on a pallet by his bedside, and bade him rise ; "for," said the King, "I will get up, I have a great work to do this day." He then gave orders what clothes he would wear, and said to his attendant, "Let me have a shirt on more than ordinary, by reason the season is so sharp[1] as probably may make me shake, which some observers will imagine proceeds from fear. I would have no such imputation. I fear not death — death is not terrible to me. I bless God, I am prepared." Soon after the King was dressed, Bishop Juxon came to him, according to his appointment the night before. He remained an hour in private with him, when Herbert was called in, and the Bishop prayed with the King, using the prayers of the church, and then read the 27th chapter of St. Matthew, which so beautifully describes the passion of our Saviour. The King thanked the Bishop for his choice of

[1] The day was so piercing that the King, at the persuasion of Bishop Juxon, wore a cloak till the moment of his death.

the lesson ; but he was surprised and gratified to learn that it was the lesson for the day according to the calendar.

About 10 o'clock Colonel Hacker knocked at the King's chamber door, and, being admitted by Herbert, came in trembling, and announced to the King that it was time to go to Whitehall, where he might have further time to rest; and soon afterwards the King, taking the Bishop by the hand, proposed to go.   Charles then walked out through the garden of the palace into the Park, where several companies of foot waited as his guard; and, attended by the Bishop on one side, and Colonel Tomlinson on the other, both bare-headed, he walked fast down the Park, sometimes cheerfully calling on the guard to " march apace." As he went along, he said, " he now went to strive for an heavenly crown, with less solicitude than he had often encouraged his soldiers to fight for an earthly diadem."

At the end of the Park, the King [1] went up the stairs leading to the long gallery, and so into the Cabinet Chamber of the Palace of Whitehall. Being delayed here in consequence of the scaffold not being ready, he offered up several prayers, and entered into religious discourse with the Bishop. About twelve he ate some bread, and drank a glass of claret, declining to dine after he had received the sacrament.

[1] The late Sir Henry Englefield related a traditional anecdote, that Charles, in passing through the Park, pointed out a tree near the entrance from Spring Gardens (where the cows at present stand), saying, " That tree was planted by my brother Henry."

When Charles arrived at Whitehall, the Colonels Hacker, Huncks, and Phayer produced to Tomlinson the warrant for his execution; and in the Horn Chamber the King was delivered by Tomlinson into the custody of those officers; Charles requested Tomlinson, however, to remain with him to the last, and acknowledged his kind and respectful conduct by presenting to him a gold tooth-picker and case which he carried in his pocket. Tomlinson also introduced to him Mr. Seymour, who brought a letter from the Prince to his father, with whom the King conversed, and charged him with various messages for the Prince.

In the mean time a different scene was passing in Ireton's chamber, a small room in another part of the palace. Ireton and Harrison were here in bed; and Cromwell, Axtell, Huncks, Hacker, and Phayer were present. Cromwell commanded Huncks to draw up an order to the executioner pursuant to the warrant for the King's execution. Huncks refused; whereupon Cromwell was highly incensed, and called him a peevish froward fellow; and Axtell exclaimed, "Colonel Huncks, I am ashamed of you: — the ship is now coming into the harbour, and will you strike sail before we come to anchor?" Cromwell then went to a table, and, as it would appear, wrote the order to the executioner, and then gave the pen to Hacker, who, as one of the officers charged with the execution of the warrant, signed it.[1] Cromwell, and the rest of the

---

[1] See the evidence on the trials of Hacker, Axtell, and Hulet, State Trials, vol. v.

officers, then went out of the chamber, and, in a few minutes, Hacker came and knocked at the door of the chamber where the King was, with Tomlinson, the Bishop, Herbert, and some of his guards. Herbert and the Bishop were deeply affected at this signal for their final separation from their sovereign and master. The King stretched out his hand to them, which they kissed, falling on their knees and weeping, the King helping the aged bishop to rise. He then bade Hacker to open the door and he would follow; and he was conducted by Hacker, Tomlinson, and other officers and soldiers, through the banqueting house by a passage broken through the wall, where the centre window now is.[1]   A

[1] The street now called Parliament Street was at that time crossed by two ranges of buildings belonging to the palace of Whitehall, with wide arched gateways crossing the street, and forming the public thoroughfare.   One gateway was opposite to Privy Gardens; and there was a way over it from these gardens belonging to the palace, to pass into St. James's Park. The other building traversing the street was the sumptuous gallery of Whitehall, built by Henry VIII., the scene of so many adventures and events of various descriptions in the reigns of Elizabeth, James, and the two Charles's. Connected with this gallery was " a beautiful gatehouse," over a noble archway. Lord Leicester says, in his Journal (p. 60.), — " The scaffold was erected between Whitehall gate and the gallery leading to St. James's." Lilly asserts, that it was just at the spot where the blood of a citizen had been shed at the commencement of the rebellion, when a mob were vociferating " No Bishop" under the windows of the palace, and some cavaliers sallied out to disperse them, and one was killed.— See Observations on the Life and Death of Charles, by W. Lilly, student of judicial astrology, in Baron Maseres's Tracts.

strong guard of several regiments of horse and foot being posted about the scaffold, so that the people could not approach near enough to hear any discourse from the King, he addressed his last sentences chiefly to the Bishop, Colonel Tomlinson, and the other officers who stood near him. They were in substance as follows :—

"I shall be very little heard of any body else ; I shall therefore speak a word to you here : indeed, I could hold my peace very well, if I did not think that holding my peace would make some men think that I did submit to the guilt, as well as to the punishment : but I think it is my duty to God and my country to clear myself, both as an honest man, a good king, and a good Christian. I shall begin first with my innocency : in troth, I think it not very needful to insist long upon this ; for all the world knows that I did never begin a war with the two houses of parliament ; and I call God to witness, to whom I must shortly make an account, that I did never intend to encroach upon their privileges ; they began upon me. It is the militia they began upon ; they confessed the militia was mine, but they thought fit to have it from me : and, to be short, if any body will look to the dates of commissions, of their commissions and of mine, and likewise to the declarations, he will see clearly that they began these troubles, not I. So that as for the guilt of these enormous crimes that are laid against me, I hope in God that God will clear me of it. God forbid I should lay it upon the two houses of parliament ; there is no necessity of either : I hope they are free of this guilt ; for I believe, that ill instruments between them and me have been the cause of all this bloodshed; so that as I find myself clear of this, I hope, and pray God, that they may too: yet, for all this, God forbid I should be so ill a Christian, as not to say God's iudgments are just upon me; many times he doth pay justice by an unjust sentence — that is ordinary. I will only say this, that an unjust sentence that I suffered to take effect, is punished now by an unjust sentence upon me; so far I have said to show you that I am an innocent man.

" Now, to show you that I am a good Christian, I hope there is a good man [pointing to Bishop Juxon] that will bear me witness that I have forgiven all the world, and even those in particular that have been the chief causes of my death; who they are, God knows; I do not desire to know: I pray God forgive them. But this is not all, my charity must go further: I wish that they may repent. For, indeed, they have committed a great sin in that particular. I pray God, with St. Stephen, that it be not laid to their charge; nay, not only so, but that they may take the right way to the peace of the kingdom; for my charity commands me not only to forgive particular men, but to endeavour, to the last gasp, the peace of the kingdom. Now, Sirs, believe it, you shall never go right, nor God will never prosper you, until you give God his due, the King his due, (that is, my successor,) and the people their due: I am as much for them as any of you. You must give God his due, by regulating rightly his church, according to the Scripture, which is now out of order; to set you in a way particu-

larly now, I cannot; but only this, a national synod
freely called, freely debated among themselves,
must settle this when every opinion is freely
heard. For the King " (Then turning to a gentleman that touched the axe, he said, ' Hurt not
the axe—that may hurt me.')—Indeed I will not
———— the laws of the land will clearly instruct
you for that; therefore because it concerns my
own particular, I shall only give you a touch of
it. For the people, truly I desire their liberty
and freedom as much as any body whatsoever; but
I must tell you, *that their liberty and freedom consist in having government, in having those laws by
which their lives and their goods may be most
their own. It is not their having a share in the
government* — that is nothing appertaining to
them. A subject and a sovereign are clean different things; and therefore until you do that, I
mean, that you put the people in that liberty, as
I say, certainly they will never enjoy themselves.

" Sirs, it was for this that now I am come
here. If I would have given way to an arbitrary
way, to have all laws changed according to the
power of the sword, I needed not to have come
here; and therefore I tell you (and I pray God it
be not laid to your charge), that I am the martyr
of the people. In truth, Sirs, I shall not hold
you much longer: I could have desired a little
time longer, because I would have a little better
digested this I have said, and therefore I hope
you will excuse me; I have delivered my conscience; I pray God you take those courses that
are the best for the good of the kingdom and
your own salvation."

The Bishop. Though your Majesty's affections may be very well known as to religion; yet it may be expected that you should say something thereof for the world's satisfaction.

The King. I thank you heartily, my Lord, for that I had almost forgotten it. In troth, Sirs, my conscience in religion, I think, is very well known to all the world; and therefore I declare before you all that I die a Christian, according to the profession of the Church of England, as I found it left me by my father; and this honest man, I think, will witness it.

Then to Colonel Hacker he said, " Take care that they do not put me to pain: and, Sir, this and it please you ———"

But a gentleman coming near the axe, the King said, " Take heed of the axe, pray take heed of the axe."

Then speaking unto the executioner, he said, "I shall say but very short prayers, and when I thrust out my hands ———"

Then turning to the Bishop, he said, " I have a good cause, and a gracious God on my side."

The Bishop. There is but one stage more, this stage is turbulent and troublesome, it is a short one; but you may consider it will soon carry you a very great way, it will carry you from earth to heaven; and there you will find a great deal of cordial joy and comfort.

The King. I go from a corruptible to an incorruptible crown, where no disturbance can be, no disturbance in the world.

The Bishop. You are exchanged from a temporary to an eternal crown; a good exchange.

Then the King said to the executioner, "Is my hair well?" and took off his cloak and his George, giving his George to the Bishop, saying, "Remember."[1] Then he put off his doublet, and being in his waistcoat, he put on his cloak again; then looking upon the block, he said to the executioner, "You must set it fast."

Executioner. It is fast, Sir.

The King. When I put out my hands this way (stretching them out), then —— After that, having said two or three words to himself, as he stood with his hands and eyes lift up, immediately stooping down, he laid his neck upon the block.[2] And then the executioner again putting his hair under his cap, the King, thinking he was going to strike, said, "Stay for the sign."

Executioner. Yes, I will, and please your Majesty. — After a little pause, the King stretching forth his hands, the executioner at one blow severed his head from his body, and held it up and showed it to the people, saying, "Behold

[1] According to Oldmixon and Hume, this injunction (which excited much curiosity) referred to the King's order to convey the George to the Prince, with a charge to forgive his father's murderers. Juxon is said to have stated this before the Council of State. Rushworth states, that the King merely reminded the Bishop that the George was to be conveyed to the Prince. Clarendon and Whitlock do not explain the word "Remember."

[2] It being doubted whether the King would submit to the executioner, staples were driven into the block, and hooks prepared, in order, if necessary, to confine his head forcibly to the block. On the trial of Hugh Peters in 1660, it was sworn that this was done by his orders given on the scaffold to one Tench, a joiner in Houndsditch. See State Trials, vol. v.

the head of a traitor!¹   At the instant when
the blow was given, a dismal universal groan

¹ Though Joyce and Hugh Peters have been suspected
of inflicting the murderous blow on Charles, and though
another claimant for this infamous distinction is put forward in the Gentleman's Magazine for 1767, there seems
little doubt that Richard Brandon, the common hangman, assisted by his man, Ralph Jones, a ragman in Rosemary Lane, in fact perpetrated the deed.   Among the tracts
relative to the Civil War presented to the British Museum
by George III., in 1762, are three on this subject, which
are fully noticed in a note to Mr. Ellis's Letters on English History, vol. iii. (second series.)   It appears, by the
register of Whitechapel Church, that Richard Brandon was
buried there on the 24th of June, 1649; and a marginal
note (not in the hand of the Register, but bearing the mark
of antiquity), states, " This R. Brandon is supposed to have
cut off the head of Charles I." — One of the tracts, entitled " The Confession of Richard Brandon, the Hangman,
upon his Death-bed, concerning the Beheading of his late
Majesty," printed in 1649, states, " During the time of his
sickness, his conscience was much troubled, and exceedingly perplexed in mind; and on Sunday last, a young
man of his acquaintance going to visit him, fell into discourse, asked him how he did, and whether he was not
troubled in conscience for cutting off the King's head.   He
replied yes, by reason that (upon the time of his tryall) he had
taken a vow and protestation, wishing God to punish him,
body and soul, if ever he appeared on the scaffold to do the
act, or lift up his hand against him.   He likewise confessed
that he had 30l. for his pains, all paid him in half crowns
within an hour after the blow was given; and he had an
orange stuck full with cloves, and a handkircher out of the
King's pocket, so soon as he was carried off the scaffold;
for which orange he was proffered twenty shillings by a
gentleman in Whitechapel, but refused the same, and afterwards sold it for ten shillings in Rosemary Lane.   About
eight o'clock at night he returned home to his wife, living
in Rosemary Lane, and gave her the money, saying, it was
the dearest money he earned in his life, for it would cost

was uttered by the people (as if by one consent) such as was never before heard[1]; and as soon as the execution was over, one troop of horse marched rapidly from Charing Cross to King Street, and another from King Street to Charing Cross, to disperse and scatter the multitude.

When the body was put into a coffin at Whitehall, says Rushworth, " there were many sighs and weeping eyes at the scene; and divers strove to dip their handkerchiefs in the King's blood." A general gloom and consternation pervaded London on the day of this atrocious perpetration;

---

him his life. About three days before he died, he lay speechless, uttering many a sigh and heavy groan, and so in a desperate state departed from his bed of sorrow. For the burial whereof great *store of wines were sent in by the sheriff of the city of London*, and a great multitude of people stood wayting to see his corpse carried to the churchyard, some crying out, ' Hang him, rogue ! '—' Bury him in the dunghill.'— Others pressing upon him, saying they would quarter him for executing the King, insomuch that the churchwardens and masters of the parish were fain to come for the suppressing of them; and with great difficulty he was at last carried to Whitechapel churchyard, having (as it is said) a branch of rosemary at each end of the coffin, on the top thereof, with a rope crosse from one end to the other. A merry conceited cook, living at the sign of the Crown, having a black fan (worth the value of 30*s.*), took a resolution to rent the same in pieces ; and to every feather tied a piece of packthread, dyed in black ink, and gave them to divers persons, who, in derision, for a while wore them in their hats."— See Ellis, *ubi supra.* The second tract states, that the first victim Brandon beheaded was the Earl of Strafford.

[1] Described by Philip Henry, a spectator. Ellis's Letters, vol. iii. p. 323.

many of the chief inhabitants either shut themselves up in their houses, or absented themselves from the city. On that day none of the courts of justice sat; and on the next, Whitelocke, one of the commissioners of the Great Seal, says, " The commissioners met, but did not think fit to do any business, or seal any writs, because of the King's death." Whitelocke says, " I went not to the House, but stayed all day at home in my study, and at my prayers, that this day's work might not so displease God as to bring prejudice to this poor afflicted nation."[1] Evelyn, in his Diary writes, " I kept the day of this martyrdom as a fast, and would not be present at that execrable wickedness, receiving the sad account of it from my brother George and Mr. Owen, who came to visit me this afternoon, and recounted all the circumstances."[2] Archbishop Usher came out to witness the scene from his house at Whitehall; but he fainted when the King was led out on the scaffold.

The Journals of the Commons show, either that nothing was done, or that it was thought fit to enter nothing on these eventful days. On the

---

[1] There is, I am informed, a tradition in Westminster School, that South, the celebrated divine, was the boy whose turn it was to read prayers on the day of Charles's death; and that he read the prayer for the King as usual.   South at that time must have been about fourteen years of age. Five years afterwards, when the loyal and learned divine was at Christ Church, Oxford, we find his name to a copy of Latin verses, addressed to the Protector on his conclusion of a treaty with the States of Holland.   This, no doubt, was a mere college exercise.   See *Musæ Oxonienses*, 1654.

[2] Vol. i. p. 233.

day of the execution there is only the following remarkable entry : —

" Ordered, *That the common post be stayed until to-morrow morning* 10 *o'clock.*"

On the 31st, Commissary-general Ireton reports a paper of divers particulars touching the King's body, his george, his diamond, and two seals. The question being put, that the diamond be sent to Charles Stuart, son of the late King, commonly called Prince of Wales, *it passed with the negative.* The same question was then put, separately, as to the garter, the george, and the seals : as to each, it passed in the *negative.*

When the news of the decapitation of the King reached Scotland, that loyal people were moved with horror and indignation. Most of the gentry put on mourning ; the chair of state in the parliament house, the uppermost seats in the kirks, and almost all the pulpits, were clothed in black.

The body of the King being embalmed, under the orders of Herbert and bishop Juxon, was removed to St. James's. The usurpers of the government refused permission to bury it in Henry the VII.'s Chapel, from a dread of the indignation of the crowds who would assemble on so solemn and interesting an occasion; but, at last, after some deliberation, the council allowed it to be privately interred in St. George's Chapel at Windsor, provided the expenses of the funeral should not exceed five hundred pounds. The last duties of love and respect were (according to Charles's express desire) paid to their sovereign's corpse by the Duke of Richmond, the Marquis of Hertford, Lord Southampton, Lord Lindsey, the Bishop of London, Herbert, and Mildmay, who, on producing a vote of the Commons, were admitted by Whichcote, the Governor of Windsor Castle, to the chapel.   When the body was carried out of St. George's Hall, the sky was serene and clear ; but presently a storm of snow fell so fast, that before it reached the chapel the pall and the mourners were entirely whitened.   When the bishop proposed to read the burial service according to the rites of the Church of England, this fanatical governor roughly refused, saying, "that the Common Prayer Book was put down, and he would not suffer it to be used in that garrison where he commanded."   Clarendon thus describes, with graphic simplicity, the sad scene to its close : —

" But when they entered into it (the chapel), which they had been so well acquainted with, they found it so altered and transformed, all inscriptions and those landmarks pulled down, by which all men knew every particular place in that church, and such a dismal mutation over the whole, that they knew not where they were ; nor was there one old officer that had belonged to it, or knew where our Princes had used to be interred.   At last there was a fellow of the town who undertook to tell them the place where, he said, ' there was a vault in which King Harry the Eighth and Queen Jane Seymour were interred.' As near that place as could conveniently be they caused the grave to be made.   There the King's body was laid, without any words, or other ceremonies, than the tears and sighs of the few beholders.   Upon the coffin was a plate of silver fixed, with these words only, ' *King Charles,*

1648.' When the coffin was put in, the black velvet pall that had covered it was thrown over it, and then the earth thrown in; which the governor stayed to see perfectly done, and then took the keys of the church." [1]

A report of the proceedings of the " High Court of Justice " being made to the parliament, they resolved, " that the persons employed in that important service had discharged their trust with courage and fidelity; that the parliament was well satisfied with their account of their

[1] Owing to the privacy of this interment, doubts were at the time current as to its having actually taken place. It was asserted that the King's body was buried in the sand at Whitehall; and Aubrey states a report, that the coffin carried to Windsor was filled with rubbish and brick-bats. These doubts were entirely removed by the opening of the coffin (which was found where Clarendon described it,) in the presence of George the Fourth, then Prince Regent, in April, 1813 — of which Sir Henry Halford has published an interesting narrative. On removing the black pall which Herbert described, a plain leaden coffin was found, with the inscription " King Charles, 1648." Within this was a wooden coffin, much decayed, and the body carefully wrapped in cerecloth, into the folds of which an unctuous matter mixed with resin had been melted, to exclude the external air. The skin was dark and discoloured — the pointed beard perfect — the shape of the face was a long oval — many of the teeth remained — the hair was thick at the back of the head, and in appearance nearly black — that of the beard was of a redder brown. The head was severed from the body. The fourth cervical vertebra was found to be cut through transversely, leaving the surfaces of the divided portions perfectly smooth and even; — " an appearance," says Sir H. Halford, " which could have been produced only by a heavy blow inflicted with a very sharp instrument, and which furnished the last proof wanting to identify King Charles I."

proceedings, and ordered it to be engrossed and recorded amongst the Rolls of Parliament, in order to transmit the memory thereof to posterity; and resolved, that the commissioners of the Great Seal should issue a certiorari to their clerk to record those proceedings in the Chancery." The Rump of the Commons had already virtually annihilated the House of Peers, by declaring themselves the supreme power, and by legislating respecting the King's trial, and other matters in direct opposition to the voice of that assembly. The resolution, which they now formally passed for their abolition, was little more than a form. They voted that "*the House of Peers was useless and dangerous, and ought to be abolished;*" and that they would no longer " take advice of them in the exercise of legislative power;" and an act for their abolition was immediately passed accordingly. They next proceeded to resolve, " *that the office of a king is unnecessary, burdensome, and dangerous to the liberty, safety, and public interest of the people, and therefore ought to be abolished;* and they will settle the government of the nation in the way of a Commonwealth." The forms of the old constitution were, of course, altered and adapted to the new scheme òf government. The old Great Seal, which had been broken to pieces by workmen in the House of Commons during its sitting, and the fragments given to Widdrington and Whitlocke, the two new commissioners, was now replaced by a new seal, which was, according to the design of the notorious Henry Marten, engraved on one side with the arms of England and

the harp and arms of Ireland, and the words,
" The Great Seal of England;" and on the reverse
side with a representation of the Rump Parliament sitting, and the legend, " In the first year
of freedom, by God's blessing restored." One of
the first offices to which this new seal was applied
was the sealing of a patent for confirming the acts
of trustees who had been appointed to *sell certain
Bishops' lands*[1], for the benefit of the army and
the state. All grants, writs, and other records
were ordered to run in the names of the " cus-
todes libertatis Angliæ auctoritate Parliamenti,"
instead of the name of the King. The dates of
legal proceedings were to be, " the year of our
Lord, and no other." Jurors were to be termed
" juratores pro republicâ," instead of " juratores
pro domino rege;" and all indictments to conclude " *contra pacem publicam*," instead of " contra pacem, dignitatem, *et coronam nostram*."

Remarks. — The extraordinary proceeding described in the foregoing pages, though eminently
instructive to the student of history and politics,
and the observer of human passions, cannot, in
any sense, be looked upon as a judicial proceeding
illustrative of the laws of England. Its deep interest, and the imposing scenes which it displays, can
alone justify the insertion in a collection of English
" Trials" of a procedure which had not the impartiality or legitimate authority of a trial, still less
any of the forms or attributes of a trial according

[1] " I would not monarchy destroy,
But as the only way t' enjoy
The ruin of the church." Denham.

to English law. If the kingly office was not to confer immunity from criminal responsibility, and if Charles's conduct was such as to justify a departure from ordinary rules, at least the principles of substantial equity and right should have been adhered to in the manner and spirit of the proceeding. But the violators of the forms of justice still more atrociously trampled upon its spirit. An *ex post facto* ordinance, passed in defiance of one branch of the legislature, by a small junto formed by a forcible reduction of the other, created the new and unheard-of crime for which a king was to be brought to judgment by his subjects; and constituted a packed court to try the accused, composed of all his bitterest enemies, whose escape from the consequences of their own treasons absolutely depended on his extinction. To call this a *trial,* is a flagrant abuse of terms, and to see in it the spectacle of a united people deliberately proceeding to a judicial punishment of their king (which to some eyes may appear edifying or sublime), is to indulge in the merest speculation and fancy, in disregard of the plainest and most unquestionable facts of history. Charles was not tried by his people, but murdered by the officers of a few regiments, and a small knot of fanatical republicans and rebels. The whole House of Lords, the great majority of the Commons, a large portion of the army, and the great mass of the English and Scotch nations, either abhorred and repudiated the proceeding, or remained wholly passive while it was effected by irresistible force. The truth is, the King's perpetual imprisonment, his assassination, or his destruction by means of an *ex post facto* law, and a packed tribunal, were the only modes open to the officers and the republican leaders, of at once completing their work of sedition and treason, and ensuring their own safety. The first alternative was evidently dangerous and objectionable. The second might have defeated their own ends, and might have immediately re-established royalty in the kingdom; while it was certainly contrary to the spirit of the nation and the age, and in its execution must probably have concentrated in one or two individuals a responsibility which was divided among a very large number by the course which was actually pursued. A judicial proceeding, however flimsy its pretensions to fairness or impartiality, was calculated to satisfy the scruples of some, and to impose on the imaginations of more. When such a man as Mr. Fox can write as follows of the mock trial, which we have followed in detail, who can wonder that it should dazzle the understandings of many enthusiasts in the inflamed period when it took place, and that it should not be, even now, universally regarded in the light in which alone we consider it — as the mere mode adopted for accomplishing, with certainty and safety, the predetermined destruction of the King?

" After all, however, notwithstanding what the
" more reasonable part of mankind may think
" upon this question, it is much to be doubted
" whether this singular proceeding has not, as
" much as any other circumstance, served to
" raise the English nation in the opinion of
" Europe in general. He who has read, and

" still more he who has heard in conversation,
" discussions upon this subject by foreigners,
" must have perceived that, even in the minds
" of those who condemn the act, the impression
" made by it has been far more that of respect
" and admiration than that of disgust and horror.
" The truth is, that the guilt of the action,—that
" is to say, the taking away of the life of the King,
" —is what most men in the place of Cromwell
" and his associates would have incurred : what
" there is of splendour and magnanimity in it,
" —I mean the publicity and solemnity of the
" act,—is what few would be capable of dis-
" playing."

As Mr. Fox seems to admit that " the more
reasonable part of mankind" think differently of
this proceeding from those " foreigners" who, he
asserts, regard it with " respect and admiration;"
we incline to hope that, as sounder views upon
most historical questions gradually become more
prevalent, the sort of hallucination which (at
least according to Mr. Fox) has partially prevailed upon this will be more and more dispelled
—that what he characterises as " splendour and
magnanimity" in the proceeding will become gradually to be regarded merely as effrontery and
audacity; and that, if Cromwell and the other
regicide commissioners escape the odious character of secret assassins, they will remain indelibly
stamped with that of public murderers.   In order
to merit the appellation of *judges*, they must have
placed the King at the bar of a fairly constituted
court, proceeding to investigate a definite and in-
telligible accusation, grounded, if not on positive

law, at least on the most obvious and undoubted principles of moral justice. But the charge against Charles was as unfair as the tribunal was partial and hostile. By being narrowly confined to " levying war against the parliament and people," according to the words of the Commons' ordinance, it evaded all the real merits of the contest between the King and the parliament, and laid the foundation for a judgment against the King, founded on the mere naked proof of being seen at the head of his forces when blood was shed in battle with the parliamentarians. That this was the construction put upon the charge by the Court itself is evident; for though the accusation of levying war is mixed up with verbose allegations of intents to subvert the constitution and liberties of the people, &c. which are largely descanted upon in Cook's speech, yet the evidence received is confined to the dry fact of warlike acts, without the least attempt to prove the motives ascribed, or to connect the acts of military hostility with those designs against the liberties of the nation, which are so copiously declaimed upon by Cook and by Bradshaw. To say that the scantiness of the proof is to be ascribed to the King's denial of the Court's authority, and that fuller proofs would have been required had the King pleaded and joined issue with his prosecutors, is a gratuitous assumption. If the King's course of conduct rendered proofs unnecessary, the Court should have required none. But as they thought fit to go into proofs, they must be presumed to have called for such as, in their judgment, established the charge. To convict the King of treason against the English constitution and people, on proof of his being seen at the head of his cavalry at Naseby, at Newbury, and Edge Hill, was much less fair than it would be to hang a man for murder on a mere indictment and proof that he was sometimes seen with a drawn dagger in his hand.[1]

Whether a king, in any circumstances, should admit the jurisdiction of his subjects to try him, and join issue on a charge preferred by those who owe him allegiance, we will not pretend to determine; but that Charles (whether acting by the advice of Hale or not) showed both wisdom and dignity in rejecting the authority of Bradshaw and the commissioners, few persons will dispute. The character and constitution of the Court, and the novelty, vagueness, and unfairness of the accusation, left him no alter-

---

[1] Mr. Hallam, who, with sound impartiality, decides that Charles could not be charged with being the author of the war, says, " We may contend, that when Hotham shut the gates of Hull against his sovereign, when the militia was called out in different counties by an ordinance of the two Houses, both of which preceded by several weeks any levying of forces by the King, the bonds of our constitutional law were by them and by their servants snapped asunder; and it would be the mere pedantry and chicane of political casuistry to enquire, even if the fact could be better ascertained, whether at Edge Hill or in the minor skirmishes the first carabine was discharged by a Cavalier or a Roundhead. The aggressor in a war is not the first who uses force, but the first *who renders force necessary*." — Vol. ii. Those who wish to see the vague, and inconclusive reasonings, to which an able writer is driven in support of the opposite view of the question, may peruse the conclusion of Mr. Godwin's second volume of his History of the Commonwealth.

native. To have acknowledged the Court, would have placed him absolutely at the mercy of his direst enemies — would have at once lowered his dignity and impeached his consistency, without augmenting the very slight chances of his deliverance. The proceeding being founded on a subversion of all positive law, Charles would have involved himself in a struggle against his most exasperated foes, without the protection of a single precedent, without one legal rule, or principle, or authority to shield him from their irresponsible power and prejudiced hate. He would have been bound hand and foot under that "law of tyrants"—judicial discretion, which, according to Lord Camden's well known saying, "in the best of judges is oftentimes caprice; in the worst, every vice, folly, and passion to which human nature is liable." With such judges, and such a mode of proceeding, the King's only course was that which he adopted. But had the tribunal been impartially composed (if indeed that were possible), and had the proceeding been warranted by the opinions of the majority of the people, it is difficult to see how Charles could have acted otherwise than he did. The course of submitting to plead would, under any circumstances, have been inconsistent with his character and principles, and with those notions of the kingly office in which (whether they were wrong or right) he had been educated, and to which he had always consistently adhered. Charles must also have felt (what very few indeed will deny), that his were not those acts of wilful and cruel tyranny which could warrant the overthrow of all positive law, and sanction a resort to a wild proceeding, under the name of natural justice, for their punishment. Supported in his principles and conduct by almost all the peers, by a large body of the commons, and by probably at least half of the nation, it would have been a gross abuse of victorious power in his enemies to treat him as a delinquent, and to apply to him the severities of municipal law, even had all his political opponents concurred in such a course, and had the procedure been as much marked by equity and impartiality as it in fact was by malice and vindictiveness.

All writers agree that the demeanour and conduct of the King during the proceeding were eminently distinguished by good sense, dignity, and temper, — equally remote from pusillanimity and arrogance. His sufferings had evidently softened his disposition and manners (which, though benevolent and upright, were not always gracious or conciliating); and, as he says in an excellent letter to the prince, from the Isle of Wight, " he had learned to busy himself by retiring into himself, and therefore could the better digest what befel him." The humiliation of his position never once made him forget himself; he was never betrayed by insult into unfit passion or acrimony; he received the indignities of the military rabble " more in sorrow than in anger," and retorted on his overbearing judges with self-collected acuteness and ready good sense, without any thing of insult or undue asperity. Echard hints, that he had not been always ready in speech; but, both in the Isle of Wight and at Westminster, the excitement of his situation appears to have entirely freed him from embarrassment. His answers to, and reasonings with, Bradshaw are marked by closeness and precision, by a well-considered sense of his kingly station, and a noble determination not to compromise its dignity. The learned serjeant at law was, indeed, placed in a position in which a much feebler disputant than Charles would easily have triumphed in the discussion. Whereever Bradshaw makes the slightest attempt at defending the jurisdiction of the Court on grounds of reason, the King readily foils him; and the president is driven back, discomfited, to entrench himself behind the Court's absolute decree, that their authority shall not be disputed. Thus, he has the absurdity to tell the King, that he is bound to obey the authority of the people of England, " of which you *are elected* King." " No, Sir, I deny that," says the King: upon which Bradshaw, defeated, replies, " If you acknowledge not the authority of the Court, they must proceed." The King, warm with his success, proceeds—" I do tell them so; England was never an elective kingdom; but an hereditary kingdom for near these thousand years," &c. Bradshaw again exposes himself, by saying— " They sit here by the authority of the Commons of England; and all your predecessors, and you, are responsible to them." The King sees his advantage—" I deny that; show me one precedent:" when poor Bradshaw has no answer but,

" Sir, you ought not to interrupt while the Court is speaking to you;" and presently after, when Charles says, " Show me that jurisdiction, where reason is not to be heard," Bradshaw, with amusing *naïveté*, replies—" Sir, we show it you here—the Commons of England." That Charles, though not betrayed into violence or irritability, was not wanting in expressing his just scorn and natural indignation at the proceedings of the Court, appears by the energy of some of his answers and interjections, and by his dignified reply when Bradshaw impudently told him—" Sir, it is not for prisoners to require." " Prisoners! Sir, *I am not an ordinary prisoner!*"

The conduct of Charles during his last moments may, by those who most pity and condemn his fate, be safely left to be gathered from the uncontroverted facts of history, or to be described by those most hostile to his conduct. Mr. Godwin (who generally writes from the best authorities) says: — " Through the whole of this critical scene, Charles deported himself with great composure, and with a carriage wholly free from affectation: he was undisturbed, self-possessed, and serene." And in acknowledging (with something of regret) that this execution " did not conciliate the English nation to republican ideas, and it shocked all those persons in the country who did not adhere to the ruling party," Mr. Godwin adds, " This was in some degree owing to the decency with which Charles met his fate. * * * I am afraid that the day that saw Charles perish on the scaffold, rendered the restoration of

his family certain."[1]   Andrew Marvel, the friend
of Cromwell and of Milton, and the tutor to
Cromwell's nephew, who may probably have witnessed what he describes, writes of this scene: —

" He nothing common did nor mean
  After that memorable scene ;
    But with his keener eye
    The axe's edge did try :
Nor call'd the gods, with vulgar spite,
To vindicate his helpless right ;
    But bow'd his comely head
    Down as upon a bed."
            Ode to Cromwell, on his Return
              from Ireland.

[1] History of the Commonwealth, vol. ii. 692.

MEMOIR OF HENRY IRETON.

HENRY IRETON, one of the most active agents
in accomplishing the death of Charles, who was
never absent from any private or public sitting
of the Court, and who, had he lived, must have
been one of the most distinguished supporters or
opponents of the rule of Cromwell, was born in
1610, and was the son of German Ireton, Esq., a
gentleman of good family at Attenton, in the county
of Nottingham. He was entered a gentleman
commoner of Trinity College, Oxford, in 1626;
and took his degree of Bachelor of Arts on the
10th of June, 1629. Anthony Wood says he
left the University without completing his degree
in arts, and that " he had the character of a stubborn and saucy fellow towards the seniors ; and,
therefore, his company was not wanting." From
Oxford, Ireton removed to the Middle Temple,
where it appears, by the Society's books, he entered as a student on the 24th of November,
1629 ; but he was never called to the bar. He,
however, studied the law for a short time in
London, and then went to reside on his family
estate in Nottinghamshire. He was the kinsman and close friend and neighbour of Colonel
Hutchinson, and, according to Mrs. Hutchinson,
" a very grave, serious, religious person. " Mrs.
H. describes him just before the commencement
of the King's war with the parliament. " Mr
Ireton, being very active in promoting the par-

liament, and the godly interest in the country, found great opposition by some projectors and others of corrupt interest that were in the commission of the peace: thereupon making complaint at the parliament, he procured some of them to be put out of the commission, and others better affected to be put into their roomes, of which Mr. Hutchinson was one; but he then forbore to take his oath, as not willing to launch out rashly into public employments while such a storm hung threatening over-head."[1]   At the commencement of the war, Ireton was one of the seventy-five persons who undertook each to raise a troop of horse for the parliament, and was one of the very few gentlemen of Nottingham-shire (Sir Thomas Hutchinson and his son the colonel were others) who were opposed to the King.   The Earls of Newcastle and Kingston, Lords Chesterfield and Chaworth, the Savills, the Eyres, the Digbys, the Palmers, the Cowpers, the Cartwrights, and almost all the nobility and gentry of that county, sided with Charles. The Birons of Newstead were," says Mrs. Hutchinson, "passionately the King's." Ireton, who was esteemed in his county a man of learning, understanding, and abilities, became the active promoter of the parliamentary interest; but when the King raised his standard in the midst of his friends at Nottingham Castle, all that Ireton could do " was to gather a troop of those godly people which the cavaliers drove out," and with these, being then a single man, he joined the

[1] Memoirs of Colonel Hutchinson, p. 80.   Col. Hutchinson at this time was only 23 years old; Ireton about 29.

standard of the Earl of Essex, the commander of the parliamentary forces.

After the battle of Edge Hill, in 1642, the King sent Sir John Digby, the sheriff, to endeavour to secure the county of Nottingham in his support; and the nobility and gentry were summoned. But the town and castle of Nottingham were now in the hands of the parliament; the roundheads in the county were zealously putting themselves into a posture of defence. The militia was raised; and Ireton (among other officers) was desired to return with his troop of horse to defend his native county. He was now major of the regiment; and in the commission issued by the parliament for raising troops and contributions, seizing delinquents, sequestering estates of the "malignants," in the county, Ireton was named commissioner with the Hutchinsons and a few other gentlemen. At this time Sir John Meldrum, who commanded for the parliament at Nottingham, was ordered by Lord Essex to march, with all the forces he could raise, to the relief of the town of Gainsborough, in Lincolnshire, where Lord Willoughby of Parham was besieged by the Earl of Newcastle and the King's troops. Colonel Hutchinson was left by Sir John in command of Nottingham Castle; and when the forces were about marching, he ordered the guns on the town works to be moved up to the castle, which was a signal for a tumultuous mutiny amongst the townsmen, who were chiefly warm cavaliers, and who threatened to demolish and set fire to the castle. Drury, an alderman of the town, and fourteen more citizens were hereupon seized, and sent prisoners to Derby, whither Ireton and his troop conveyed them. Ireton with his regiment (of which the gallant Thornhagh was colonel) then marched with the other forces, and, joining Colonel Oliver Cromwell's regiment, arrived before Gainsborough. They soon routed the King's troops, killed Sir Charles Cavendish the commander, relieved the place before Lord Newcastle's forces came up, and then retired honourably to Lincoln. Here the Nottinghamshire troops were separated and dispersed into different services in the parliamentary cause. Ireton's connection with his county regiment now ceased: and this appears to have been the commencement of his close and constant union to the fortunes of Cromwell, which produced such important influence on national events. Mrs. Hutchinson says, " Major Ireton quite left Colonel Thornhagh's regiment, and began an inseparable league with Colonel Cromwell, whose son-in-law he after was." Ireton, though eleven years younger than Cromwell, and only a captain of horse up to the time of the new model of the army, when Cromwell, as lieutenant-general to the Earl of Manchester, was the second military man in the kingdom, besides being a member of the house, appears, according to Whitlock, to have always exercised considerable ascendancy over him. " No one could prevail so much with Cromwell, nor order him so far as Ireton could." Mr. Godwin says, " Cromwell felt the curb of his virtue, and of the clearness of his spirit, and submitted." Cromwell doubtless saw

the services which either the public cause or his
own personal views might derive from the zeal
and capacity of such a character as Ireton. Their
objects and principles at this time were the same:
Ireton's military knowledge was equal, if not
superior, to Cromwell's; and the ardent, sanguine
temperament of Cromwell met, in the stern resolution and rigid firmness of Ireton, that degree of
contrast which so much more promotes union than
a closer resemblance in qualities. The self-deny-
ing ordinance, and the new model of the army,
which were passed at this time, by removing Essex,
Manchester, Waller, and Denbigh from the command of the army, opened to Cromwell, Ireton,
and other energetic men of their stamp and
station, the avenue to the control of the army,
and the power and influence which they soon
attained. Fairfax became commander-in-chief;
Cromwell, lieutenant-general; Skippon, major-
general; Ireton, Desborough, Harrison, were at
first among the inferior officers. Ireton, indeed,
accepted the appointment of captain in the regiment of horse commanded by Algernon Sydney,
who was at least seven years younger than himself: but he soon rose from that humble office to
be a colonel of horse, and, at Cromwell's express
request, was nominated commissary-general of
horse, being the next officer in authority under
Cromwell.

On the 11th of June, 1645, Fairfax, wrote to
Cromwell, by order of the parliament, to join
him, with his horse, near Northampton, in ex-
pectation of a battle with the King; concluding,
" They are, as we hear, more horse than foot,
and make their horse their confidence; *ours*

shall be in God." Three days after, the great battle of Naseby was fought.   Here Ireton was distinguished for his courage and military capacity. The parliamentary army was commanded, on the right wing, by Cromwell; in the centre by Fairfax and Skippon; and on the left wing, at Cromwell's express desire, by Ireton.   After a vigorous combat, Ireton's wing was defeated by Prince Rupert. He himself received two wounds in the face, and was made prisoner; but when Rupert, by rashly pursuing the parliamentarians, lost the advantages of his success, and when the valour and skill of Fairfax and Cromwell had turned the fortune of the day, Ireton made his escape. He was now, as commissary-general, nominally the fourth officer in rank in the army; but Ireton and his extraordinary father-in-law were, in truth, the pivots on which all its movements turned. The General, Fairfax, (though a consummate officer, and a brave and high-minded man,) suffered himself to be outwitted or overpersuaded on all occasions by these more designing and energetic colleagues.   In the beginning of 1646, the King's affairs being at a very low ebb, he took the decisive step of departing from Oxford, and throwing himself into the hands of the Scots before Newark. He then removed with the Scotch army to Newcastle, where a commission of lords and commons was sent down to lay before him propositions for peace; as to which, however, they had no authority to treat: on learning which Charles said, " Then, saving the honour of the business, an honest trumpeter might have done as much."

About this time the union between Cromwell

and Ireton was rendered closer and more inti-
mate, by Ireton's marrying, on the 15th January,
1647, Bridget, the eldest daughter of Cromwell,
by whom he had one son (Henry, married to
the daughter of Henry Powle, afterwards Speaker
of the House of Commons and Master of the
Rolls,) and four daughters.[1]

The two Houses now voted that Holdenby
House, a royal mansion[2], built by Sir Christopher Hatton, in Northamptonshire, was a fit
residence for the King; and three peers and
six of the commons were named commissioners
to receive Charles from the Scots, and bring
him to that manor. He arrived there about
the middle of February, 1647, and remained
till June following. He was received with
loyalty and affection by the gentry and country people, who assembled about the mansion;
and he resided at Holmby with dignity and
comfort[3], keeping up his cheerfulness and equa-
nimity, riding in the neighbourhood, reading
much, according to his custom[4], and amusing

[1] An account of their families is given in Mr. Noble's
Memoirs of the Cromwell Family.

[2] This royal mansion, as well as others at Richmond,
Oatlands, Theobalds, &c. were pulled down to raise money
to pay the arrears of some regiments of the revolutionary
army.

[3] Charles was, however, refused the presence of his chaplains by the presbyterians. Ashburnham and Legge, his
attendants, were now also removed; and Sir Thomas Herbert, author of the Memoirs, and Sir John Harrington,
author of the Oceana, were substituted in their places.

[4] April 15—25. 1647, P. Killigrew went to Holmby
with some books for the King's use. He brought back
another note under the King's hand for more books, the
first whereof was " The Crown of Thorns." He says the

himself occasionally at the game of bowls at the neighbouring seats of Harrowden and Althorp.

It is difficult to trace the exact part which Ireton and his father-in-law took in the dissensions which, in 1647, commenced between the victorious army of Fairfax and the parliament. The presbyterians in the House, actuated by religious animosity, and urged on by the citizens of London, and by their own imprudent leaders, Hollis and Stapleton, proposed to disband great part of the army without indemnity, or an adequate provision for their pay; to send the remainder to Ireland; to reduce all officers above the rank of colonel, with the single exception of Fairfax; and to force the army to accept the covenant. To suppose that twenty thousand brave and enthusiastic troops would calmly acquiesce in such treatment, was the height of

King looks better than at Newcastle, and outwits still all about him, refusing to meddle with affairs of state till he come a free man to London. — Extract of a Letter from London to Mr. Secretary Nicholas in France.   Append. to Clarendon's State Papers, vol. ii.   When Charles was in the Isle of Wight, Sir Thomas Herbert, who was then his attendant, says, " The Sacred Scripture was the book he most delighted in : he read often in Bishop Andrews' Sermons, Hooker's Ecclesiastical Polity, Dr. Hammond's Works, Villalpandus upon Ezekiel, Sands's Paraphrase of King David's Psalms, Herbert's Divine Poems, and also Godfrey of Bulloigne, writ in Italian by Torquato Tasso, and done into English heroic verse by Mr. Fairfax, — a poem his Majesty much commended; as he did also Ariosto, by Sir John Harrington, a facetious poet, much esteemed, &c., and Spenser's Fairy Queen, and the like, for alleviating his spirits after serious studies." — Memoirs, 62.

madness. They expressed their dissatisfaction,
by advancing their quarters nearer to London;
a measure which could not have been adopted
without the concurrence of Fairfax, their general,
who was governed by Ireton and Cromwell.   A
deputation from the House was sent to the army
at Saffron Walden, to negotiate with their officers
as to drawing off a portion of their numbers for
the Irish service; and also to announce a con-
cession made by the parliament, in voting 60,000*l.*
per month for their pay.[1]   But the officers declined concluding any arrangement without full
satisfaction as to their arrears, an indemnity for
past service, and security for their future subsistence.   Before the convention separated,
a petition to this effect, from the army, was
prepared, to be presented by the general to
the parliament.   Ireton, if not Cromwell, was
present and active at these conventions; but
the details of what took place are not known.
They were also both members of the House of
Commons[2]; and when the commissioners sent to
the army reported in the House the result of
their mission, and adverted incidentally to the
petition then in progress from the army, Waller
says that Ireton at first denied its existence,
but afterwards admitted it.   The House ordered
General Hammond, and his nephew, Colonel
Robert Hammond (the gaoler of the King at Carisbrook), Colonel Lilburne, and Colonel Grimes, to
the bar, where they intended to interrogate them,

---

[1] The arrears were now 331,000*l.*; a bill for paying the
arrears had been lost in the Lords a few weeks before.

[2] Ireton appears to have been returned for Appleby.—
Noble.

and also Ireton and Pride, respecting the petition, and late at night, when the members were exhausted, and the House was thin, the intemperate Holles penned a resolution on his knee[1], and had it carried, declaring that all who, for the future, promoted the petition should be proceeded against as enemies to the state, and disturbers of the public peace. This resolution was little short of a declaration of war against the army.

The summoned officers were examined by the House; the famous Pride was especially censured; and they were enjoined to return to the army, and endeavour to suppress the petition. The House now sent a second deputation, headed by the popular Lord Warwick, to Saffron Walden, to endeavour to engage a part of the troops to agree to serve in Ireland: but the deputation was attended with no success; and the Parliament, indignant at the report made by the deputation, summoned several officers to the bar, voted that those refusing the Irish service should be disbanded with six weeks' pay; and forbade the officers to encourage the soldiers' discontents, or to assist them in their efforts for redress. The officers, under the guidance of Cromwell and Ireton, had too much sagacity not to see that, by ostensibly complying with these commands of the parliament, and abstaining from encouraging the soldiers' schemes, their discontent would only be more effectually inflamed, and their exertions stimulated. Those officers who were members of the House, accordingly, attended with

[1] Ludlow.

diligence in their seats; others, under different
pretexts, absented themselves from the army.
The soldiers, who were, in general, freeholders,
farmers, yeomen, and tradesmen, with fervent
religious feelings and acute minds, who had taken
up arms (according to their own notions) for liberty and conscience, now felt the necessity of
acting for themselves. They disdained to be
treated as mercenaries or machines. They held
consultations, elected deputies, and established
those singular councils of agitators which afterwards gave them such prodigious influence,—
which controlled their officers when they dis-
agreed with them,—and which gave them an
ardent, energetic support while their objects
agreed, such as could not have been derived
from men coldly obeying the orders of a despotic
commander. That Cromwell and Ireton, and
the other superior officers, had a secret understanding with the soldiers in all these proceedings, is a fact of which there is little doubt.
Desborough, a major, and Berry, a captain, in
Fairfax's regiment of horse, were zealously instrumental in stimulating these movements of the
troops. Desborough was Cromwell's brother-in-
law; and Berry, who had been a gardener, was one
of his earliest friends and adherents. Berry was,
from the first, president of the council of agitators.

On the 28th of April, 1647, the agitators
presented letters to Fairfax, Cromwell, and Skippon, complaining of the treatment they had
received, demanding an indemnity for their
services in the war, and denouncing the Irish
expedition as a plan for ruining and breaking to

pieces the army. On the 30th of April, Cromwell and Skippon produced these letters in the House of Commons, and stated that the three private soldiers, Sexby, Allen, and Shepherd, who had delivered them were then at the door of the House. When they were called in, they stated that the letters originated in a rendezvous of several regiments, and that few of the officers knew any thing of the proceeding. Major-General Skippon bore testimony to the fidelity and active services of the three men against the royalists. Some violent members, however, proposed to commit them to the Tower; when Cromwell rose, and made one of those bold, vehement, and hypocritical harangues by which, without any approach to regular eloquence, he always produced a powerful impression on his hearers. He protested that the army was calumniated and misunderstood; that they would willingly conform to all that the parliament required of them ; and that, if the House commanded them to disband, they would pile up their arms at the door of the assembly.[1] The result was, the House was duped ; the messengers were allowed to depart ; and Skippon, Cromwell, Ireton, and Fleetwood (the latter three being the real authors and fomentors of the discontents) were named commissioners

---

[1] " So Cromwell, with deep oaths and vows,
     Swore all the Commons out o' th' House ;
     Vow'd that the red coats would disband.—
     Ay, marry, would they at their command ;
     And troll'd them on, and swore and swore,
     Till th' army turn'd them out of door."
                    Hudibras, part ii. canto 2.

to repair to head-quarters and quiet the dis-
tempers of the army.   The House made some
concessions, which these commissioners were to
communicate to the troops.   They agreed to indemnify them by an act for all their proceedings
in the war; to pay a portion of their arrears on
their disbanding; and the remainder as early as
the necessities of the kingdom would admit.
They still, however, adhered to their purpose of
disbanding them.

 When the four commissioners presented
themselves to the officers at Saffron Walden,
the latter demanded a week's delay, in order
to take the sense of all the regiments as to
the proposals of the House.   At the end of the
week a general council of war, accordingly, assembled at Bury St. Edmund's, when the officers
produced a petition from the council of agitators,
expressing their amazement and disgust that a
disbandment should be proposed without redress-
ing their grievances, and entreating the General
Fairfax to appoint a speedy rendezvous of the
whole army.   The council of war, consisting of
about 200 officers, almost unanimously recommended the general in chief to listen to the
representations of the army; and Ireton was at
the head of those who were deputed by the officers to draw up advice to the general to this
effect.   Matters now approached a crisis.   The
house had actually proceeded to appoint the
days for disbanding the several regiments.   Fairfax's regiment of foot was to be disbanded at
Chelmsford on the 1st of June.   But when Lord
Warwick, with the other commissioners, pro-

ceeded thither for the purpose, with money to pay off a portion of the arrears, the regiment was ordered by Fairfax to another place, in order to approach the general rendezvous; and Skippon produced a letter from the general, stating that it would be impossible to proceed in the matter of the disbanding till the house had considered the report he had just made to them of the result of the council of war at Bury. In the mean time Colonel Rainsborough's regiment, who were on their march to embark for Jersey, mutinied at Petersfield, with the connivance of their colonel, took up their colours and marched to Oxford, to which place the famous Joyce, a cornet in Cromwell's regiment, repaired at the same time, by orders from Cromwell, Ireton, and other officers, who held a meeting at Cromwell's house in London. Joyce, pursuant to his orders, seized all the artillery and ammunition laid up at Oxford, in order that the army might not be unprepared should they be obliged to defend themselves by arms against the Houses. He then proceeded to accomplish the master-stroke of the energetic council of the army. He marched, on the 3d of June, with 700 horse, to Holdenby House, where Charles resided. The guards who attended the King refused to make any resistance to their brother soldiers; and Joyce, without opposition, made himself master of the person of Charles, who proceeded the next day under his escort, along with the parliamentary commissioners, to Hinchinbrook House, the seat of Colonel Edward Montagu. There is little doubt that Cromwell and Ireton were the contrivers of this extraordinary plot for placing Charles in the custody of the army. Fairfax, the general, was ignorant of it; and when he learned it, sent Colonel Whalley with two regiments to restore the King to his former position, and to apologise for this daring insult. But Charles, who was on his road to Hinchinbrook, peremptorily refused to return, deluding himself with the vain notion that the agitators and soldiers were friendly to him, and were worthy of his confidence.

The struggle for predominance was now every day growing more energetic and earnest between the independent party and the victorious army on the one side; and the presbyterians, who ruled the House of Commons, and had the voices of the majority of the country, and of the corporation and citizens of London, on the other. The acquisition of the King's person was of the highest importance to the independents and the army. The negotiations, which they carried on with the parliament on the one hand, and with Charles on the other, were conducted by Cromwell and Ireton. The skill, resources, and daring duplicity which characterised their proceedings, would alone stamp them as men of the most powerful minds, and the most accommodating moral principles. The declaration of the army at St. Alban's, calling for the punishment of "delinquents" (adherents of the King), for the suspension of some of the principal enemies of the army in the house, and for fixing a definite period when the house should be dissolved, was the production of Ireton. Whitlock says, " In these declarations and transactions of the army Colonel Ireton was chiefly employed, or took upon him the business of the pen; and having been bred in the Middle Temple, and learned some grounds of the laws of England, and being of working and laborious brain and fancy, he set himself much upon these businesses, and therein was encouraged and assisted by Lieutenant-General Cromwell, his father-in-law, and by Colonel Lambert, who had likewise studied in the Inns of Court, and was of a subtle and working brain." [1]   The next day the heads of charge, drawn by the same pen, were presented against Denzil Hollis, Stapleton, and the eleven leaders of the presbyterian party.   The presbyterian majority in the house refused to suspend them.   The army, which was then at Berkhampstead, instantly advanced to Uxbridge, and some regiments pushed their way to Harrow and Brentford.   The house was in consternation, and the eleven members immediately absented themselves from their seats.   The house then demanded on what terms the troops would recede farther from London; and Ireton presented them with a paper requiring as conditions that the declaration inviting the soldiers to desert should be withdrawn, the raising of more forces stopped, the maintenance of the army voted, and that Charles should not be desired to reside nearer London than the head-quarters of the army might be at the time.

While Cromwell and Ireton thus successfully maintained the interests of the army against the parliament, they had with consummate ad-

[1] Memorials, June 16. 1647.

dress, in long and daily interviews, acquired something of the favour, if not of the confidence, of the King. The parliament had disgusted Charles by their intolerant rigour in depriving him of his chaplains, and of the free exercise of the rites of the Church of England. Cromwell, Ireton, and the Council of War (who were independents), disclaimed any such severity, and allowed Sheldon (afterwards Archbishop of Canterbury) and Hammond (the King's favourite divine) to have free access to him; they at the same time permitted Charles an unrestrained intercourse with the Duke of Richmond, Sir John Berkley, Ashburnham, Denham (the poet), and others of his royalist friends. Cromwell and Ireton, with their usual artifice and address, persuaded these attendants on the King that his restoration was an object very near their hearts, and for which they would zealously labour, if he would only repose confidence in them.[1] These Machiavelian politicians then touched one of the most potent chords in Charles's breast. They procured him permission from the parliament for an interview with his children; Fairfax and the officers pledging their honour that they should afterwards return safely to their former abode. Charles had not seen the

---

[1] The narratives of Sir John Berkley and of Ashburnham (especially the former) detail these transactions. Berkley's memoirs derive confirmation from being incorporated for forty pages into Ludlow's Memoirs, p. 195. to 236. Ludlow considered Berkley as the dupe of Cromwell and Ireton, which was doubtless the case as to all the royalists introduced by them to the King.

Duke of Gloucester (now seven years old) and the Princess Elizabeth (of the age of twelve) since January, 1642, when he left London, at the commencement of the war; nor the Duke of York (now fourteen years old) since he quitted Oxford to repair to the Scottish army at Newark. On the 15th of July, 1647, the children were conducted from St. James's by the Earl of Northumberland, their governor, to Maidenhead, to meet their father. The people flocked to see them, and strewed their way with boughs and flowers. The King came from Caversham, near Reading, where he resided at a seat of Lord Craven's, and dined with his children at the Greyhound Inn; and in the evening they all accompanied their father back to Caversham, and remained for two days under the same roof with him. The army was now at Reading; and Cromwell, who witnessed these scenes of domestic happiness and endearment, told Sir John Berkley " he had seen the tenderest sight that ever his eyes beheld, which was the interview between the King and his children; and wept plentifully at the remembrance of it, saying, that never man was so abused as he in his sinister opinions of the King, who, he thought, was the uprightest and most conscientious man of his three kingdoms. He wished God would be pleased to look upon him according to the sincerity of his heart towards his Majesty." When Berkley related this to the King, " he seemed not well edified by it." Charles, doubtless, distrusted the ready tears and exaggerated professions of Cromwell. Ireton (who, though engaged in the crooked intrigues

of his father-in-law, often spoke with a severe honesty and frankness,) had indeed, not long before,
hinted to Charles their real intentions towards
him. — " Sir, you have an intention to be the arbi-
trator between us and the parliament, and we
mean to be so between you and the parliament."
And when Charles said to him, " I shall play my
game as well as I can," Ireton retorted, " If your
Majesty have a game to play, you must give us
the liberty to play ours."

Ireton's pen was now employed in drawing up
the celebrated proposals of the army for the
King's restoration, and the settlement of a plan
of future government.   Berkley, who, with Ashburnham, was the principal negotiator for the
King with the council of the army, sat up near
a whole night with Ireton, perusing them before they were presented to the King, and was
permitted by Ireton to make some material
changes.   Charles was suffered privately to in-
spect them at Woburn Abbey several days before
they were presented to him in public.   He strongly
objected to the exception of seven of his friends
(not named) from pardon, to the exclusion of the
royalists from the next ensuing parliament, and
the absence of any provision for the maintenance
of Church government.   Berkley, sensible of
the great difficulties of his position, earnestly
counselled the King to accept the terms; but
Charles broke off from him, saying, that "he should
see them glad, ere long, to accept more equal
terms."   Charles, encouraged by favourable messages from the presbyterian party and the corporation of London, and buoyed up by the sanguine

counsels of Ashburnham [1] and other royalists, appears at this period to have greatly over-rated his strength; and when the proposals were formally presented to him, the King, to the astonishment of Ireton and the officers, as well as of Berkley, rejected them with disdain, and used "very tart and bitter discourses" to the army commissioners; saying, he would have no man suffer for his sake; and that he repented of nothing so much as the bill against Lord Strafford; and that he would have the Church established according to law. " You will fall to ruin," said he, " if I do not sustain you." Berkley whispered to him — " Sir, your Majesty speaks as if you had some secret strength and power that I do not know of; and since your Majesty hath concealed it from me, I wish you had concealed it from these men also." The King recollected himself, and " began to sweeten his former discourse with great power of language and behaviour." [2] But it was too late. The news of the conference had been carried by Rainsborough, a desperate agitator, to the army at Bedford, who were indignant at the King's rejection, and still more at the manner in which it was conveyed: and when Berkley hastened thither, and, in a conference with Ireton and the officers, endeavoured to soften

[1] The courtly Ashburnham fell into the error of despising the army agitators: he said, " he was always bred in the best company, and could not converse with such senseless fellows as the agitators were; that if they could gain the officers sure to the King, there was no doubt but they would be able to command their own army." — Berkley's Memoirs.   [2] Berkley.

the angry impression, he was told plainly, that if
the King accepted the proposals, they should be
presented to the parliament; if he rejected them,
they would not say what they would do. The
proposals were never again tendered to the King.

Immediately after Fairfax's entry with the
army into London, the head-quarters were fixed
at Putney, and Charles was removed to Hampton
Court, where he lived with regal splendour and
dignity, and was surrounded by the nobility and
his personal friends. During this period the
greatest degree of intercourse appears to have
existed between Charles and Cromwell, Ireton,
and the principal officers of the army. Fairfax,
when he waited on the King, kissed his hand;
but Cromwell and Ireton appear to have declined
that ceremonial. Charles also complained to
Berkley that these men were backward in receiving from him any specific grace or advantage;
a complaint that confirms the common rumour,
that offers of preferment were made to them by
the King. Cromwell himself told Berkley that
Lady Carlisle had propagated a report that he
was to be made Earl of Essex, and Captain of the
Guard to the King: and Hollis states, in his
Memoirs, that it was affirmed Cromwell was to
be a Knight of the Garter; his son to be of the
Bedchamber to the Prince; and Ireton to have
some great office in Ireland. Whether such offers
were ever made, or whether these were mere ru-
mours spread either by the royalists or the republicans for their own purposes, will ever be a matter
of uncertainty. The mere existence of such reports, however, shows the footing on which Crom-

well and Ireton then stood with the King and his
party.

The well known story of the letter from Charles
to his Queen, said to be intercepted by Cromwell
and Ireton, who seized the messenger at the Blue
Boar Inn in Holborn, also relates to this period.
It has been often adduced as a proof of Charles's
perfidy, and also as forming the real ground which
influenced Cromwell and Ireton to break with
the King, and to resolve on his ruin. But Hume
discredits the story; and Baron Maseres, an
acute judge, with opposite principles to Hume's,
gives no credence to it. The story in Lord
Orrery's Memoirs is, that Lord O. (then Lord
Broghill) riding with Cromwell and Ireton at the
head of his troops, in Ireland, the conversation fell
on the King's death; and Cromwell observed, that
" if the King had followed his own judgment, and
had been attended by none but trusty servants,
he had fooled them all." Lord Broghill, finding
Cromwell and Ireton in good humour, and no
other person being within hearing, asked them,
" 1st, Why they once would have closed with the
King? and, secondly, Why they did not?" Cromwell very freely told him he would satisfy him in
both his queries. " The reason," says he, " why
we would once have closed with the King was
this: — We found that the Scots and the presbyterians began to be more powerful than we;
and if they had made up matters with the King,
we should have been left in the lurch; therefore
we thought it best to prevent them, by offering
first to come in upon any reasonable conditions.
But while we were busied with these thoughts.

there came a letter from one of our spies, who
was of the King's bedchamber, which acquainted
us on that day our doom was decreed; that he
could not possibly tell what it was, but we might
find it out, if we could intercept a letter from
the King to the Queen, wherein he declared
what he would do. The letter, he said, was
sewn up in a skirt of a saddle; and the bearer of
it would come with the saddle upon his head
about 10 o'clock that night to the Blue Boar Inn
in Holborn; for there he was to take horse, and
go to Dover with it. This messenger knew nothing of the letter in the saddle, but some persons in Dover did. We were at Windsor when
we received the letter; and immediately upon
the receipt of it, Ireton and I resolved to take one
trusty fellow with us, and with troopers' habits
to go to the inn in Holborn, which accordingly
we did; and set our man at the gate of the inn,
where the wicket only was open, to let people in
and out. Our man was to give us notice when
a person came there with a saddle; while we, in
the disguise of common troopers, called for cans
of beer, and continued drinking till about ten
o'clock: the sentinel at the gate then gave notice that the man with the saddle was then come
in. Upon this we immediately rose, and as the
man was leading out his horse saddled, came up
to him with drawn swords, and told him we were
there to search all that went in and out there;
but as he looked like an honest man, we would
only search his saddle, and so dismiss him. Upon
that we ungirt the saddle, and carried it into the
stall where we had been drinking, and left the

horseman with our sentinel: then ripping up one of the skirts of the saddle, we there found the letter of which we had been informed; and having got it into our hands, we delivered the saddle again to the man, telling him he was an honest man, and bidding him go about his business. The man, not knowing what had been done, went away to Dover. As soon as we had the letter, we opened it; in which we found the King had acquainted the Queen, that he was now courted by both factions, the Scotch presbyterians and the army, and which bid fairest for him should have him; but he thought he should close with the Scots sooner than the other, &c. Upon this," added Cromwell, "we took horse and went to Windsor; and finding we were not likely to have any tolerable terms from the King, we immediately from that time forward resolved his ruin."

Mr. Godwin truly observes, that it does not follow that Cromwell had ever actually intended to close with Charles, even if he made such a statement to Lord Broghill. Still less can this account (related by Lord Orrery's chaplain on *memory* of what Lord Orrery also *remembered*) be taken as evidence of Charles's perfidy, or of the real cause of Cromwell and Ireton breaking with him. It surely discovered no perfidy in the vanquished and half-dethroned king to receive the overtures of both parties, and to be willing to close either with the Scots or with the army, according as the offers of the one or the other were most advantageous. Nor can it be supposed that Cromwell and Ireton resolved on abandoning him merely on the contents of a letter which, in

truth, discovered to them little more than what
they must well have known before they per-
used it.   But another still more doubtful version
is given of this letter, which, if true, would certainly evince perfidy in Charles, and show sufficient reasons for Cromwell and Ireton's alteration
of their conduct towards him.   In a book called
" Richardsoniana," a *posthumous* publication of
Richardson the younger, the painter (1776), it is
stated, that Lord Bolingbroke told Richardson
and Pope in conversation, in 1742, that the second Lord Oxford told him, he had had in his
hand a letter from Charles to the Queen, in answer to one from her reproaching him with " having made those villains, Cromwell and Ireton, too
great concessions;" in which letter Charles said
" *she should leave him to manage, and in due
time he should know how to deal with the rogues,
who, instead of a silken garter, should be fitted
with a hempen cord.*"   That a letter from Charles
to Henrietta Maria was intercepted by Cromwell
and Ireton at the inn, is not improbable; and
that its contents were something to the effect
which is stated by Lord Broghill, seems very
credible.   The probability appears to be, that the
account of Lord Orrery's chaplain is erroneous in
making Cromwell assign this letter as the sole
cause of their giving up the King.   The second
story, quoting the contents of a letter on hearsay
at second hand, seems very questionable; and the
two versions of the letter differ materially as to
the King's intentions expressed in it.   The rhe-
torical and antithetic passage which, by Lord
Bolingbroke is ascribed to Charles, is wholly unlike

the style of all the King's letters and writings, and of itself is sufficient to excite suspicion; while the glaring improbability of an experienced man like the King, surrounded by spies and living in the custody of his enemies, gratuitously committing such a design, so expressed, to a letter, is sufficient to destroy all the verisimilitude of this version of the tale.

In June, 1648, while Cromwell was engaged in opposing the Scots, Ireton was actively co-operating with Fairfax in quelling the insurrections of the royalists and presbyterians in the southern counties, and was detached by Fairfax to reduce Canterbury, which was in the hands of the Kentish insurgents. The city surrendered on the 8th of June; when Ireton rejoined Fairfax in Essex, and was second in command at the memorable and protracted siege of Colchester, where General Goring, the Lord Capel, Sir Charles Lucas, and Sir George Lisle made a last noble and heroic exertion on behalf of the King and the monarchy. The siege lasted ten weeks, and was conducted with all the skill and sagacity of which Fairfax and Ireton were eminently possessed. The garrison and the suffering inhabitants looked in vain for relief from the Scottish army; and were disappointed in their hopes that the treaty between the King and the parliament would be concluded in time to protect them from their conquerors. They were reduced to eat horse-flesh, to fire the suburbs of the town, and to drive out the women and children. The gallantry and obstinacy of this defence, prolonged after the rest of the kingdom had been reduced to sub-

mission by the army, roused the indignation of
the parliament and of the besiegers. All favourable terms of capitulation were refused; and when
the garrison was driven to surrender, on the 27th
of August, the more distinguished prisoners were
shut up in the Town Hall; and the council of
war resolved on the military execution of Sir
Charles Lucas, Sir George Lisle, and Sir Ber-
nard Gascoigne. Lord Capel and the other prisoners insisted on sharing the fate of their com-
rades, but Lucas and Lisle alone were shot;
Gascoigne, being a foreigner, was spared. Clarendon asserts, that this barbarity was generally
" imputed to Ireton, who swayed the General, and
was on all occasions of an unmerciful and bloody
nature." But it must be remembered that Clarendon was abroad at this time, and writes from the
reports of the royalists, who were naturally exasperated against Ireton. Fairfax, in the post-
script to his own Memoirs, takes the responsibility
of the transaction on himself, and makes his own
apology. This circumstance, however, is not conclusive that he did not act by Ireton's advice. The
prisoners were delivered, he contends, *on mercy,*
" which is to be understood, that some are to
suffer, and others to go free;" and he says that
the Lords Capel, Norwich, &c. being men of
considerable estates and families, he thought fit
to transmit them to the civil judicature for trial;
but that, Lucas and Lisle being mere soldiers
of fortune, and falling into his hands by the
chance of war, it was fitting to execute them; —
a feeble and unsatisfactory defence of an act of
severity so little necessary, and so little in harmony

with Fairfax's feelings and general conduct. Mr.
Godwin observes truly, " It was one of those acts
which would never be perpetrated but where victory has pretty sufficiently secured the actors
from retaliation."

It is but justice to Ireton, whom Clarendon as
well as Lord Broghill charges with inhumanity,
to notice the exertions which he made, in con-
junction with Colonel Hutchinson, to save Sir
John Owen, one of the insurgents, who, with the
Duke of Hamilton, Lords Holland, Capel, and
Goring, was condemned to death by the second
High Court of Justice, — a tribunal formed on the
bad precedent of that which tried Charles. The
parliament intended to spare some of these prisoners, and great efforts were made for each
nobleman by his friends in the house. " While
" there was such mighty labour and endeavour for
" these Lords, Colonel Hutchinson observed that
" no man spoke for this poor Knight ; and sitting
" next to Colonel Ireton, he told him that ' it
" pitied him much to see, that, while all were la-
" bouring to save the Lords, a gentleman that
" stood in the same condemnation should not find
" one friend to ask his life ; and so,' said he, ' am
" I moved with compassion, that if you will se-
" cond me, I am resolved to speak for him, who
" I perceive is a stranger and friendless. Ireton
" promised to second him ; and accordingly en-
" quiring further whether he had not a petition
" in any member's hands, he found that his keep-
" ers had brought one to the Clerk of the House,
" but the man had not found any one that would
" interest themselves for him, thinking the Lords'

" lives of so much more concernment than this
" gentleman's. This the more stirred up the Co-
" lonel's generous pity; and he took the petition,
" delivered it, spoke for him so nobly, and was
" so effectually seconded by Ireton, that they car-
" ried his pardon clear." *

That Ireton's stern nature was not inacces-
sible to emotions of pity, is also shown by what
Ludlow relates of his treatment of Lady Honoria
O'Brien in Ireland. Ireton having granted his
passport of safety to that lady, she abused it for
the protection of the cattle and goods of Irish rebels, declaring that they were her own. Ireton
charged her with this perfidy, when she burst
into tears, implored forgiveness, and assured him
she would not repeat such conduct. When she
retired, Ludlow, at her entreaty, interceded with
Ireton to continue his favour to her; to which
Ireton answered, " As much a cynic as I am,
the tears of this woman moved me;" and he gave
orders that her safeguard should be continued.

We have seen by what machinations Charles
was driven to fly to the Isle of Wight, and to in-
trust himself to the custody of the Governor
Hammond, the son-in-law of Hampden, the dear

---

¹ Mrs. Hutchinson's Memoirs, p. 310. Ludlow says of
this matter, " Ireton moved the house to consider that Sir
John Owen was a commoner, and therefore more proper to
be tried in another way by a jury; whereupon the house
reprieved him." He does not name Colonel Hutchinson,
who in this, as in all other stories, is the hero of his wife's
narrative. Ludlow's omission may, however, have been
intentional; for Hutchinson and he had bitterly quarrelled,
though both were republicans and independents, and opponents of Cromwell's ambition.

friend of Cromwell and Ireton, and one who was
regarded by them as a trustworthy promoter of
all their objects and designs. In November,
164S, the army presented their famous remonstrance to the house, recommending the immediate breaking off of the treaty with the King,
and demanding that he should be brought to justice as the source of all their grievances. The
council of war now found it necessary to be entirely
secure of possessing Charles's person; and in order
to prevent his attempts at escape, they resolved
on removing him from Carisbrook to the hopeless
and miserable dungeon of Hurst Castle. To
their astonishment and annoyance, their friend
and comrade, Hammond, now professed scruples
of conscience, which made him hesitate to dispose of the King, except under orders from the
parliament, by whose authority he had hitherto
kept him in confinement. Fairfax (the general
in chief) immediately wrote to him, summoning
him to appear before him at head-quarters, and
sent Colonel Ewer, an inveterate republican, to
assume the command of the island. Cromwell
and Ireton, at the same time, despatched long
letters to Hammond, endeavouring to remove his
scruples by subtle reasoning and accomplished
casuistry. These letters are truly characteristic
of the men, and also of the style prevalent among
the puritans and independents of the day. Ireton's letter is as follows : —

" DEAR ROBIN,

" Thou wilt receive herewith a letter from the
General, by which thou wilt see what tenderness
there is here towards thee. I shall not at this
distance undertake a dispute concerning our

ground or proceedings ; but leave thee for the one to our remonstrance, for the other to further trial of us. I shall only, in the love of a friend and brother, speak a word or two to that, which I found the ground of thy scruples, against what hath been from hence desired, or rather of thy declared resolution to the contrary.

" Thou lookest on thyself as a servant under trust ; and so both in honour and conscience obliged to discharge that faithfully. And thus far thou art in the right. But the only measure of that discharge thou takest to be the mere formal observance of commands ; and those carrying but that name of power from which thou apprehendest it was committed to thee. As to the first part, the faithful discharge of the trust, the Lord forbid that I should tempt thee from it. Nay, I will charge and challenge it at thy hands, that, with all faithfulness and singleness of heart, as before the Lord, thou perform thy trust to those persons by whom, and to those public ends and interests for which, it was committed to thee.

" But for these things I shall appeal to the witness of God in thy conscience, as follows : —

" 1. For the persons, trusting whether thou didst receive thy present place from the affections or trust of the formal parliament only, even as then it stood ; or whether of the General or army ? And whether, so far as thou seemest to have the formality, by way of confirmation from the parliament, it were from any affection or trust of that sort or generation of men, which now, through accident, bear the sway and name ? or whether from them, whose judgment and affections are most opposite to the present proceedings there ?

" 2. For the end whether thou receivedst thy trust in order to the ends now carried on by the prevailing party there? or whether, in confidence of thy faithfulness to some other higher and more public ends? Whether for the kings, and the present prevailing factions; or for the public interest, and the generality of honest men that have engaged for the same? Upon the answer of thy conscience in these I propound further; in case such persons as neither did nor would have committed any such trust unto thee, but only gaining since the name of that power, from which thou hadst the formal compliment of the trust, and yet but partly that, shall require things destructive to, or not to the best advantage of, those public ends for which really thou receivedst thy trust, and at the same those from whose affection and confidence in thee thou hadst the matter and power of thy trust, shall desire and expect from thee other things necessary for the security, or but really for better advantage, of those public ends for which thou wert trusted, and for the common benefit and interest of that people, for which all pretend their employments and interest; in this case, I say, I shall appeal further to thy conscience, or thy ingenuity, to determine to which of these several persons, and according to which commands and expectations, thou art to exhibit and approve thy faithfulness in the trust: and which part to observe and follow is the more real and substantial performance before God and reasonable men.

" I shall not press upon thee, but thus plainly lay thy case before thee, only desiring thee not to slight it, but seriously to weigh it, as thou tenderest the approving thyself to God and his people. And I hope, he will not give thee up to such delusion, as to follow an air of honour, or mere form or shadow of faithfulness, to the rejection or neglect of that which is the reality and substance of both, as surely thou wouldst, if in the present case thou shouldst neither do the thing expected thyself, nor leave it to any other. Dear Robin, I will yet hope God hath better endued thee with truth and judgment in the inner parts, and more sense of his righteous judgments appearing abroad in this age and nation. So I leave thee to his gracious guidance; and the weight of what I have writ, lying not in authority to indemnify thee, but reason to lead thee. I shall not need subscribe other name than what I must desire to be known by unto thee.

" Thy most dearly
  " Affectionate and faithful
    " Friend to serve thee,
" Nov. 24th, 1648.   HENRY IRETON.

" For my dear friend Colonel Hammond
  Governor of the Isle of Wight."

Cromwell's letter is much longer. It is less formal, and has less pretensions to logical reasoning. It has more of bold hypocrisy, and of the conventual phrases of puritanism : —

" DEAR ROBIN,
" No man rejoyceth more to see a line from thee than myself. I know thou hast long been under tryal. Thou shalt be no loser by it. All must work

for the best. Thou desirest to hear of my experiences. I can tell thee I am such a one as thou didst formerly know, having a body of sin and death; but I thank God through Jesus Christ our Lord there is no condemnation, though much infirmity, and I wait for the redemption; and in this poor condition I obtain mercy and sweet consolation through the Spirit; and find abundant cause every day to exalt the Lord,—abase flesh. And herein I have some exercise.

" As to outward dispensations, if we may so call them, we have not been without our share of beholding some remarkable providences and appearances of the Lord. His presence hath been amongst us, and by the light of his countenance we have prevailed. We are sure the good will of him who dwelt in the bush has shined upon us; and we can humbly say, we know in whom we have believed, who is able, and will perfect what remaineth, and us also in doing what is well-pleasing in his eyesight.

Because I find some trouble in your spirit, occasioned first, not only by the continuance of your sad and heavy burthen, as you call it, upon you; but by the dissatisfaction you take at the ways of some good men, whom you love with your heart, who through this principle, that it is lawful for a lesser part (if in the right) to force, &c.

" To the first: call not your burthen sad nor heavy. If your Father laid it upon you, he intended neither. He is the Father of lights, from whom cometh every good and perfect gift; who of his own will begot us, and bad us count it all joy when such things befall us; they bring forth

M 2

the exercise of faith and patience; whereby in the end (James 1st) we shall be made perfect.

" Dear Robin, our fleshly reasonings ensnare us. These make us say, heavy, sad, pleasant, easy. Was not there a little of this, when Robert Hammond, through dissatisfaction too, desired retirement from the army, and thought of quiet in the Isle of Wight? Did not God find him out there? I believe he will never forget this. And now I perceive, he is to seek again, partly through his sad and heavy burthen, and partly through dissatisfaction with friends' actings. Dear Robin, thou and I were never worthy to be doorkeepers in this service. If thou wilt seek, seek to know the mind of God in all that chain of providence, whereby God brought thee thither, and that person to thee: how before and since God has ordered him, and affairs concerning him. And then tell me, whether there be not some glorious and high meaning in all this, above what thou hast yet attained. And laying aside thy fleshly reasoning, seek the Lord to teach thee what that is; and he will do it.

" You say, 'God hath appointed authorities among the nations, to which active or passive obedience is to be yielded. This resides in England in the parliament. Therefore active or passive,' &c. Authorities and powers are the ordinance of God. This or that species is of human institution, and limited, some with larger, others with stricter bands, each one according to his constitution. I do not, therefore, think the authorities may do any thing, and yet such obedience due; but all agree there are cases in which it is lawful to resist. If so, your ground fails, and so likewise the inference. Indeed, dear Robin, not to multiply words, the query is, whether ours is such a case? This ingeniously is the true question. To this I shall say nothing, though I could say very much; but only desire thee to see what thou findest in thy own heart as to two or three plain considerations. First, Whether *salus populi* be a sound position? Secondly, Whether in the way in hand, really and before the Lord, before whom conscience must stand, this be provided for; or the whole fruit of the war like to be frustrated, and almost like to turn to what it was, and worse? And this contrary to engagements, declarations, implicit covenants with those who ventured their lives upon those covenants and engagements, without whom perhaps, in equity, relaxation ought not to be. Thirdly, Whether this army be not a lawful power called by God to oppose and fight against the King upon so stated grounds; and being in power to such ends, may not oppose one name of authority for those ends as well as another? the outward authority, that called them, not by their power making the quarrel lawful; but it being so in itself. If so, it may be, acting will be justified *in foro humano*. But truly these kind of reasonings may be but fleshly, either with or against; only it is good to try what truth may be in them. And the Lord teach us."

Ireton is regarded by Whitlock as an *instigator* of the violence offered to the House of Commons by Colonel Pride and his troops, immediately

previous to the trial of the King; and his representation is probably correct.   At the same time,
according to Ludlow and Mrs. Hutchinson, it is
clear, that Ireton was, some months earlier, averse
to violent proceedings by the army against the
parliament, when Cromwell, Ludlow, and others
thought them expedient.   Ludlow says, " that
he himself went down to the siege of Colchester,
in which Fairfax and Ireton were engaged, and
proposed to them that the army should interpose
against the house."   Fairfax readily agreed; but
Ireton demurred to interfering till the King and
the presbyterians should have actually agreed,
and the body of the nation have been convinced
of the iniquity of their coalition.   The project
was for that time abandoned.   But when Colchester had surrendered, when the Scots were
defeated, the insurrections in the counties quelled,
and when the house was proceeding to the actual
conclusion of the treaty with the King, Ireton's
reasons for delaying the violence were probably
removed; and there can be no doubt (notwithstanding the contrary assertion of the editor of
Mrs. Hutchinson's Memoirs) that, if not an *instigator*, Ireton was a party actively concurring in
the outrage of the 6th of December.   It appears, from Ludlow, that the day after the house
resolved that the King's concessions were ground
for a future settlement, three officers of the army,
and three members of the house, (Ludlow being
evidently one, and it is rather to be inferred that
Ireton was another,) met together privately, and
arranged the plan of forcibly excluding the obnoxious members, and agreed on the list of those
who were to be suspended; and Ludlow adds ex-

pressly, that Ireton went to Sir Thomas Fairfax and acquainted him with the necessity of this extraordinary proceeding. On the following day *Pride's purge* was put in operation. Whitlock, writing shortly afterwards, (on the 24th of February, 1648,) says, with his usual simplicity, " From the council of state Cromwell and his son Ireton went home with me to supper, and they told me *wonderful observations of God's providence* in the affairs of the war, and in the triumph of the army's coming to London and *seizing the members of the house.*"[1]

We have seen the active part which Ireton took in the trial and execution of the King At the time of the trial, and for a short time subsequently to the King's death, the executive powers of the state were exercised by a committee sitting at Derby House; and on the 9th of July, Ireton, with Marten, Ludlow, Lord Grey, and seven others, chiefly of the Judges of the King, were added to this council. On the 10th of February following, when the first Council of State of forty were elected by votes in the parliament, the names of Harrison and Ireton were negatived on the previous question. It is impossible to conjecture the cause of this singular circumstance. A few months afterwards, Cromwell[2] was named Lord Lieutenant-General and

[1] Memorials, p. 384.

[2] On the 10th of July he set out on his journey himself, in a coach drawn by six Flanders mares, whitish grey, with several other coaches and great officers attending him, his life guard consisting of eighty persons in stately habits, some of them colonels, and the meanest field-officers or esquires.—Cromwelliana, p. 62.

General Governor of Ireland, and Ireton Major-General of the forces; and 12,000 men were ordered by the Council to be drafted for the service. It appears from Ludlow, however, that the army did not land in Ireland till September, 1649, when Cromwell and his suite were received at Dublin with great joy. In a campaign of great activity and splendid success, he reduced, before December, Wexford, Kilkenny, Clonmel, Cork, and the principal places in the south of Ireland.

Munster was now conquered by the instrumentality of Lord Broghill and the gentry of the province; and Ireton was immediately appointed by the parliament Lord President of the province; while Cook, the regicide solicitor, was named, by Cromwell, Chief Justice of Munster; in which situation, his friend Ludlow affirms (with the peremptoriness of a military man deciding on matters out of the sphere of his knowledge), "by proceeding in a summary and expeditious way, he determined more causes in a week than Westminster Hall in a year." In January, 1650, when Cromwell was recalled from Ireland to command the expedition against the Scots, Ireton was appointed his successor, with the title of Lord Deputy; and Cromwell, Ireton, Ludlow, with Colonel John Jones, and Mr. Miles Corbet (two of the King's judges), were named a committee for the administration of the civil affairs in Ireland. The Lady Ireton (Cromwell's daughter) embarked with the commissioners, and joined her husband at Waterford.

However much his principles and conduct are

to be reprobated, it cannot be doubted that Ireton was actuated in his proceedings by other motives than those of personal interest and ambition. While Cromwell, long before his protectorate, willingly received votes of 6500*l.* per annum in land, a handsome residence at Whitehall, the use of the palace at Hampton Court, and other provisions from the parliament, Ireton refused the only pecuniary grant which was made to him. When the news was brought to him in Ireland that the parliament had settled 2000*l.* per annum on him, he said, " They had many just debts which he desired they would pay before they made such presents; that he had no need of their land, and would not have it; and that he should be more contented to see them doing the service of the nation than so liberal in disposing of the public treasure."[1]   Ludlow, who was his colleague, describes Ireton to have conducted the military and civil affairs of Ireland with great ability, and with unbounded devotion to the public service. He says, he accompanied him on a visit to the garrison of Killalo, and to order a bridge between the counties of Tipperary and Clare, when " he left his guard to refresh themselves, and rode so hard that he spoiled many horses and hazarded some of the men ; but he was so diligent in the public service, and so careless of every thing that belonged to himself, that he never regarded what food or clothes he used, what hour he went to rest, or what horse he mounted." The hardships and fatigues endured by the deputy and his officers are co-

[1] Ludlow, 159.

piously described by Ludlow, who was himself
affected by the plague raging in Limerick, which
the army were then besieging.   After several
days' hard riding among bogs and over rocks in
the county of Limerick, making reconnoissances,
and ordering garrisons and winter quarters for
his troops, Ireton was exposed to a violent
storm of wind, rain, and snow, by which he took
cold, and was seized with illness on his return to
his quarters.   He, however, refused to go to bed
till he had determined a cause that was before
him, as president of a court-martial, upon an officer
accused of doing some violence to the Irish.   Ludlow, after an absence of a few days, returned to
him, and found him " grown worse, having been
let blood, and sweating exceedingly, with a burn-
ing fever at the same time.   Yet, for all this, he
ceased not to apply himself to the public business,
settling garrisons, and distributing winter quarters.   I endeavoured to persuade him, as I had
often done before, that his immoderate labours
for his country would much impair, if not utterly
destroy him: but he had so totally neglected
himself during the siege of Limerick, not putting
off his clothes all that time, except to change his
linen, that the malignant humours which he had
contracted, wanting room to perspire, became
confined to his body, and rendered him more
liable to be infected by the contagion."   He
insisted on Ludlow leaving him, in order to meet
his own family, who were then arriving at Dublin.
In two days afterwards Ireton died of the plague,
on the 26th of November, 1657, at the age of 41.
   The tidings of his death, according to Whit-

lock, struck a great sadness into Cromwell; and Ludlow says he "was universally lamented by all good men; more especially because the public was thereby deprived of a most faithful, able, and useful servant." Mrs. Hutchinson, in alluding to the ambitious views of Cromwell, which had ripened after the battle of Worcester, mentions that Ireton "would not be wrought to serve him, but hearing of his machinations, *determined* to come over to England to endeavour to divert him from such destructive courses; but God cut him short by death," &c.[1] We are not aware that this *intention* of Ireton is mentioned by any other writer; but from the intimacy and relationship which existed between Ireton and Colonel Hutchinson, they were doubtless in correspondence as to public affairs, and Colonel Hutchinson alone might be in possession of Ireton's secret intentions. Whitlock regrets Ireton's death, on account of the influence he had over the mind of Cromwell; and there can be no doubt (as Clarendon seems to think) that, whether he had formed any intentions or not in his lifetime, he must, if he had lived, and if Cromwell had pursued the same course, have joined with Ludlow, Harrison, and the other republicans, in opposing that selfish ambition which threatened destruction to all their favourite schemes of government. It is remarkable, that, only two days after Cromwell received the news of Ireton's death, he opened a conference with some of the leading members of the house, on the question *whether they would*

[1] Memoirs, p. 328.

establish in England a republic or a government
of mixed monarchy.[1]

The remains of Ireton were, by order of the
house, and by desire of Cromwell, transported
to England, where they lay in state at Somerset
House, and were then interred with much pomp,
at the public expense, in Henry the Seventh's
Chapel in Westminster Abbey; Cromwell walking as chief mourner, attended by many members of the house dressed in black. The celebrated John Goodwin, Dean of Christ Church,
preached his funeral sermon, on the text in
the 12th chapter of Daniel, verse 13th :—" But
go thou thy way till the end be : for thou shalt
rest, and stand in the lot at the end of the days."
Anthony Wood says, " Elegies were made on his
death ;" and a splendid monument, with a relief
representing himself and his wife, was placed
on his grave in the Abbey. These pompous
obsequies of his son-in-law were among the
indications, more or less distinct, which now
appeared of the aspiring views of Cromwell.
Ludlow says, with a mournful eloquence, that,
" if Ireton could have foreseen what was done,
he would certainly have made it his desire that
his body might have found a grave where his
soul left it. So much did he despise those
pompous and expensive vanities ; having erected
for himself a more glorious monument in the
hearts of good men, by his affection to his country, his abilities of mind, his impartial justice,

[1] Whitlock, who was present, describes the conference
fully : and see *post*, in the Memoir of Harrison.

his diligence in the public service, and his other
virtues; which were a far greater honour to his
memory than a dormitory amongst the ashes of
kings."[1]   Ireton was a consistent democrat and
cynic, and would doubtless have despised the
honours bestowed on his remains as much as he
hated living kings; but Ludlow's unqualified
panegyric will be approved by few who reflect on
the bloody act which stands conspicuous in the
history of Ireton's conduct.   Cromwell, who appears before this time to have neglected Colonel
Hutchinson, probably knowing him to be a determined republican, not reconcileable to his own projects, omitted to send him mourning, or an invit-
ation to his kinsman's funeral ; which the Colonel,
according to his wife's account, seems to have re-
sented with some littleness of mind :—" Such was
the flattery of many pitiful Lords, and other gentlemen parasites, that they put themselves into
deepe mourning ; but Colonel Hutchinson, that
day, put on a scarlett cloak very richly laced,
such as he usually wore, and coming into the
room where the members were, seeing some of
the Lords in mourning, he went to them to enquire the cause ; who told him, they had put it on
to honour the General ; and asked why he, that
was a kinsman, was in such a different colour?
He told them, because the General had neglected
sending to him, when he had sent to so many
that had no alliance, only to make up the train ;
he was resolved he would not flatter so much
as to buy for himself, although he was a true
mourner in his heart for his cousin, whom he

[1] Memoirs, p. 164.

had ever loved, and would therefore go and take his place among the mourners. This he did, and went into the room where the close mourners were, who, seeing him come in as different from mourning as he could make himself, the Alderman[1] came to him, making a great apology," &c. Mrs. Hutchinson adds:—" Cromwell, who had ordered all things, was peeked horribly at it, though he dissembled his resentment at that time," &c. Ireton's costly tomb in the Abbey could not preserve his body from that vengeance which, whether well or ill judged, must be anticipated by men who have outraged humanity by staining their hands with the blood of their sovereign. At the restoration it was disinterred, exposed on a gibbet at Tyburn, the trunk thrown into a pit, and the head set upon a pole.

Ireton has naturally shared the fate which belongs to all men who act so conspicuous a part in the transactions of an eventful and passionate period of history. He has been unsparingly abused by the royalists and presbyterians, and as vehemently extolled by the independents and republicans. Some of the charges against him are certainly groundless. Clarendon insinuates more than once that he was wanting in courage; saying, that Hollis, " one day upon a hot debate, and some rude expressions that fell from the Colonel, challenged him to fight;" and that, " Ireton replying that his conscience would not allow him to fight a duel, Hollis pulled his nose, telling

---

[1] John Ireton, Alderman of London, and Henry Ireton's brother.

him, that if his conscience would keep him from giving men satisfaction, it should keep him from provoking.them ;" a rule, certainly, which ought to be most strictly observed by all persons who, on the ground of religion, refuse a compliance with the existing usages of society. Even supposing this account were correct, still Ireton's conduct at Naseby, at Gainsborough, in Nottinghamshire, at Colchester, and in Ireland, would be sufficient to place his courage beyond all doubt. But Hollis, in his Memoirs, which are certainly not wanting in bitterness against Ireton and Cromwell, does not hint at the affair. Clarendon wrote as to it only from hearsay; while Ludlow, who was a member of the house, speaking of the same transaction, says, " that several members, observing the quarrel, sent the Serjeant-at-arms to command Hollis and Ireton to attend; when he found them taking boat to go to the other side of the water; and on their return to the house they were compelled to give promises to forbear all acts of hostility to each other." [1]

The skill and capacity of Ireton as a military man have never been questioned. Indeed, the officer whom Cromwell selected to be either near himself, or, when absent, to be intrusted with the most difficult posts during the war, — whom Fairfax relied on, and Hutchinson, Harrison, and Ludlow admired, — must obviously have been a man of no common capacity in the affairs of war. Whitlock, in his famous speech in defence of his own profession, when some

[1] This account of the matter is confirmed by Mrs. Hutchinson, and by the Journals of the House of Commons.

member proposed to exclude lawyers from parliament, mentions Ireton as one of the distinguished instances of services of the sword rendered to the state by lawyers, who had laid aside the gown when called upon by their country. Nor are his abilities as a politician and negotiator matter of doubt. He was the chosen associate and instrument of Cromwell in governing the council of officers, in duping and ruling the agitators and soldiers, in negotiating with the King, and in secretly directing the influence of the independents and republicans in the parliament. The numerous papers drawn up by him on behalf of the army display much sagacity, acuteness, and forethought, and a skilful command of language. His management of the civil affairs of Ireland is highly praised by Ludlow, and admitted to be vigorous and efficient by his enemy, Clarendon. This historian says, " Others thought his parts lay more towards civil affairs, and were fitter for the modelling of that government (a republic) which his heart was set upon, (being a scholar, conversant in the law, and in all those authors who had expressed the greatest animosity and malice against the regal government,) than for the conduct of an army to support it." He preserved strict discipline in the army, and rigorously administered what he deemed justice towards the Irish and his own officers. In one instance, a boat full of soldiers, moved either by fear or a promise of life, surrendered to the English; notwithstanding which, some of them were put to the sword. Ireton was much troubled at this severity, considering that they would not have quitted their means of preservation except upon some terms of advantage. He directed a strict enquiry into the matter by a court-martial, and the Colonel who had ordered the execution was cashiered. An obstinate adherence to his own purposes and resolutions was a conspicuous feature in Ireton's character. Clarendon says " he was of a melancholick, reserved, dark nature, who communicated his thoughts to very few; so that, for the most part, he resolved alone, but was never diverted from any resolution he had taken; and he was thought often, by his obstinacy, to prevail over Cromwell himself." According to Ludlow, in his latter years he was cured of this extreme pertinacity, which had been his greatest infirmity. — That Ireton, as well as his father-in-law, made abundant use of hypocrisy, and every art of perfidious deception in their dealings with the King, the parliament, and the army, is a fact beyond contradiction. Considerable mystery and doubt obscure their proceedings, from the King's seizure by the army to his flight to the Isle of Wight. If they were sincere in the professions which they then made of a desire to restore Charles, they grossly deceived the officers and agitators of the army; if these professions were only intended to lull the King and the royalists to sleep, they were treacherous to the King and his friends; if, as seems probable (though more so as to Cromwell than to Ireton), they played the game of working out their own safety and power by dexterous management, and by a readiness to side with that party which should preponderate, there is little

N

doubt that they alternately duped and deceived the King, the republicans, and the soldiers, as the circumstances and intrigues of the day demanded. Mr. Godwin, their admirer, offers an apology for their conduct, which resolves itself into the worn-out casuistry, that they conceived the ends they sought sanctified the means which they used. " Having once sworn to deceive, the dimensions of their minds enabled them immediately to stand forth accomplished and entire adepts in the school of Machiavel. They were satisfied that the system they adopted was just, and they felt no jot of humiliation and self-abasement in the systematical pursuit of it." We are aware that the essence of such an excuse is, not that the objects at which they aimed were, in fact, just and righteous, but that they conscientiously believed them to be so. But in judging of such obliquities of proceeding, the world are ever tempted to ask, what, in truth, were the ends which were thus deemed sufficient to justify the departure from all morality and honesty of proceeding ? No one can deny, that selfish ambition and personal aggrandisement entered largely into the objects of Cromwell. We acquit Ireton of selfish and personal views. Ireton played the dark and accomplished hypocrite, as he afterwards became the bloody regicide, in order to realise his vain dream of erecting a political and religious republic on the ruins of the monarchy and hierarchy of England.

We have seen Clarendon's charge against Ireton, of being bloody[1] and unmerciful. Lord

[1] Sir Philip Warwick, who of course hated him as the enemy of the King, says "he died in a delirium, cry-

Broghill, a licentious soldier of fortune, says that when he marched against a certain barony in Ireland, " he gave orders to kill man, woman, and child," and said that the Irish " did not deserve to live;" but he admits that his own expostulations induced Ireton to relax these severe orders. Ireton, in giving them, acted on the notion that the Irish were a conquered people rebelling against their governors, and waging exterminating war against all Protestants. When Limerick surrendered to Ireton after a long siege, twenty-two persons of influence in the city were excepted out of the capitulation; and of these, five, including the Mayor, the Catholic bishop, an incendiary friar, and the deputy governor, were executed by order of a court-martial, of which Ireton, Ludlow, and others, were members. The governor, O'Neal, saved his life by showing that he had earnestly recommended a timely surrender of the city. This proceeding, though severe, was, according to Ludlow, the act of all the members of the court-martial, adopted after great consideration, and an attentive hearing of each prisoner. It derives some palliation from the peculiar circumstances of the country, and the cruelties which had been committed on the English by the rebellious Irish; it is certainly not to be compared for injustice and hardship with the execution of Lord Derby and the other prisoners after the battle of Worcester, or with the shooting of Lucas and Lisle, at Colchester, under the orders of Fairfax. Cook (the regicide coun-

---

ing out, *Blood! blood! blood!*" As if this proved any thing as to his ferocity of character.

sel) extols Ireton as "a patron, father, and husband to the fatherless and widow;" and Whitlock,
a much more unobjectionable witness, gives him
credit for humanity.   His rule was undoubtedly
rigid and despotic in Ireland; but the circumstances of that unfortunate country seem to
have required it.   His severe character inclined
him to stern discipline, and to an uncompromising execution of justice on all who offended;
but there is little evidence of his showing any
disposition to wanton and gratuitous cruelty; and
the instances before cited evince that his stern
nature could at times relent under the influence
of compassion.

MEMOIR OF JOHN BRADSHAW.

JOHN BRADSHAW, the President of the Court
which condemned Charles, was of a respectable
gentleman's family, settled at Marple, in Cheshire,
and was baptized at Stockport, on the 16th of
December, 1602.   He was the son of Henry
Bradshaw, of Marple and Wyberslegh. His grand-
father, Henry Bradshaw, first purchased those
considerable estates from Sir Edmund Stanley,
knight of the Bath, a few years after John Bradshaw's birth.   Bradshaw received his school education at Bunbury, in Cheshire, and Middleton,
in Lancashire; as he was the youngest son of his
father he was articled to an attorney at Congle-
ton, and afterwards entered as a student of law
in Gray's Inn, where he appears diligently

to have studied his profession. [1] Clarendon says " his fortune was of his own making," and that at the time of his being appointed President of the Court " he was not much known in Westminster Hall, though of good practice in his chamber, and much employed by the factious. He was not without parts, and of great insolence and ambition." He was associated [2] with the famous William Prynne and Mr. Nudigate, as counsel appointed by the parliament to prosecute Lord Maguire and Hugh Ogee Macmahon, in 1645, for their treason and massacre in attempting to seize Dublin Castle, and destroy the Lords Justices and council. But he appears to have acted only as a junior counsel among many, for his name is not mentioned in the report of the trial; and the great question in the cause as to Lord Maguire's liability as an Irish peer to be tried for treason in the English Court of King's Bench, and not by his peers in Ireland, was successfully argued by Prynne (with a triumphant display of learning and pedantic zeal), and by Serjeant Rolle (afterwards Chief Justice), for the Crown, and by Hale (afterwards Sir Matthew) and Twisden (afterwards a Judge of the King's Bench) for the prisoners. In 1646, Bradshaw, by a vote of the Commons, in which the peers were desired to acquiesce, was joined with Sir Rowland Wandesford and Sir Thomas Bedingfield, as Commissioners of the Great Seal for six months;

[1] The books of Gray's Inn do not give any traces of Bradshaw, as they are not complete further back than the Restoration.

[2] Whitlock's Memorials.

N 3

and in February, 1646-7, he had sufficient influence to procure his appointment by both houses as Chief Justice of Chester,—a situation peculiarly agreeable to him, from its connection with his native county.

In June, 1647, Bradshaw, together with Oliver St. John, the Solicitor-General, Serjeant Jermyn, and Prynne, was ordered by the Commons to prosecute the aged, intrepid, and learned champion of royalty, Judge Jenkins, who had been committed to the Tower for his adherence to the King; who had refused to kneel when brought to the bar of the house; and who constantly exposed in his writings, with legal learning and acumen, the want of all legitimate authority in the two houses without the King. Bradshaw's nomination for this business, jointly with these other eminent counsel, shows that he was then in some estimation as a lawyer; for the loyal old Judge was not less formidable by his knowledge, than by his invincible courage, to the parliament, and the parliamentary lawyers of the day. The House of Commons, among other royal functions, at this period usurped that of ordering calls of Serjeants at law; and in October, 1648, Bradshaw, together with Sir Thomas Widdrington (afterwards Keeper of the Great Seal), Sir Thomas Bedingfield, Mr. Keble, and Mr. Thorp (one of the King's pretended Judges, who refused to sit), was by order of the two houses called to the degree of the coif.[1]

Though Bradshaw was a man of some talents

[1] These Serjeants do not find a place in Dugdale's Chronica Series, who does not deign to notice any legal ap-

and professional knowledge, and had attained to some distinction among his party, even according to Clarendon, yet circumstances contributed quite as much as any merits of his own to raise him to the " bad eminence "of trying his sovereign. The Judges of the realm (headed by the learned Rolle, Chief Justice of England, and St. John, Chief Justice of the Common Pleas) positively declined to be parties to the proceeding. Prynne, Widdrington, Whitlock, Maynard, and all the parliamentarian lawyers kept aloof. It was first determined that Bradshaw, Serjeant Nicholas, and Steel, should be " *assistants* " only. The two latter, however, made excuses for non-attendance. Of eight lawyers who were named commissioners in the ordinance constituting the court only four ever sat on the trial ; viz. Bradshaw, Miles Corbet, and Bradshaw's two assistants or assessors, Say and Lisle. That the President should be a practical lawyer was obviously expedient; and Bradshaw was the most eminent and efficient of the few desperate members of the long robe who would consent to partake the guilt of the proceeding. Milton, in his extravagant panegyric on his kinsman and republican friend, says, " Tandem uti Regis judicio præsidere vellet, a Senatu rogatus, provinciam sane periculosissimam non recusavit." Bradshaw was certainly an intrepid as well as an ambitious man; and any remote dangers which were likely to attend the part he was going to act were,

---

pointments after 1645; inscribing his subsequent pages in large letters, " *Dominante Perduellione Justitium.*" Widdrington and Bedingfield were again called Serjeants by the King's Writ at the Restoration.

no doubt, soon thrown into shade in his mind by the dazzling dignity of Lord President of the High Court of Justice, the Deanery House at Westminster for a permanent residence, 5000*l.* for outfit, a seat in the council of state, and 4000*l.* per annum in land, which the house voted to be settled on him and his heirs. The lands were those plundered from the Earl of St. Alban's and the Lord Cottington, and an exact survey was ordered to be made of them. In six months after the King's death Bradshaw was also appointed Chancellor of the Duchy of Lancaster,—a place which the Parliament had determined to abolish, but which was retained solely to reward his pre-eminent merits.

Clarendon (who, however, only speaks from report) says he " with great humility accepted the office of President, which he administered with all the pride, impudence, and supercili-ousness imaginable." Milton loads his con-duct with a splendid but vague and hyperbolical eulogy. " For he brought to the study of the law an enlightened capacity, a lofty spirit, and spotless manners, obnoxious to none ; so that he filled that high and unexampled office, ren-dered the more dangerous by the threats and daggers[1] of private assassins with a firmness, a gravity, a dignity, and presence of mind, as if he had been designed and created by the Deity ex-pressly for this work, which God in his wonder-

---

[1] Bradshaw's " broad brimmed hat," which was a thick high-crowned beaver lined with plated steel, was worn as a protection in case of violence. It was sent by Dr. Blisse, preacher at the Rolls, to the Museum at Oxford. 3 Ken-nett's Comp. Hist. 181. note (a).   (Second edition).

ful providence had appointed to be done in this nation, and by so much eclipsed the glory of all former tyrannicides, by how much it is more humane, more just, and more majestic, to try a tyrant than to slay him untried.[1]" It is remarkable that Ludlow, who sat every day on the trial, and who shortly relates the course of the proceedings, does not bestow a single epithet of approbation or description on the President's conduct in his office. Judging from the report of the trial, we think that Clarendon's epithets are not less warranted by the audacity of Bradshaw in accepting the office, than by the peculiar manner in which he discharged its functions. He seems to have acted fully *up to* the extraordinary part he had assumed, and for which his friend Milton thought him peculiarly created. He had consented to be President and organ of an assembly met without authority either from the constitution or the nation, to act the part of Judges of their vanquished King, and to prepare the way for his destruction; and he shrunk not from executing a lawless function with all the bullying effrontery and cold-hearted insolence, which it demanded of him. The difficulties of the office certainly required to be met by much talent, judgment, and readiness, and, above all, by an impenetrable assurance. This last quality almost alone is remarkable in the conduct and speeches of Bradshaw, which exhibit few traces either of well applied learning, of acuteness, or of that eloquence which Milton extolled. His la-

[1] Secunda Defensio pro Populo Anglicano. Milton's Prose Works, vol. ii.

boured address to the King on pronouncing
sentence is pedantic, sophistical, and canting,
without the redeeming qualities of ingenuity
of reasoning, or felicity of elocution.   When
we compare Bradshaw's harangues with the
speeches and legal arguments of Whitlock, St.
John, Hale, Prynne, and other lawyers of the day, the
regicide Judge makes but an insignificant figure.
Noble[1] says, that Bradshaw was offended that his
Sovereign should not be uncovered in his presence.   "The *offence* was pardoned the first day
of the King's appearance, but order was taken
respecting it in future."   This is wholly inaccurate; for it was expressly resolved in the
Painted Chamber before the trial, not to insist on
the King's taking off his hat; and Charles remained covered during every day of the trial,
as well as the President.   The King's rejection
of the authority of the Court was a cause much
more likely to gall the pride of Bradshaw and
his accomplices: while the manifest superior-
ity of Charles in argument, and the expressions
of sympathy shown to him by the audience, were
well calculated to exasperate the temper of his
Judges.

Bradshaw's office did not expire with the com-
pletion of the wickedness for which it was erected,
— and he was also immediately elected by the
Commons one of the Executive Council of State of
Forty, who were appointed to carry on the government, when the King and the House of Peers were
voted to be useless, dangerous, and burdensome.

Bradshaw was the only member not of the

---

[1] Lives of the Regicides, vol. i.

House of Commons, unless, perhaps, we except
Rolle, St. John, and Wild (formerly Serjeant
Wild), the three Chief Judges.   At first, the
Council had a different President at each sitting; but on the 16th of March, Bradshaw was
appointed permanent President; which, considering that Whitlock, St. John, Rolle, Vane,
Haslerig, besides five peers, were members, (we
reckon nothing of the lesser herd of regicides
who had sat as mutes in the mock trial at Westminster, and who now became State Counsellors,)
certainly shows the consideration he enjoyed
among his party.   Milton, who was three days
later appointed Secretary for foreign tongues, to
the Council (that body having decreed that they
would neither write to other states, nor receive
answers, but in that tongue which was fittest to
record great things! [1]) of course extols the
stateman-like qualities of his kinsman the President and Mr. Godwin naturally follows him.
But Whitlock, who was an acute judge, and a
a member of the Council, says Bradshaw seemed
but little versed in such business, and spent much
of the members' time " in urging his own long
arguments, which are inconvenient in state matters.   His part was only to have gathered the
sense of the Council, and to state the question,
not to deliver his own opinion."   He, however,
remained President in the Councils of 1649, 1650,
and 1651, and was a member of the committees on the law and for examinations.   Mr.
Godwin [2] says — " Bradshaw, by his office, was

---

[1] Toland's Life of Milton.   [2] Vol. iii. p. 185.

in some measure the first man in the nation.[1] He was to receive foreign ambassadors, and to represent, in his own person, upon occasions of public solemnity, the executive government of the Commonwealth of England." In the third year of the Commonwealth he applied to resign his office; but, as he states it, " could not obtain that favour." In the fourth year the mode of proceeding was altered, and the office of President was appointed to continue only for one month of twenty-eight days; Bradshaw was the first President, commencing on the 1st of December, 1652; and he was followed in the office by Whitlock, Haslerig, Lord Lisle, John Lisle (the regicide), Chief Justice Rolle, Sir Henry Vane, Lord Pembroke, &c.

Bradshaw was a stern republican, who, having destroyed his legitimate sovereign, had no inclination to submit to an usurper; agreeing with his friend Henry Marten, that " if they were to be governed by a single person, Charles was as proper a gentleman for it as any in the kingdom." As Cromwell's ambitious views matured themselves, it was natural, therefore, that a cordial disgust should grow up between the usurper and the Lord President. — Bradshaw saw with hatred the projects of a powerful man threatening to eclipse his own consequence, and to crumble to dust the fabric of government which he had mainly contributed

---

[1] When Evelyn went to France in April, 1649, he says he " got a passe from the rebell Bradshawe, then in great power," but that he found silver quite as useful to him at Dover as Bradshaw's hand and seal. — *Diary.*

to raise: and Cromwell knew the impracticable character of the President too well to hope to cajole him by his wonted hypocrisy, or to gain him by his rare art of persuasion. It was clear that a violent breach must take place between these two remarkable men; and it occurred in April, 1653, on the day on which Cromwell forcibly broke up the sitting of the Long Parliament. After Oliver, with Harrison and his troopers, had seized the "bauble," the mace, driven out the members, and locked the doors of the house, he made his appearance in plain black clothes, with grey worsted stockings, attended by Lambert and Harrison, at the Council of State at Whitehall. Bond's month of presidency had just expired, and Bradshaw was in the chair of the Republic. Cromwell entered the Council Chamber, and addressed the members: "Gentlemen, if you are met here as private persons, you shall not be disturbed: but if as a Council of State, this is no place for you: and since you cannot but know what was done in the morning, so take notice that the parliament is dissolved." Bradshaw intrepidly answered, — "Sir, we have heard what you did at the house in the morning, and before many hours all England will hear it; — but, Sir, you are mistaken to think that the parliament is dissolved: for no power under heaven can dissolve them but themselves; therefore take you notice of that." After some words to the same purpose from Sir Arthur Haslerig, Mr. Love, and Mr. Scot, the Council, perceiving themselves to be under the same violence

as the House, broke up and withdrew.[1]   The
closing scene of the English Monarchy has been
depicted in the foregoing pages.   This was the
last act of the first English Republic.   To Bradshaw, who had performed the principal part in destroying royalty, it devolved to make the last
expiring protest on behalf of the Commonwealth.
Mr. Godwin, who has described this scene with a
sorrowful enthusiasm, worthy of Bradshaw or Ireton themselves says, "Perhaps no man was ever
placed in so illustrious a situation as that which
Bradshaw occupied at this moment * * * * *.—
Cromwell was backed by all his guards, and by
an army of the highest discipline, and the most
undaunted and prosperous character.   Bradshaw
appeared before him in the simple robe of his
integrity.   The Lord General was the most reso-
lute of men, and who could least endure an idle
show of opposition.   The parade of contradiction,
and the pomp of declamation, would have been
useless.   A few words — a brief and concentred
remonstrance—were enough.   They were uttered,
and Cromwell ventured on no reply.   Abashed
the traitor stood !"

Neither in the new Convention or Parliament,
(which went by the name of Praise God Barbone's), nor in Cromwell's new Council of State,
was Bradshaw's name to be found; though we
find it inserted among the thirty-three com-
missicners of the new High Court of Justice,
which was erected on the 10th of August, 1653,
for trial of the persons who were conspiring
to bring in Charles the Second: but Heath

---

[1] Ludlow, p. 195.

says Lisle was made President, Bradshaw, as a great Commonwealth-man, and enemy to a single person, being laid aside; and it does not appear that he ever consented to sit. Cromwell now, to the great disgust of Bradshaw, and his friends Ludlow, Scot, Haslerig, and other friends of a republic, had secured his road to the throne of England, with the title of Lord Protector. Barbone's convention, influenced by the manœuvres of Cromwell and his creatures, Whalley, Sydenham, and other officers of the army, went with the Speaker, Rous (who had been Provost of Eton), to Whitehall, and formally surrendered up their authority to the usurper. Cromwell presented his new " instrument of government," and was sworn in as Lord Protector in the Court of Chancery, in the presence of the Judges, Council, Commissioners of the Seal, the Lord Mayor and Aldermen, and the Generals and other officers. He was proclaimed throughout the kingdom; and all writs were altered from the name of the " Keepers of the liberties of England" to that of " Protector." Ludlow, who had a command in Ireland, states that he hindered the proclaiming of him for a fortnight in that country; and when it was carried by one in the Council, he refused still to sign the order. And in speaking of the ceremony, he says discontentedly, " the artillery, which was at the command of Lieutenant-General Fleetwood (Cromwell's son-in-law), wasted some powder belonging to the public, the report of which was very unwelcome music to me, who, desiring to be as far from this pageantry as I could, rode out of the

town that afternoon." [1] The new Protector dined,
amidst regal splendour, with the citizens at Gro-
cers' Hall; and, as a first act of royal grace, knighted
Viner the Lord Mayor.   He acted the part of
King in all its details; received the sword from
the Mayor and Aldermen at Temple Bar, and
graciously returned it.   He was harangued by
the Recorder; and the Lord Mayor bareheaded
rode with the sword before him through the city.
The people did not perform equally well the part
of subjects; for they gazed in stupid wonder and
silence, entirely withholding those cheers and
greetings which they had on all such occasions
bestowed on their legitimate monarchs.

According to the promise contained in the
instrument of government, writs were now issued
for electing a parliament; and notwithstanding
Cromwell's party " endeavoured to promote the
election of such as would concur in adoring the
idol lately set up," Bradshaw, together with
Haslerig, Scot, and other republican malcon-
tents, were returned members.[2] This parliament
met on Sunday the 3d of September, 1654-5,
having first twice attended divine service with
the Protector in Westminster Abbey.   When
they had assembled to the number of 300, Lambert came and informed them the Protector
was in the Painted Chamber, and required their
presence; the members, notwithstanding some
cried " *Sit still* [3]," adjourned to comply with his
Highness's pleasure.   Cromwell received them

---

[1] Page 204.
[2] Bradshaw appears to have been returned for Cheshire.
[3] Introduction to Burton's Diary.

standing bareheaded, on a throne raised for the
purpose, and with a short speech dismissed them
to meet for business on the following day.   On
the next day they met at the Abbey, the Protector being attended with three maces and the
sword of state, which was carried by General
Lambert.   " Some hundreds of. gentlemen and
officers,"says Whitlock, " went before, bare, with
the lifeguards, and next before the coach his
pages and lacqueys richly clothed.   On the one
side of the coach went Strickland, one of the
council and Captain of his guard, with the Master
of the Ceremonies, both on foot.   On the other
side went Howard, Captain of the Lifeguards.
In the coach with him was his son Henry, and
Lambert ; both sat bare.   After him came Clay-
pole, Master of the Horse, with a gallant led
horse, richly trapped.   Next came the Commissioners of the Great Seal and of the Treasury,
and divers of the Council in coaches, and the
ordinary guards.   He alighting at the Abbey
door, the officers of the army and the gentlemen
went first ; next them, four maces : then the
Commissioners of the Seal, I carrying the purse ;
after, Lambert, carrying the sword, bare ; the
rest followed.   His Highness was seated over
against the pulpit, and the members on both
sides." [1]   Thomas Goodwin, the famous independent divine, a fellow of Eton College, and
favourite of Cromwell, who made him President
of Magdalen College, Oxford, preached the sermon.   After the sermon the members met Crom-

---

[1] Memorials, p. 582.

well in the Painted Chamber, where, according
to Whitlock, " he made a large and subtle
speech to them," and then they proceeded to
elect a Speaker. Bradshaw was put in nomination and warmly supported by the republicans,
in opposition to Lenthal, the old Speaker.   The
latter, however, was re-elected, on account of his
great experience and knowledge, and probably as
being less disagreeable to the new Protector.
After appointing a fast, reading an act against
fairs and markets on the Sabbath and other
matters, the house adjourned till the next day.

On Thursday the 7th commenced the memorable debate, of which it is to be regretted that
no detailed report exists, on the vital question,
" whether the government by a single person
and a parliament should be approved!"   A preliminary point was first debated, and carried in
the affirmative, viz. that the house should resolve
itself into a committee for the debate.   On the
division on this question Bradshaw and the republicans voted with the " Yeas," and Bradshaw
was their teller.   The great question was then
discussed from nine in the morning till seven
at night for three successive days.   Ludlow says,
" Bradshaw was very instrumental in opening the
eyes of many young members, who never before
heard their interest so clearly stated and asserted;
so that the Commonwealth party increased daily,
and that of the sword lost ground."   On Monday the 11th, the debate was once more adjourned at night.   Cromwell and his officers
resolved that it should never be resumed.   The
next morning, when the members repaired to the

house, they found the doors locked, guards in the lobby, Commissary-General Whalley had carried away the mace, and they were told they were to attend the Protector shortly in the Painted Chamber! The Speaker and members were to be seen walking up and down Westminster Hall in great confusion, waiting for his arrival. At ten o'clock Cromwell came in his barge from Privy Gardens to Westminster, with his lifeguards, officers, and halberdiers; and in a speech of an hour and a half duration, explained to them, that before any member could enter the house again, he must sign a recognition of his authority, engaging not to consent to alter the government as it was settled in a sole person and the parliament. The courtiers and officers of the army immediately subscribed the instrument. When the house adjourned at twelve o'clock there were 100 signatures.

Goddard and the other Norfolk members dined together to hold consultation, and, except three, they all determined to sign, as the best course left to peaceable men in the dreadful perplexities and agitations of the time. Ludlow states, that most of the eminent asserters of liberty withdrew themselves. There is no doubt that Bradshaw was among the number. The house, thus purged after the approved precedents of the time, met again on the 14th of September, and sat till the 22d of January; when Cromwell, finding even their very limited freedom of debate offensive, and disgusted that they reserved to themselves the nomination of his successor in the Protectorate, dissolved them in a very uncourteous speech, studded with scriptural allusions.

Bradshaw appears to have been excluded, probably by the contrivances of Cromwell, from sitting in any subsequent parliament. Before the election of that which met on the 17th of September, 1656, Bradshaw, Sir Harry Vane, Colonel Rich, and Ludlow, were summoned by Oliver to attend the Council at Whitehall. Vane coolly told the messenger he should be at his house at Charing Cross on a certain day, if he was wanted. Bradshaw, Rich, and Ludlow, attended. As soon as Cromwell saw Bradshaw, he required him to take out a new commission from him for his office of Chief Justice of Chester. Bradshaw peremptorily refused, alleging that he held his office by a grant from the parliament *quamdiu bene se gesserit,* and he was ready to submit his conduct to a trial by any twelve men whom Cromwell should appoint. He then withdrew, and resolved, notwithstanding what had passed, to go the summer circuit as usual, unless prevented by force. Cromwell, unwilling to draw on himself the dislike of the lawyers, did not on this occasion, as he did on many others, interrupt the ordinary administration of justice. He allowed Bradshaw to proceed on the circuit; but wrote earnest letters to Cheshire, to desire that he might be opposed at the election for the county. One of these came into the hands of Bradshaw's friends, who publicly read it at the election, and Bradshaw was returned by the sheriff a knight for the county. It seems, however, that he never took his seat.

In 1655, Bradshaw, with Haslerig and other republicans, appears to have been a party to

Colonel Overton's conspiracy against the Protector's government. Overton, the great friend of Milton, who was second in command to Monk in Scotland, was to seize that General's person, and to march with his troops to England, where Haslerig, Bradshaw, and others were to join him, and where they were sure of reinforcements from the partisans of Charles the Second. The plot was detected by Cromwell, and Overton was sent to the Tower. Mr. Noble, who is perpetually inaccurate, charges Bradshaw, as well as Lord Grey, with being a party to the plots of Venner and the other mad enthusiasts who aimed at setting up the "fifth monarchy" of our Saviour on earth, supported by themselves and other saints. But there appears no authority for the statement, either as to Bradshaw or Lord Grey.

After the death of Oliver Cromwell, and the proclamation of Richard as his successor, many of the republicans, who still held the Long Parliament to be in existence, as not having been legally dissolved, met at Sir Harry Vane's, and after mature deliberation resolved that it was both their duty and policy, if fairly elected to the new Protector's parliament, to sit in the assembly, and to use their best endeavours to serve the public. Ludlow, Haslerig, Scot, Weaver, &c. were returned, and took their seats. Bradshaw was returned by the sheriff for the county of Chester; but in consequence of another person being also returned, he did not sit — at least, during the early sittings; and we do not find his name as a Speaker in the Protector Richard's Parliament, in Mr. Burton's Diary. He was appointed by the parliament, soon afterwards, one of the ten members of the new Council of State, not of the House. Fairfax, Lambert, Desborough, Colonel Berry, Sir Ashley Cooper (afterwards Lord Shaftesbury), were also of that number. Soon afterwards, Bradshaw, with Serjeant Fountain and Serjeant Tyrrell (afterwards a Judge), were named Commissioners of the Great Seal. He was ordered by the parliament to take the oaths of office on the 21st of June, 1659; but his health having decayed for some time, he begged to be excused the duties of his office, and his attendance was accordingly dispensed with during his illness. Owing to the same cause he did not hold the Spring Assizes at Chester, in 1659, but appointed Ratcliffe, the Recorder of Chester, his deputy for that occasion.

We have seen Bradshaw's vehement denunciation of Oliver Cromwell's violent dissolution of the Long Parliament. The last act which we find of his public conduct was in protesting against a similar military outrage committed by Richard Cromwell's generals and officers on the parliament in his reign. The officers of the army assembled at Wallingford House, presented an address to the house, stating a multitude of grievances, and praying that a commander-in-chief might be appointed immediately,—that no officer might be dismissed without court-martial,—that the Protector's debts might be paid, and his revenue enlarged; and when the parliament were with some vigour and resolution debating on this proceeding, and taking measures for resistance to the conspiracy of officers, Lambert, Sydenham, and others, at the head of their troops, in spite of opposition from other regiments, invested the house, placed guards at the doors and in the avenues, and prevented the approach of the members. The Speaker was stopped in his coach in Palace Yard by Colonel Dukenfield, compelled to return up Parliament Street, and nearly forced to drive into Wallingford House[1], where the council of officers sat. He insisted on proceeding, however; and was allowed to go home. Sydenham, one of the Protector's council, attempted to justify this outrageous proceeding at one of its meetings, declaring that they were driven to the measure " by a particular call of the Divine Providence." But the Lord President Bradshaw, who was present, " though by long sickness very weak, and " much attenuated, yet animated by his ardent " zeal and constant affection to the common cause, " upon hearing those words stood up, and in- " terrupted him, declaring his abhorrence of that " detestable action, and telling the Council, that " being now going to his God, he had not patience " to sit there to hear his great name so openly " blasphemed; and, therefore, departed to his " lodgings, and withdrew himself from public " employment."[2] He did not live many days; dying on the 22d of November, 1659, of a quartan ague, from which he had suffered more than a year. He was buried with great pomp in Westminster Abbey. His body was disinterred,

---

[1] On the site of the present Admiralty.
[2] Ludlow, p. 307.

with those of Cromwell and Ireton, at the Restoration, and exposed on a gibbet at Tyburn, and then thrown into a pit.

Whitlock drily sums up his character thus : " a stout man, learned in his profession, no friend to monarchy ;" and this sentence probably expresses every quality which can on certain grounds be ascribed to Bradshaw.[1] His eloquence, which Milton so much extols, does not manifest itself in the imperfect account we possess of his speeches on the King's trial,—the only speeches of which we know any thing, except the short energetic remonstrances to Oliver Cromwell and to Colonel Sydenham.   John Lilburne, however, in his relation of his sufferings in the Star Chamber, bears testimony to the same quality.   That he was an undaunted and intrepid man, and to all appearance conscientiously bent on establishing and preserving a republican government, must be admitted.   Indeed, Bradshaw, Ireton, Ludlow, Haslerig, Scot, appear to have belonged to a class of stern democrats, who were less influenced in their proceedings by personal ambition, and by that fanatical enthusiasm which actuated many others, than by a determined hatred to monarchy, and a resolution to destroy it at all hazards.   This impracticable steadfastness of purpose alone was sufficient to give to Bradshaw some importance in the agitated times in which he lived ; add to this, his respectable knowledge of his profession, an impressive elocution and manner in public, an iron intrepidity, and the distinction of having judged

---

[1] Mrs. Hutchinson speaks of him as *hot* and *stout-hearted.*

and condemned his sovereign, and there is sufficient to account for the authority and influence
which he enjoyed among the enemies of monarchy
up to his death.[1]   That Bradshaw, without chil-

[1] John Bradshaw, Serjeant at Law and Chief Justice of
Chester, bequeaths all his manors, &c. in the counties of
Kent and Middlesex, to his wife, Mary Bradshaw, for life, in
lieu of dower; and devises to her his manors, &c. in Kent,
with liberty, in her life-time, to disparke the parke at
Somerhill, for her subsistence and making provision for
her kindred, " God not having vouchsafed me issue."
He further devises his manors in the counties of Berks,
Southampton, Wilts, and Somerset, with his reversions
in Middlesex, in trust, to his friend, Peter Brereton, Esq.,
his nephew, Peter Newton, and his trustie servant Thomas
Parnell, and their heirs, for payment of debts, &c.; to
expend 700*l.* in purchasing an annuity for maintaining
a freeschool in Marple, in Cheshire; 500*l.* for encreasing
the wages of the Master and Usher of Bunbury School;
and 500*l.* for amending the wages of the Schoolmaster
and Usher of Middleton school, in Lancashire (in which
two schools of Bunbury and Middleton I had part of
my education, and return this as part of my thankful
acknowledgment for the same); these two sums of 500*l.* to
be laid out in purchasing annuities.
 After this follows a bequest of an annuity of 40*l.*, for
seven years, to Samuel Rowe, Gent., his secretary, for
maintaining him at Gray's Inn, and remunerating his assistance to his executors; various legacies to friends; and
250*l.* to the poor of Founthill, Stopp, Westminster, and
Feltham; a bequest of the impropriation of Feltham, for
the use of a proper minister to be established there; a bequest of an annuity of 20*l.* for providing a minister at Hatch,
in Wiltshire, charged on his estate there; legacies to his
chaplain, Mr. Parr; Mr. Strong, the preacher at the
Abbey; and Mr. Clyve, a Scottish minister; and his houses
and lodgings at Westminster to the governors of the alms-
house and school there.
 A codicil, dated March 23. 1653, bequeaths all his law

dren, and with relations in easy circumstances con-
descended to amass a large private property by
his career of rebellion and crime, is clear from the
terms of his will, which is given below.   The
regicide, who began life as a poor student of
Gray's Inn, died at the age of 57, possessed of
considerable estates in six counties, a house in
London, and a beautiful seat and park in Kent.
These estates were, within a year after Bradshaw's death, revested, on the Restoration of
Charles the Second, in their rightful owners.
The beautiful park of Somerhill (which the regicide's wife by his will was to have liberty to
dispark, in order to provide for herself and her
relations), was restored to Lord Clanrickard, and
became the scene of some of those amusing adventures of Charles's Court, which are described
in the Memoirs of Grammont.   Bradshaw left no
issue by his wife (Mary the daughter of Thomas
Marbury, of Marbury, in Cheshire), and the small
remains of his ill-gotten wealth ultimately devolved on his nephew, Henry Bradshaw, who, in
1693, purchased an estate called Bradshaw Hall.

---

books, and such divinity, history, and books as shee (his
wife, the executrix,) shall judge fit for him, to his nephew,
Harrie Bradshaw.

A second codicil, dated September 10. 1655, in which
the testator is also styled Chief Justice of Chester, annuls
several legacies, and appoints others (among them to *Mr.
John Milton* 10*l.*); appoints a legacy of 5*l.* each to all his
servants living at the time of his decease, and makes several
additional legal provisions.

Will proved at London, December 16. 1659, by Henry
Bradshaw, Esq., the nephew of the testator.

But this, as well as the Cheshire property, appears to have passed, early in the eighteenth century, into the family of Isherwood, of Bolton-le-Moors, in Lancashire, by a marriage with the niece of the regicide, the heiress of the Bradshaw family.

MEMOIR OF THOMAS HARRISON.

THOMAS HARRISON, whose courageous defence of his conduct on his trial, and undaunted endurance of his last sufferings, were not less remarkable than the fanatical extravagances of his life, was the son of a grazier, near Newcastle under Line, according to some writers; of a butcher, near Nantwich, in Cheshire, according to Clarendon. The former is the more probable account. In the Register of Newcastle under Lyne is an entry of "Thomas Harrison, baptized July 16. 1606." And tradition points out an old house in the Lower Street of that town as having belonged to the regicide. It is certain that he came to London young, and was placed under an attorney in Clifford's Inn, of the name of Hoselker; "which kind of education," says Clarendon, "introduces men into the language and practice of business; and if it be not resisted by the great ingenuity (ingenuousness) of the person, inclines young men to more pride than any other kind of breeding, and disposes them to be pragmatical and insolent, though they have the skill to conceal it from their masters, except they find them (as they are too often) inclined to cherish it." When the students of the Inns of Court, infected with the insubordinate spirit of the times, formed themselves into companies at the commencement of the civil war, Harrison was among the number; and served under Sir Philip Stapylton in the body guard of the General the Earl of Essex. Clarendon says he "first obtained the office of a Cornet; and got up, by diligence and sobriety, to the state of a Captain." He served as a Major at the battle of Marston Moor in 1644. Baillie, after the battle, writes, " We were both grieved and angry that your in- dependents there should have sent up Major Harrison to trumpet over all the city their own praises to our prejudice; making all believe that Cromwell alone, with his unspeakably valorous regiments, had done all the service."[1] But he appears to have attracted no particular notice till the new modelling of the army, and the self- denying ordinance in 1645·— a scheme which gave a spring to the fortunes of so many inferior aspirants who afterwards played conspicuous parts. In the list of officers next to the Colonels, Harrison's name is then found along with those of Ireton, Desborough, Huntington, and others. He was sent by Fairfax to give the parliament a particular account of the battle of Langport, when the House ordered him two good horses for his service; and in October of the same year, when Colonel Fleetwood was appointed Governor of

<hr>

[1] Letters, vol. ii. 40.

Bristol, Harrison was named Colonel of his regiment. In 1646 he was one of the commissioners to receive possession of the palace of Woodstock, which had surrendered to the parliamentary army; and in the following year, when Philip Lord Lisle (the brother of Algernon Sidney, and the friend of Dryden) went to Ireland, as Lord Lieutenant, Harrison was one of the persons voted by the Commons at his request to attend him. That his services in this employment were considered meritorious, appears from the fact, that when Lord Lisle and his colleague, Sir John Temple, reported to the parliament the state of Ireland, Harrison (together with Colonel Algernon Sidney) was included by the Houses in the vote of thanks bestowed on the Lord Lieutenant and Sir John Temple.

When the King's person was seized at Holdenby House by Joyce, in 1647, Harrison was a Colonel of horse — Cromwell having found him, according to Clarendon, " of a spirit and disposition fit for his service, much given to prayer and preaching, and otherwise of an understanding capable to be trusted in any business to which his clerkship contributed very much. He was looked upon as inferior to few, after Cromwell and Ireton, in the council of officers, and in the government of the agitators[1] (adjutators); and there are few men with whom Cromwell more communicated, or upon whom he more depended for the conduct of any thing committed to him."

[1] See *antè*, p. 5. note.

Harrison, with his regiment, accompanied the army (which had now the signal advantage over the parliament of possessing the person of the King) to the general rendezvous at Newmarket, and at Triploe Heath, near Royston. Here, together with Cromwell, Ireton, the two Hammonds, Desborough, Pride, Waller, and other officers, Harrison was active and energetic in resisting the disbandment [1] of the army which had been proposed by the parliament; and in exciting and directing the fermenting spirit of the common soldiers, and of the council of agitators, against the authority of the Houses. On the evening of the meeting at Triploe Heath (where Vane and the other parliamentary commissioners read to the regiments the propositions of the parliament, to which an officer from each regiment coolly replied, they must be submitted to the councils of officers and agitators chosen by the soldiery), a letter was despatched from the army from Royston to the Corporation of London, announcing their intention of approaching the metropolis in order to obtain a redress of their grievances, and warning the citizens against offering them resistance. Harrison's name was signed to this letter, along with those of Fairfax, Cromwell, Ireton, and the thirteen principal officers of the army. The Lord Mayor summoned a common council; and on the petition of the alarmed citizens, an order was sent by the Houses to the General-in-chief, Fairfax, not to approach within forty miles of London, — an injunction little heeded, for on the follow-

1 See *antè*, the Memoir of Ireton.

ing day the head-quarters of the army were removed from Royston to St. Alban's, within twenty miles of the capital.

The King was now removed from Newmarket to Royston, then to Hatfield, and afterwards to Richmond and Windsor Castle, travelling and lodging with a comfort and state scarcely inferior to what had always attended a royal progress through the kingdom. The army had pushed their head-quarters to Uxbridge, but afterwards retired to Wycombe, where the council of war appointed ten persons — Cromwell, Ireton, Fleetwood, and Harrison being of the number — to meet Lord Nottingham, Vane, Skippon, and the other parliamentary commissioners; and to treat for a settlement of the disputes between the army and the Houses. In the active and energetic struggles and intrigues for mastery which now took place between the Presbyterian party (with a majority in the Commons) and the independents, backed by the army, the support of the King became the eager object of desire to each contending party. To Cromwell and Ireton (the arch politicians of the republicans and independents) was intrusted the delicate task of winning Charles by hypocritical professions and subtle cajolery. Harrison appears to have been a zealous fanatic and bold officer, well suited to execute the plans of superior minds, but who never himself displayed any capacity for negotiation or intrigue. He was with the army, however, and aiding in the schemes of Cromwell and his son-in-law, during all its shiftings from Wycombe to Reading, to Aylesbury, to Woburn, to Bedford; and he marched with his regiment to London, when the army, having overcome their Presbyterian opponents, were met by the Speaker and numerous members at Hounslow, and entered London in triumph under Fairfax.

When the Scotch, commanded by the Duke of Hamilton, invaded England, and made an effort to arrest the military domination which was threatening all the civil and religious institutions of the country, Harrison was sent to the north to oppose the invaders, and his troops defeated the Duke at Preston, in Lancashire. In this service Harrison received a wound. This invasion and all the insurrections in the counties being defeated, Cromwell and the Council of War were established in full authority at Whitehall, where Oliver already began to occupy one of the King's rich beds, and, reclining on it, gave audiences to some of the most considerable persons in the kingdom. The House now underwent its memorable purification by Colonel Pride and Lord Grey, which has been before described; and on the 16th of December, 1648, Harrison was despatched by the Council of War to conduct the King from Hurst Castle to London, in order to his trial. He made the preparations for the King's journey, and remained two nights at Hurst, without, however, seeing Charles, probably owing to the prejudice which the King had conceived against him. The King left this wretched prison, escorted by a troop of horse, and attended by Sir Thomas Herbert, who has minutely described the journey. Between Alresford and Farnham another troop was drawn up, by which the King passed on

horseback, attended a little behind by Herbert.
" At the head of it was the Captain, gallantly
mounted and armed. A velvet monteir was
on his head, a new buff coat on his back, and
a crimson silk scarf about his waist, richly fringed ;
who, as the King passed by with an easy pace
(as delighted to see men well horsed and armed),
the Captain gave the King a bow with his head,
all *à soldade*, which his Majesty requited." This
being the first time the King saw the officer,
who was Harrison, he called Herbert to him,
and on being told who he was, viewed him
more narrowly, and · said to Herbert, " He
looked like a soldier, and that his aspect was
good, and found him not such a one as was
represented ; and that having some judgment in
faces, if he had observed him so well before, he
should not have that ill opinion of him."[1]

Burnet's statement[2], that when it was in doubt
whether to kill the King, or bring him to an
open trial, Harrison offered to assassinate him,
seems to be wholly without foundation. Charles
had, indeed, entertained such a suspicion of
Harrison; and, when the Colonel came to Hurst
Castle, had expressed it to Herbert. When the
King was at Farnham, a little before supper he
took Harrison by the arm, and led him aside to
the window, and discoursed for half an hour, and
told Harrison of the information he had received
to his prejudice. Harrison assured him it was
not true, and that what he had really said was,
" that the law was equally obliging to great and

---

[1] Herbert's Memoirs, p. 140.   [2] Hist. vol. i.

P

small, and that justice had no respect of persons;"
which Herbert says, not unnaturally, " his Majesty found *affectedly spoken*, and to no good end,
and left off further communication, and went to
supper, being all the time very pleasant; which
was no small rejoicing to many there, to see him
so cheerful in that company and in such a condition." [1]

We have seen the zealous part which Harrison
took in the proceedings in Westminster Hall.
He never was absent from any sitting of that
Court, and from very few of the meetings in
the Painted Chamber.   Harrison, together with
Ireton, Henry Marten, Miles Corbet, Scot, Lisle,
and others, were appointed a committee to concur with the Counsel in settling the charge,
adjusting the evidence, and preparing general
rules for expediting the business of the Court.
This unflinching republican was also appointed,
with Marten, Scot, Ireton, and others, to draw
up the sentence of the Court, leaving a blank
for the manner of death.   He signed the warrant
of execution; and was present at the last extraordinary scene in Ireton's bedchamber, at
Whitehall, when Cromwell and Hacker together
prepared the order to the executioner.   Though
Harrison was a vehement fanatic, (Bishop Burnet
calls him a " fierce and bloody enthusiast,") and
distinguished for praying, preaching, and expounding [2] on all occasions, yet Hume's story of

[1] Memoirs, p. 142.
[2] This union of the military with pastoral functions was
very common at this period.   In the Appendix to Clarendon's State Papers, vol. ii., a letter to Mr. Secretary

his designedly engaging Fairfax in prayer till the decapitation of the King was at an end is hardly to be credited. That Fairfax was disgusted at the trial and the sentence is beyond doubt. He never attended any meeting, public or private, of the Court: and Sir Thomas Herbert states, that when Bishop Juxon and himself were conducting the King's corpse to be embalmed, they met Fairfax in the Long Gallery at Whitehall, when he enquired how the King did, being ignorant of his death, and having resolved with his own regiment to prevent it ; and Herbert states, that Fairfax had just come from Colonel Harrison's apartment, where he had been at prayer with the officers. Hume represents that Cromwell and Ireton, in order to remove Fairfax's repugnance to the proceedings, endeavoured to persuade him that God had rejected the King ; and counselled him to seek, in prayer, direction from Heaven on this important occasion. Harrison was appointed to pray with him, and prolonged his effusions till the fatal blow was struck; when he rose from his knees, and insisted that this event was the miraculous and providential answer of Heaven, sent to their devout supplications. Harris[1] thinks this story inconsistent with the bold and artless character

Nicholas from a Cavalier states, " There was lately a fast at head-quarters for the uniting of the army; when the Lieutenant-General (Cromwell) and the Commissary-General (Ireton) prayed publicly in the assembly, which, (my godly author tells me) was such sweet music as the heavens never knew before."

[1] Life of Cromwell, 208.

of Harrison. But this would not alone be a sufficient ground for rejecting it: for Harrison's zeal knew no bounds; and men not less open and frank than Harrison in their general character, at that time, scrupled not to accomplish their ends by the most refined duplicity and hypocrisy. The fact most opposed to the story is, that Harrison was proved, on Colonel Hacker's trial, to have been in Ireton's bed-room, with Cromwell, Ireton, and others, up to the moment of the execution, and for some time previous. Nor is this evidence inconsistent with so much of Hume's story as rests on the unexceptionable authority of Sir Thomas Herbert; for Herbert only says that the General Fairfax had been in prayer with the officers in Harrison's apartment, without asserting that Harrison was present there himself. That Fairfax should have been ignorant of the execution till he met Herbert and the Bishop is certainly most extraordinary, and is by some deemed incredible. It could only have arisen from some artful contrivances on the part of Cromwell and his party. But Herbert's statement can hardly be doubted, nor can it be supposed that Fairfax told Herbert a falsehood. The artifice practised on Fairfax must, however, have been of some other kind, and not that which is ascribed by Hume to Harrison.

Considering the services of Harrison, his sturdy republicanism, and puritanical zeal, it is inexplicable that he (and also a more considerable man, Ireton) should have been negatived as one of the new executive Council of State, to which the sceptre of the kingdom was intrusted after the

King's death. Lisle, Holland, Scot, Ludlow, and Robinson, were appointed to nominate forty to the Rump of the Commons for their approval. Eighteen of those chosen were men who had taken no part in the trial of Charles. There was only one division in the House on the names; it was on that of the Earl of Pembroke, who was elected by fifty to twenty-five. Both Ireton and Harrison were negatived by the previous question.

In May, 1649, Fairfax, with all the chief officers of his army, visited Oxford; where they were received with much festivity and honour, and quartered in the lodgings of the Warden of All Souls. The Vice-Chancellor had previously been sent to prison, and all the royalist heads of houses removed, and replaced by men well affected to the new Commonwealth. The honorary degree of Doctor of Laws was, on this occasion, bestowed on Cromwell and Fairfax; that of Master of Arts on Harrison, Waller, Ingoldsby, and eleven officers, seven of whom had sat in judgment on the King.

In 1650, Harrison was raised to the rank of Major-General, and served with Cromwell (the new Lord Lieutenant) and Ireton in Ireland. Previous to their departure, Whitlocke relates, " three ministers prayed, and (Colonel) Goffe and Harrison expounded some places of Scripture excellently well, and pertinent to the occasion." Whitlocke was present at this characteristic scene; but it does not appear clear whether it took place in the House of Commons, or at the Council at Whitehall, or in what other place. According to the testimony of Mrs. Hutchinson, Harrison by no means neglected his worldly fortunes;

and while he read long and fervent lectures to Colonel H. and others upon the worthlessness of "outward estate," he provided for himself and his family with a very unsaintly anxiety. "For at that time the Major-General, who was but a mean man's sonne and of a meane education, and no estate before the war, had gathered an estate of two thousand a year, beside engrossing great offices, and encroaching upon his under officers, and maintained his coach and family at a heighth as if they had been born to a principality." This lady's statements on this point must, however, be taken with some allowance, as Harrison, as well as Cromwell and Ludlow, was evidently an object of her and her husband's resentful feelings.

The attention of the Parliament and the Council of War was now directed to the storm which was threatening them from the loyal and presbyterian Scottish nation; who, though ardently bent on supporting their own religious establishment, partook of none of the republican and king-killing doctrines which had just overthrown the monarchy of England. We have seen that the Scots endeavoured to close with the King in the Isle of Wight, and solemnly protested against the murderous proceedings of his executioners. They proclaimed Charles II. his successor, and invited that Prince from Holland to assume his northern throne. It was obvious that a war with the Scots must ensue; and the House and the Council looked to Fairfax and Cromwell to avert these gathering perils. Cromwell was hastily recalled from Ireland, and Harrison returned with him;

Ireton being left, as Lord Deputy, to finish the
war which Cromwell had successfully commenced.
A small circumstance now contributed materially
to the sole ascendancy of Cromwell. Fairfax's
wife, who was a rigid presbyterian, surrounded
by presbyterian ministers, had assisted in preventing the General from staining his hands with
his sovereign's blood — she now prevailed on him
to refuse the command of the expedition against
the Scots. The Council of State, much disappointed at his hesitation, appointed Cromwell,
Harrison, General Lambert, Whitlocke (the Lord
Commissioner of the Seal), and St. John (the
Chief Justice), to endeavour to remove his scruples. Whitlocke and Ludlow both describe their
conference; the former with the minute detail of
one who participated in it. They met on the 22d
of June, and "being shut up in a room in Whitehall, they went first to prayer that God would
direct them in this business; and Cromwell began, and most of the committee prayed, after
which they discoursed." Cromwell and Fairfax
were the principal speakers. Whitlocke closely
seconded Cromwell's reasoning and persuasions,
which were earnest, and apparently sincere.
Harrison said but little; what he uttered was in
his usual style of unction and enthusiasm.

Harrison.—It is indeed, my Lord, the most
glorious cause that ever any of this nation appeared in; and now, when we hope that the
Lord will give a glorious issue and conclusion
to it, for your Excellency then to give it over,
will sadden the hearts of many of God's people."

Lord General Fairfax.—What would you have me do?   As far as my conscience will give way, I am willing to join with you still in the service of the Parliament : but where the conscience is not satisfied, none of you (I am sure) will engage in any service; and that is my condition in this ; and, therefore, I must desire to be excused."

An act was immediately passed, constituting Cromwell Captain-General and Commander-in-Chief of all the forces of England.   Exactly a month after this conference, Cromwell crossed the Tweed with his army.   His principal officers were, Fleetwood, his son-in-law, Lieutenant-General ; Lambert, Major-General ; Whalley, his first cousin, Commissary-General ; Monk, Pride, and Overton.   Harrison remained in London ; and, on the 22d of October, we find him reviewing, in Hyde Park, 8000 troops of the regiments of Middlesex and the city trainbands. In place of a king and queen, and a glittering court, who had been used to grace such exhibitions, the Speaker of the House of Commons, in his robes and wig, and many of the members, attended the review, and, according to Whitlocke, were " received with great shouts, and vollies of great and small shot."

That Harrison's spiritual character was by no means exempt from a certain carnal love of admiration, which his portly and martial figure (applauded even by so critical a judge as Charles) was calculated to excite, appears from a story related of him by Mrs. Hutchinson.   " About the same time a great ambassador was to have public audience in the House (of Commons) ; he came from the King of Spain, and was the first who had addressed them, owning them as a republic.   The day before his audience, Colonel Hutchinson was set in the House near some young men handsomely clad, among whom was Mr. Charles Rich, since Earl of Warwick; and the Colonel himself had on that day a habit which was pretty rich, but grave, and no other than he usually wore. Harrison, addressing particularly him, admonished them all, that now the nations sent to them, they should labour to shine before them in wisdom, piety, righteousness, and justice, and not in gold and silver, and worldly bravery, which did not become saints; and that the next day, when the ambassadors came, they should not set themselves out in gorgeous habits, which were unsuitable to holy professions.   The Colonel, although he was not convinced of any misbecoming bravery in the suit he wore that day, which was but of sad coloured cloth trimmed with gold, and silver points and buttons; yet because he would not appear offensive in the eyes of religious persons, the next day he went in a. plain black suit, and so did all the other gentlemen: but Harrison came that day in a scarlet coat and cloak, both laden with gold and silver lace; and the coat so covered with *clinquant,* that scarcely could one discern the ground; and in this glittering habit set himself just under the Speaker's chair; which made the other gentlemen think that his godly speeches, the day before, were but made that he alone might appear in the eyes of strangers. But this was part of his weakness; the Lord at last lifted him above the poor earthly elevations which then and some time after prevailed too much with him." [1]

On the 11th of February, 1650, Harrison was one of the twenty new members balloted into the executive Council of State; and on the 18th of March following he was sent with a force of horse and foot to repress the conspiracies in Lancashire and the northern counties in aid of the Scots. He advanced as far as Cumberland; whence he wrote to the Parliament, announcing the advance of the Scots, and concluding his epistle with a requisition of "some provision of four or five hundred godly men for two or three months, if I can get them mounted." [2] This curious letter is dated after the manner of the Quakers, "7th of the 6th month, 1651, at 11 o'clock forenoon." Harrison, who tried every shade of fanaticism, and was by turns an independent, an anabaptist, and a fifth-monarchy man, appears at that time to have been captivated with the novel doctrines and customs of the Quakers.

Harrison commanded a brigade of horse at the decisive battle of Worcester; and wrote to the Parliament a spirited account of the pursuit. This brilliant victory, — the " crowning mercy" of Cromwell, — while it annihilated for the time the cause of the royalists, and drove Charles the Second into exile, gave at the same time a destructive blow to the young republic — the idol of Harrison, Ludlow, Scot, Marten, Whalley, and of almost all the officers of the army Cromwell advanced to London, nourishing kingly

[1] Mrs. Hutchinson's Memoirs.
[2] Whitlocke's Memorials.

ambition, and was received with almost kingly honours. Hampton Court was voted for his residence; and 4000*l.* in land given him in addition to 2500*l.* per annum which had been formerly granted. The Keepers of the Seal (Whitlocke and Lisle), Chief Justice St. John, and Sir Gilbert Pickering, met him at Aylesbury to offer him the ardent thanks of the Parliament; and Cromwell, with the munificence of a sovereign conqueror, presented each commissioner with a horse and two Scottish captives. [1] The militia and volunteers were now disbanded by Cromwell, probably as not being yet sufficiently under his control and management. Peters, Ludlow, and the other republicans, from this time saw through his designs. A few months afterwards the news arrived of Ireton's death in Ireland; which, Whitlocke says, struck a great sadness into Cromwell. But while Cromwell grieved for his attached friend and coadjutor, Harrison, Ludlow, and the other sturdy republicans, mourned an irreparable loss in this champion of their principles, who, while he lived, must ever have presented a formidable obstacle to the ambition of his father-in-law. Only two days after the news arrived, Cromwell, in order to sound the minds of men of influence, desired a meeting of members of parliament and the chief officers of the army at the Speaker's house. Whitlocke was present, and has given an interesting account of the conference, in which Harrison took part. In his usual style, Harrison

---

[1] Whitlocke says, his horse was a handsome, gallant young nag, of good breed; and one of his prisoners a gentleman of quality. He gave both prisoners their liberty, and passes for Scotland.

says, " I think that which my Lord General **hath** propounded, is to advise as to a settlement both of our civil and spiritual liberties; and so that the mercies which the Lord hath given us may not be cast away;— how this may be done is the great question."

Whitlocke.—It is a great question, indeed, and not suddenly to be resolved;— I should humbly offer, in the first place, whether it be not requisite to be understood in what way this settlement is desired, whether of an absolute republic, or with any mixture of monarchy.

Cromwell. — My Lord Commissioner Whitlocke hath put us upon the right point; and, indeed, it is my meaning, that we should consider whether a republic or a mixt monarchical government will be best to be settled; and if any thing monarchical, then in whom that power shall be placed.

Sir Thomas Widdrington. — I think a mixt monarchical government will be most suitable to the laws and people of this realm, — and if any monarchical, I suppose we shall hold it most just to place that power in one of the sons of the late King.

Colonel Fleetwood. — I think the question between a republic and a mixt monarchical government not easily determined.

Chief Justice St. John. — It will be found that the government of this nation, without something of monarchical power, will be very difficult to be so settled, as not to shake the foundation of our laws and the liberties of the people.

Speaker. — It would breed a strange confusion

to settle a government of this nation without something of monarchy.

Colonel Desborough (with the temerity of a soldier) says, " I beseech you, my Lords, why may not this, as well as other nations, be governed in the way of a republic ? "

Whitlocke. — The laws of England are so interwoven with the power and practice of monarchy, that to settle a government without monarchy in it, would make so great an alteration in the proceedings of our law, that you have scarce time to rectify, nor can well foresee, the inconveniences which will arise thereby.

Colonel Whalley. — I do not well understand matters of law ; but it seems to me the best way not to have any thing of monarchical power in the settlement of the government; and if we should resolve upon any, whom have we to pitch upon ? The King's eldest son hath been in arms against us, and his second son is likewise our enemy.

Sir Thomas Widdrington. — But the late King's third son, the Duke of Glo'ster, is still among us, and too young to have been in arms against us, or infected with the principles of our enemies.

Whitlocke suggested, that a day might be given to the King's eldest son, or the Duke of York, to come in to the Parliament, and upon such terms as should be thought fit.

Cromwell. — That would be a business of more than ordinary difficulty ; but if it might be done with safety to their rights as Englishmen and Christians, he thought a settlement of somewhat with monarchical power in it would be very effectual.

"Generally," says Whitlocke, "the soldiers were against any thing of monarchy, though every one of them was a monarch in his regiment or company. The lawyers were generally for a mixt monarchical government, and many were for the Duke of Glo'ster to be made King ; but Cromwell *still put off that debate and came off to some other point,* and the company parted without coming to any resolution at all ; only Cromwell discovered, by this meeting, the inclinations of the persons that spake, for which he fished, and made use of what he then discovered."

Cromwell steadily pursued his purpose, and bent all his machinations towards accomplishing the dissolution of the Long Parliament, which presented an insuperable obstacle to his plans of despotic rule. On the evening of the 7th of November, 1652, in a long conference with Whitlocke in St. James's Park, Cromwell opened his mind as to terminating the Parliament and making himself King. Whitlocke observed to him, that the great controversy had been, whether the government of the nation should be in a monarchy or a republic; and most of their friends had engaged with them in hopes of the latter, and for that had undergone all their hardships and difficulties. " Now, if your Excellency should take upon yourself the title of King, this state of the question will be wholly determined; and the matter that remains will only be, whether a Cromwell or a Stuart shall be our king." Whitlocke then turned Cromwell's thoughts to Charles II., and hinted to him that the Prince, being in a low condition, might be restored on any terms favourable to Cromwell and the nation; on which Cromwell was displeased, and abruptly ended the conversation.

Cromwell now brought about various meetings between the chief officers of the army and the leading members of the Parliament, for the purpose of convincing the latter of the necessity of putting a speedy end to their sittings. Harrison, who was one of his confiding dupes and active agents, attended these meetings and furthered his schemes. From the moment of his taking his seat after the battle of Worcester, Cromwell had incessantly pressed on the Parliament, that they should consider the question of dissolving themselves, and of calling another House under such rules and qualifications as should be judged expedient; and he at length induced them to fix, as a limit to their existence, the 3d of November, 1654, which was afterwards altered, in order to gratify his impatience, to the 3d of November, 1653. Cromwell had, in the mean time, with matchless art and hypocrisy, persuaded the army that the Parliament was composed of interested men, " baleful unclean birds," persons of loose morals, who, without sharing the soldiers' hardships, desired to use them as tools; while he himself desired only moderate measures and a free republic, and would never resort to violence against the House, except under the clearest necessity and for the public good. The leaders of the republican party in the House—Vane, Bradshaw, Haslerig, Marten—in introducing the Bill which was now under discussion for dissolving the Parliament, had carefully provided for the constitution and election of future Parliaments, and for the government of the nation by a Council of State chosen by the House in the intervals of its sittings.   At the last meeting of the officers with the members of Parliament, (on the 19th of April, 1653,) at which Whitlocke, Widdrington, and St. John were present, as well as Major-General Harrison and the other officers of note, the military men had frankly stated their disapprobation of this Bill, especially of the clause continuing the present House till November, and providing that the present members should be members of the new Parliament without re-election.   This they regarded as a perpetuation of the present Parliament.   They desired that the Parliament should at once pronounce their dissolution, and devolve the whole government on a Council of forty, to be chosen by both parties.   Whitlocke and Widdrington (the Commissioners of the Great Seal) earnestly represented the fatal dangers which would attend such a course: Oliver St. John, the other eminent lawyer, sided with Cromwell, Harrison, and the rest of the soldiers.   This memorable meeting broke up without coming to any precise conclusion[1], and with an agreement to meet on the next afternoon; and it appears to have been understood that nothing further should be done in the House till the pro-

---

[1] Whitlocke says, " The conference lasted till late at night, when Widdrington and I went home weary and troubled to see the ingratitude and indiscretion of these men, and the way they designed to ruin themselves."

Memorials.

position made by the officers had been considered.
The next morning, however (the 20th of April),
the Parliament resumed the consideration of the
Bill; and as the amendments had been already
decided on, the republican members vehemently
urged that it should be immediately read a third
time and passed. This produced some debate.
Major-General Harrison expostulated with the
House, and intreated them not to adopt a course
which would so deeply offend Cromwell and the
Council of officers.

In the mean time, the members were beginning to assemble at the adjourned conference
at Whitehall, and Whitlocke had already arrived,
when Cromwell received intelligence of what was
passing in the House. He was enraged, and
abruptly broke up the Council. Those members
of Parliament who were present went down to
the House. He himself remained at Whitehall.
Presently Colonel Ingoldsby came to him, and
told him if he meant to take any decisive step he
had no time to lose. Cromwell immediately walked
down to the House, attended by Lambert (a
sworn enemy of the Parliament) and five or six
officers. He gave orders to several files of troops to
follow him. He was dressed in plain black clothes
and grey worsted stockings, and took his seat and
listened to the debate. The republicans pressed
the passing of the Act, and in their impatience
proposed to dispense with its being engrossed.
Cromwell, seeing the urgency of the crisis, beck-
oned Harrison to him from the other side of the
House, and whispered to him that " the House
was now ripe for dissolution" The Major-

General answered, " Sir, the work is very
great and dangerous; therefore I desire you seriously to consider of it before you engage in it."
— " You say well," replied Cromwell, and then sat
still for about a quarter of an hour; when, seeing
the question was about to be put, he said tc
Harrison, " Now is the time—I must do it;"
and then rose and poured forth a vehement tor-
rent of invective against the House, charging
them with corruption, self-seeking, an attachment
to presbyterians and lawyers, who supported tyranny, and with a desire to perpetuate their own
power. He told them the Lord had done with them,
and had chosen honester and worthier instruments
for carrying on his work. " This he spake with
so much passion and discomposure, as if he had
been distracted."[1]   Sir Harry Vane and Sir Peter
Wentworth stood up and expostulated with him;
but Cromwell walked up and down the House
with the air of a madman, kicking the ground
with his feet, and exclaimed, " Come, come, I'll
put an end to your prating.   You are no Parliament.   I'll put an end to your sitting.   Call them
in — call them in."   The Serjeant-at-Arms opened
the door of the House, and Colonel Worsley, with
two files of musqueteers, entered.   No resistance
was offered by the members, and no one drew the
sword which he wore.   Sir Harry Vane cried
aloud from his place, " This is not honest — yea,
it is against morality and common honesty."
Cromwell began railing at him, crying out, with a
loud voice, " Oh! Sir Henry Vane, Sir Henry

[1] Ludlow.

Vane! the Lord deliver me from Sir Henry Vane!" He then addressed the sage Whitlocke with much severity — told Vane he was a juggler, pointed to Henry Marten and Wentworth as adulterers, and called Chaloner a drunkard. Laying his hand on the mace, he said, " What shall we do with this bauble ? — take it away ! " He then ordered Harrison to remove the Speaker, Lenthal. Harrison advanced to him, and intimated it was no longer convenient for him to remain in his place. The Speaker answered, that he would not come down unless he was removed by force. Harrison laid hold of his hand, and pulled him by the gown ; and Lenthal then left the chair. Algernon Sidney, who was sitting close to him on his right hand, was one of those who refused to remove, till forced by Harrison and Colonel Worsley. Cromwell, in the mean time, was violently addressing the retiring members, who were from eighty to a hundred in number. He told them, " It is you that have forced me to this ; for I have sought the Lord, day and night, that he would rather slay me than put me upon the doing of this work." As the members withdrew, Allen, an alderman of London, ventured to say that it was not yet too late to order the soldiers out of the House, to restore the mace, and proceed with public affairs. Cromwell turned upon him with an accusation — and charged him with not having made up his accounts of some hundred thousand pounds, as treasurer of the army. Allen answered, that he had long before tendered his accounts to the House. Cromwell made no reply, and it is uncertain whether there were any grounds for his accusation. Cromwell then snatched the Act of Dissolution from the hands of the clerk, put it under his cloak, and, having commanded the doors to be locked, took the keys, and went away to Whitehall.

This unparalleled scene closed for the time the famous Rump of the Long Parliament; an assembly which, without any legitimate authority, and feared rather than loved by the English nation, had undoubtedly wielded, for four years, the sovereign authority with singular wisdom, vigour, and success. Republican writers have naturally poured forth its eulogy; but Whitlocke, in heart a friend to monarchy, and a singularly cool and sagacious man, is also eloquent in its praise. "Thus it pleased God," says he, "that this assembly, famous through the world for its undertakings, actions, and successes, having subdued all their enemies, were themselves overthrown and ruined by their own servants, and those whom they had set up now pulled down their masters; an example never to be forgotten, and scarcely to be paralleled in history, in any story, by which all persons may be instructed how uncertain and subject to change all worldly affairs are, and how apt to fall when we think them highest. All honest, prudent, and indifferent men were highly disturbed at this unworthy action."

Cromwell, assisted by Harrison, had thus rid himself of the Parliament. Of the manner in which he disposed of the Council of State, on the afternoon of the same day, we have seen some account in the Memoir of Bradshaw. But Cromwell was still far from being in the condition to declare himself King. Harrison and the Council of officers, who shared Cromwell's influence with the troops, and who had assisted his overthrow of the Parliament, were ardent lovers of a republic, and had no design of investing him with sovereign authority. He was compelled to temporise — to issue a declaration promising to call a freely chosen Parliament, and to invest the executive power in thirteen hands, nine of whom were officers of the army. Major-General Harrison, together with Lambert, Desborough, and five Colonels, were members of this Council. Its Presidents were chosen weekly, and Harrison was the third. On the 4th of July, the new assembly (commonly called Praise God Barebones) met at Whitehall to the number of about one hundred and twenty. Cromwell, in the name of the army, surrendered the authority of the state into their hands, and addressed them for three quarters of an hour, in a speech which, according to Carrington, his biographer, showed " that the spirit of God was upon him." Harrison and the inveterate republicans were again entirely duped, and exulted in their chief's display of pure patriotism and disinterestedness. The day was spent in humiliation and prayer; and the assembly resolved that Cromwell, together with Harrison, Lambert, Desborough, and Tomlinson, should sit among them as members. In a few days, a new Council of State was elected by the assembly, consisting of thirty-one members : the Lord General Cromwell's is the first name, Lambert's the second, and Harrison's the third.

It is remarkable, that one of the first objects

Q 3

which occupied this Parliament was the question,
whether the maintenance of the clergy by the
provision of tithes should be continued. The
question was referred to a committee after long
debates ; and the committee of this assembly, composed of so many men vehemently adverse to
episcopacy and to royalty, and who had joined in
destroying the King, reported that *incumbents,
rectors, and impropriators, had a legal property in
tithes, and that they ought to be continued accordingly.*[1] A debate for five whole days ensued on the
question, whether the House should agree to the
Report ; and it was at last carried by only two
voices that the House did not agree to this clause
in the Report; the numbers being fifty-six and
fifty-four.

The time had now arrived when Cromwell was
compelled to throw off the thin mask which had
concealed his designs from his easy dupes — Harrison, Ludlow, and the other zealous republicans.
Ireton was dead, Whitlocke was removed by an
embassy to Sweden, which Cromwell had pressed
upon him ; and matters were ripe for the anni-
hilation of Barebones Parliament, and the assumption by Cromwell of absolute sway. Cromwell
and his creatures had, by active calumny and falsehood, blackened the character of this assembly of
his own creation ; and Sydenham, one of his slavish
tools, proposed to the House that they should dissolve themselves, as unfit for the purposes of representation. Harrison and the small knot of
honest republicans resisted the attempt ; but

[1] Journals, July, 1653.

Rous, the Speaker, a creature of Cromwell, left the chair, and with a majority of the members proceeded to Whitehall, and resigned their authority to Cromwell, who acted the farce of astonishment, humility, and regret, with his accustomed art. The few members who obstinately remained behind, of whom Harrison was one, were under forty, the number required to form a House; and these were dispersed, after the approved fashion, by Colonel Goffe, a relation of Oliver, and his musqueteers. Four days afterwards Cromwell was sworn in as Protector in Westminster Hall; and in his new Council of State, Harrison, together with Tomlinson, Stapeley, Carew, and Bennet, were omitted. They henceforth became uncompromising opponents of Cromwell's reign. The republicans were now indeed much divided. Milton adhered steadily to Cromwell, and applauded his conduct.[1] Oliver St. John was dangerously ill at this period, but appears to have disapproved the usurper's proceedings. Harrison opposed Cromwell, not merely from that love of equality and of republican institutions which influenced Bradshaw, Vane, Haslerig, and Marten, but because he regarded monarchy as hostile to the Christian religion. The anabaptists were all determined foes to the Protector, and Harrison was now the most distinguished man in that sect. Political meetings of these sectarians were held in Blackfriars, where the Protector was denounced as an usurper and a perjured villain. Foake and Simpson, anabaptist

---

[1] Defensio Secunda pro Populo Anglicano.

ministers, were committed to prison in Windsor Castle, and the meetings were suppressed.

A few days after the establishment of the Protectorate, Harrison was summoned to the Council, and asked if he would own and act under the new government. With his usual frankness he absolutely refused; and his commission was in consequence taken from him, and shortly afterwards he was ordered to retire to his native county of Stafford. Harrison, and his anabaptist friends, appear to have still continued their speeches and machinations against the Protector's government; and in September, 1654, when Cromwell took the violent measure of excluding from the House all the members who refused to sign his " instrument of government," Harrison was considered an object of alarm, and was arrested.[1] The Dutch ambassadors in England, writing to the States of Holland, on the 15th of September, 1654, thus notice this matter:—" In the mean time, it is " said another party, called the anabaptists, under " the direction of Harrison, was busy to get the " hands to a petition to present to the Parliament; " so that his Highness was moved thereby to se- " cure Harrison at his house in the country (by " a party of horse), and to remedy what was " acting in the Parliament, and to send for the " members into the Painted Chamber, as hap- " pened on Tuesday morning, at nine o'clock, " there being several regiments of soldiers dis- " persed up and down the city, and all places well " secured. Some hundred and forty-five signed

---

[1] Goddard's Journal, prefixed to Burton's Diary, vol. i.

" presently ; and the next day some fifty more.
" There are others, without doubt, who after
" consideration will do as the rest have done —
" sign, and sit in Parliament as they ought, and
" not stand without, at the door, and be laughed
" at." [1]

Harrison's enthusiasm and activity never allowed him to remain in repose. In 1655, he appears to have been to a certain extent implicated
in the conspiracy of Colonel Overton (Milton's
friend), who was to seize on Monk, transfer
the command of the Scottish army to himself,
and march to the south to join the royalist
and republican troops, who now made common
cause against the government of Cromwell. The
plot was defeated by the prompt and vigorous
measures of Cromwell. Harrison was seized, and
conducted to the isle of Portland; and Carew,
another anabaptist and regicide, was confined at
St. Mawes, in Cornwall. Harrison was afterwards
released ; but at the commencement of the Protector's second Parliament he was sent to Pendennis Castle [2], in Cornwall. Between Cromwell
and Harrison there had existed, till Cromwell
made himself Protector, the strictest union and
friendship: Harrison displayed the most cordial

[1] See Thurloe State Papers, vol. xi. 606.

[2] Ludlow says he was sent to Carisbrook Castle; but he
appears to be wrong, as he occasionally is as to dates and
details, owing to his having written his Memoirs from
memory at Lausanne several years after the events happened. Vane was at this time sent to Carisbrook, but Harrison was confined at Pendennis.—Thurloe, vol. v. 407
Godwin, vol. iv. p. 276. Mercurius Fumigosus, a journal
of the day, 306.

devotion to his distinguished friend, and Cromwell reposed the highest confidence in Harrison. When Harrison gave him up, and plotted against his reign, Cromwell was not a man to be restrained, by his feelings, from repressing, by severe measures, the schemes of his former friend. But he bore more from Harrison than he would have endured in others; and Cromwell had a heart quite capable of feeling regret, when he ordered his former devoted ally to a distant dungeon. The following letter from Harrison, written a few years before, is characteristic of his fanatical disposition, and marks the affection and intimacy which then existed between him and Cromwell ·—

"MY DEAR LORD,

" To spare you trouble, I forbeare to give you my excuse for not waiting on you to Ware. I know you love me, therefore are not apt to except; though in this particular I had not failed, but that orders from the Councell superseded me.

" Considering under how many and great burdens yow labour, I am afraid to saie anie more, that I may not add to them; but love and duty makes me presume.

" The business you goe upon is weightie, as ever yett yow undertook: it plainly and deeply concerns the life or death of the Lord's people, his own name, and his Son's: nevertheless maie yow rejoyce in God (whose affair it is), who, having heretofore given yow numberless signall testimonies to other parts of the worke, will in mercie prosper this, that he maie perfect what he hath begun. And to omitt other arguments, that in Deut. xxxii. 27. hath much force on my heart, especially the last words, — " And the Lord hath not done all this."   I believe, if the present ene- my should prevaile, hee would as certainly re- proach God, and all that hitherto hath been done as aforesaid, even as I now write ; but the jealousie of the Lord of Hosts for his great name will not admitt it.

" My Lord, lett waiting upon Jehovah bee the greatest and most considerable business you have every daie ; reckon itt more then to eate, sleep, or councell together.   Run aside sometimes from your companie, and gett a word with the Lord. Why should not you have three or four precious souls allwaies standing att your elbow, with whom you might now and then turn into a corner ? I have found refreshment and mercie in such a waie.   Ah ! the Lord of compassion arise, pittie your burthens, care for yow, stand by and refresh your heart each moment.   Here is little newes, only Charles Vane retorned from Portugall, who left our fleet indifferently well, and that they had seized nine of the Portugall's shipps.

" The Father of Mercies visit and keep your soule close to him continually, protect, preserve, and prosper yow, is the praier of, my Lord,
" Your Excellencie's loving Servant,
" Whilst I breath,
Whitehall, 3d July, 1650.   " T. HARRISON.
" For his Excellentcy the Lord General
    Cromwell, humbly present theis."

When he was released from his confinement at Pendennis, Harrison went to live at his house at

Highgate, where Ludlow visited him. The General gives in his Memoirs a characteristic description of a conference that took place between them. "When I was acquainted with his arrival, I went to make him a visit; and having told him that I was very desirous to be informed by him of the reasons that moved him to join with Cromwell in the interruption of the civil authority, he answered, that he had done it because he was fully persuaded they had not a heart to do any more good for the Lord and his people. 'Then,' said I, 'are you not now convinced of your error in entertaining such thoughts, especially since it has been seen what use has been made of the usurped power?' To which he replied, 'Upon their heads be the guilt, who have made a wrong use of it; for my own part, my heart was upright and sincere in the thing.' His second reason for joining with Cromwell was, because he pretended to own and favour a sort of men who acted upon higher principles than those of civil liberty. I replied, that I thought him mistaken in that also, since it had not appeared that he ever approved of any persons or things, further than he might make them subservient to his own ambitious designs; reminding him that the generality of the people that had engaged with us, having acted upon no higher principles than those of civil liberty, and that they might be governed by their own consent, it could not be just to treat them in another manner upon any pretence whatsoever. The Major-General then cited a passage of the prophet Daniel, where it is said, 'That the saints shall take the kingdom and possess it.' To which he added another to the same effect—'That the kingdom shall not be left to another people.' I answered, that the same prophet says in another place, 'That the kingdom shall be given to the people of the saints of the Most High:' and that I conceived, if they should presume to take it before it was given, they would at the best be guilty of doing evil, that good might come from it; for to deprive those of their right in the government, who had contended for it equally with ourselves, were to do as we would not that others should do to us: that such proceedings are not only unjust, but also impracticable, at least for the present; because we cannot perceive that the saints are clothed with such a spirit, as those are required to be to whom the kingdom is promised; and therefore we may be easily deceived in judging who are fit for government; for many have taken upon them the form of saintship, that they might be admitted to it, who yet have not acted suitably to their pretensions in the sight of God or men: for proof of which we need go no further than to those very persons who had drawn him to assist in their design of exalting themselves, under the specious pretence of advancing the kingdom of Christ. He confessed himself not able to answer the arguments I had used; yet said, he was not convinced that the texts of Scripture quoted by him were not to be interpreted in the sense he had taken them, and therefore desired a further conference with me at another time."[1]

In 1657, by the activity of Secretary Thurloe,

---

[1] Ludlow's Memoirs.

the famous conspiracy of Venner and the **fifth-monarchy**[1] men against Cromwell's government was discovered and reported to the House, Whitlocke writes, on the 4th of February, 1657, "Divers were imprisoned on the new plot; and the Protector and his Council were busie in the examinations concerning it; and Thurloe did them good service. Major-General Harrison was deep in it." These men, not content with putting forth the doctrine of the Revelations, that the saints shall reign for one thousand years upon earth after the extinction of all worldly kingdoms, asserted their own right as saints to determine for themselves when their reign was begun, and to overpower all existing dynasties and thrones which obstructed the establishment of their present dominion. Their manifesto was contained in a tract, entitled " A Standard set up, whereto the true Seed and Saints of the Most High may be gathered together for the Lamb against the Beast and the False Prophet; or the Principles and Declarations of the Remnant who have waited for the blessed Appearance and Hope." It treated Cromwell as an apostate and a traitor, " exceeding the rage, oppression, and treason of the late King." It proclaimed a government, of which Christ had the supreme authority, " by right, conquest, election, and inheritance;" with a Council of " men of choicest light and spirit," to be elected annually by " the Lord's freemen, such as have a right and interest in the Redeemer of

---

[1] They looked on the Assyrian, the Egyptian, the Greek, and the Roman, as the four monarchies preceding that of the Saints on Earth.

mankind." The laws were to be derived solely from the Bible. There were to be neither taxes, nor tithes, nor salaries, nor imprisonment, nor excise.

On the 9th of April a general rendezvous of the conspirators was to take place at Mile End Green; to which place a party of horse was despatched. The chief conspirators, who did not assemble in any large number, were seized; some were committed to the Tower, and others to the Gate House. Harrison, Colonel Rich, Admiral Lawson, and Major Danvers, were consigned to the custody of the Serjeant-at-Arms. Mr. Godwin[1], who has a great partiality for Harrison, contends that the Major-General was not really engaged in these wild designs; but that Cromwell only made them a pretext to imprison a republican whom he feared. But Thurloe and Whitlocke expressly state that Harrison was concerned in the plot; and his conversation just related with Ludlow at Highgate shows how strongly his mind was imbued with the wild and peculiar doctrines of the insurgents. Some months after, a fresh plot of the same kind broke out, and Harrison was again seized. The proceedings relative to the seizure of Harrison, Portman, Carew, and the other insurgents, are highly characteristic of the arbitrary spirit of Cromwell's sole government, and show the sort of murmur of discontent which it excited even in his subservient Parliament. The letter from Cromwell to the Lieutenant of the Tower, ordering the seizure, seems

[1] History of the Commonwealth, vol. iv. p. 379.

to have been to this effect, written with Cromwell's own hand:—" Sir, I desire you to seize Major-General Harrison, Mr. Portman, Mr. Carew, &c. and *other eminent fifth-monarchy men.* Do it speedily, and you shall have a warrant after you have done." Portman's wife petitioned the House for her husband's discharge from the Tower; and a Committee of grievances investigated the matter. Sir John Barkstead [1] (a " Lord " of Cromwell's " other House "), who was Lieutenant of the Tower, was brought to the bar, when Colonel Terrill, the Chairman, *refused to call him Lord Barkstead;* and it was said in the House, it was not fit a Lord of the other House should be a gaoler. When Barkstead produced the warrant and letter from Cromwell, the words " other eminent fifth-monarchy men " were strongly excepted

[1] Barkstead was an active member of the Court which tried Charles, and signed his death warrant. He was originally a working silversmith, or, according to others, a goldsmith in the Strand, in little business. He belonged to the City trainbands, and got a commission as Captain; and being a useful tool of Cromwell, he became a Colonel. Oliver knighted him and made him Lieutenant of the Tower, in 1655; and in 1656, Steward of his Household; and in 1657, one of the " Lords of the other House." At the Retoration he was excepted from the Indemnity Act, and escaped to Hanau, in Germany, where he became a burgess of the city: but going into Holland with Colonel Okey and Mr. Corbet, two other regicides, they fell into the hands of the English ambassador, who sent them to England; and after a fair trial they were condemned, and suffered at Tyburn, April 19. 1662. Barkstead, under the Protectorate, amassed much wealth, and bought, at two or three years' purchase, as much *Bishop's land* as cost 10,000*l.*— See Noble's Memoirs of Cromwell, vol. ii.

against by the committee; the general sense was, that it was a high breach of the liberties of the subject; and the committee resolved that the imprisonment of Mr. Portman was unjust and illegal.

Harrison seems not to have remained long in confinement. But during the short remainder of Cromwell's life, and during the brief reign of Richard Cromwell, he was always an object of suspicion, and resided chiefly in his own county of Stafford. When the restoration of Charles II. was settled, and when the Parliament was discussing the Act of Indemnity, and the exceptions to be made in it, Bowyer, colonel of the Staffordshire militia, a zealous royalist, determined to seize Harrison. The Major-General refused to withdraw from his house and escape, as so many others of the regicides did—deeming it a desertion of the glorious cause in which he was engaged. He was accordingly seized, with all his horses and arms, and brought to London; where the House ordered that he should be committed to the Tower, and his horses taken to the Mews for the King's use. (For the details of Harrison's trial and death, see *post*.)

MEMOIRS OF OTHER REGICIDES.

VALENTINE WAUTON, who was present at all the sittings of the Court in Westminster Hall, and at most of those in the Painted Chamber, and who signed the warrant for the King's death, was of an ancient knightly family, seated at Great Stoughton in Huntingdonshire. He married Margaret, the sister of Oliver Cromwell; was returned member for the county of Huntingdon in the Long Parliament, and strenuously sided with the Parliament in the civil war. In August, 1642, he assisted Cromwell, who was then member for the town of Cambridge, and who had just raised a troop of horse against the King, in intercepting the plate of the University of Cambridge, which was sent by the University to the King at York for defraying the expenses of the war. The exploit only partially succeeded, as part of the plate appears to have reached its destination; but the Parliament thought proper to grant an indemnity to Cromwell and Wauton for what they had effected. In 1643, he was taken prisoner by the royalists, and was confined at Oxford, where (according to Noble) he experienced many kindnesses from Dr. Lawrence, Head of Baliol College, which he afterwards repaid when the Doctor was ejected from his preferments for his loyalty, by procuring the great tithes to be annexed to the chapelry of Coln on his estate in Huntingdonshire, and presenting the chapelry to the Doctor. By the exertions of the Parliament he was released from Oxford, being exchanged for Sir Thomas Lemsford, a royalist prisoner in Warwick Castle; in 1646 he was raised to the rank of Colonel; and in the following year was appointed a commissioner for preventing scandalous persons from receiving the Sacrament. He was one of the republican Council of State installed immediately after the King's death, (17th of February, 1649,) which was composed of twenty of the regicides out of forty-one members; and we find his name in all the Councils till the year 1653. During that period he was also Governor of King's Lynn, with all the level in Ely, Holland, and Marshland. Heath calls him Governor of Lynn and *Bashaw* of the Isle of Ely; and Walker, in his "History of Independency," states that he fortified several bridges and places in the island, for which arms, ammunition, and ordnance were sent him from Windsor. He was (like his friend Ludlow) a stern republican in his principles: after Cromwell's forcible dissolution of the Long Parliament, his name no longer appears in the Councils; and from the time when Cromwell assumed kingly power, he lived in retirement, and was narrowly watched by the usurper. After Richard Cromwell's deposition he again appeared on the stage, and declared himself for the Parliament, which was now mainly governed by Sir Harry Vane and Sir Arthur Haslerig, and was struggling against the army under Lambert. When Lambert, and the other leaders of the army, were cashiered by the Parliament, Colonel Wauton, with Fleetwood, Ludlow, Haslerig, Monk, Morley, and Overton, were the seven commissioners named by the Parliament for the control of the army. He was afterwards joined with Monk and three others for the government of the army, and was appointed one of the twenty-one commissioners for managing the affairs of the admiralty and navy. As soon as he perceived that Monk designed to restore Charles II., he thought it prudent to withdraw to the continent; and at first took refuge at

Hanau, where he became a burgess : but fearing that he might be delivered up, like others, to the King's agent in Holland, he left that place, and passed the short remainder of his days in obscurity. The close of his life was spent in Flanders under a feigned name, and in the disguise of a gardener; where he died, at rather an advanced age, in 1661, having first discovered himself, and desired that his relations in England might be apprised of his decease.

COLONEL EDWARD WHALLEY, who sat in the Court in the Hall at all its sittings, and attended almost every sitting in the Painted Chamber, and signed the warrant of execution, was first cousin to Cromwell, and of an ancient and honourable family in Nottinghamshire. He appears to have been originally brought up to trade, and, according to Heath, was apprenticed to a woollen-draper. He was a rigid puritan, and took arms in the parliamentary service at the commencement of the civil war, in opposition to the sentiments of his family. He was then in middle age, and soon distinguished himself by his courage and military talents, which are spoken well of both by Clarendon and Ludlow. At Naseby, in 1645, he charged and defeated two divisions of Sir Marmaduke Langdale's horse, though supported by Prince Rupert, who commanded the right wing; for which service he was, in January, 1645–6, voted by the Parliament to be a Colonel of horse. He assisted in the defeat of General Goring in Somersetshire; and was commander of the horse at the siege of Bristol, when Prince Rupert surrendered up the city. In May, 1647, he received the thanks of the House, and 100*l.* to purchase two horses, for his brilliant conduct in an action at Banbury. His pay, like that of the rest of the officers, being greatly in arrear, the House (according to a practice not uncommon) granted him for the arrears, at the rate of fifteen years' purchase, the manor of Flamborough, part of the estate of the Marquess of Newcastle, at the annual rent of 410*l.* Cromwell confided in him so much, that he was intrusted with the care of the King during great part of his residence with the army, and especially during his abode at Hampton Court. Clarendon says, speaking of his treatment of the King, " He was a man of rough and brutal temper, who had offered great violence to his nature when he appeared to exercise any civility and good manners." But Charles, when he escaped to the Isle of Wight, left behind him (among others), at Hampton, a letter for Whalley, thanking him for his attentive services while the King was in his custody. On one occasion, Whalley incensed Charles by interposing when the King was walking up and down the gallery in earnest conference with Captain Sayers, who came to deliver to him the *insignia* of the order of the Garter which had been worn by the late Prince of Orange. Charles, in his anger, is said to have pushed him away with both his hands, and even to have struck him with his cane ; but Clarendon denies that the King gave a blow.

Whalley was distinguished at the battle of Dunbar, in 1650, where he, with Monk, commanded the foot, and had two horses shot under him; and Cromwell left him Commissary-General in Scotland, with the command of four regiments. When his cousin Cromwell assumed the protectorate, he was made a Major-General, and had the command of the counties of Lincoln, Nottingham, Derby, Warwick, and Leicester; where, as he said himself, he " did not leave a vagrant in a whole county." He was member for Nottinghamshire in the Parliaments of 1654 and 1656, and seems to have sat in the Protector's Parliaments in 1658–9. We find him, according to Burton's curious Diary, an occasional and seemingly pertinent speaker. When Cromwell created his miserable mimicry of that House of Peers which he had destroyed, Whalley was made one of the " Lords" of this " other House;" an honour of which he was so proud, that, in a conversation in Westminster Hall, with Colonel Ashfield, a stout republican, Whalley threatened to cane him for speaking disrespectfully of the new House; and the Colonel defying him, Whalley, instead of executing his threat, complained against him to Richard Cromwell, then Protector. Ashfield insisted on being heard by a Council of officers; which the Protector agreed to — taking care to nominate Ingoldsby, Goffe, Howard, and others of his own creatures, who immediately awarded that Ashfield must ask the Lord Commissary-General Whalley's pardon, which the Colonel absolutely refused.

When the Restoration appeared inevitable. Whalley, seeing that he must lose his estate of Sabthorpe, purchased of the Duke of Newcastle's trustees, and also the manors in Norfolk (part of Queen Henrietta Maria's jointure,) of which he

had become possessed, and that his life was in
jeopardy, left the kingdom; and on the 22d of September, 1660, a reward of 100*l.* was offered for
his discovery. But he, with Colonel Goffe (another active regicide), his son-in-law, arrived in
America on the 27th of July, 1660, with testi-
monials from eminent puritan divines, with which
they waited at once on the Governor of Boston,
who received them courteously. For some little
time they resided at Cambridge, four miles from
Boston, attending public service, and being received with respect and hospitality by the inhabitants. But when the Act of Indemnity arrived
at Boston, in November, out of which they were
expressly excepted, the magistrates withdrew
their protection, and Whalley and Goffe retired to
Newhaven. Here they were at first treated with
respect by the ministers and magistrates; but on
the arrival of the King's proclamation against the
regicides, they were obliged to fly. The Governor issued a warrant for their seizure; the news
arrived of ten of the regicides having been executed, and a royal mandate reached the colony for
their apprehension. They lay hid at the house of
Davenport, the minister of Newhaven, till they
were removed, on the 11th of March, to one
Jones's, and from thence immediately afterwards
to a retirement called Hatchet's Harbour, in the
woods, where they remained two nights till a cave
in the side of a hill was prepared to conceal them.
To this hill they gave the name of *Providence;*
and remained some weeks in their hiding place,
sleeping, when the weather was tempestuous, in
a house near it. They behaved with great

honour towards their friends; and when **Mr.**
Davenport was suspected by the magistrates of
concealing them, they went publicly to the Deputy Governor of Newhaven to offer themselves
up; but he refused to take any notice of them,
suffering them to return again to the woods. The
pursuit of them soon afterwards relaxing, they
remained two years in a house near Milford, where
they frequently prayed and preached at private
meetings in their chamber; till, the King's commissioners coming to Boston, they were again
driven to their cave in the woods. Here some
Indians in hunting discovered their beds, which
obliged them to seek a fresh refuge; and they
went to Hadley, 100 miles distant, where they
were received by Mr. Russel, the minister, and
remained as long as they lived, very few persons
knowing who they were. Whalley's death took
place about the year 1679. They confessed that
their lives were "miserable, and constant burdens to them;" especially when their fanatical
hopes of some divine vengeance on Charles II.
and his advisers were perpetually disappointed.
They were persuaded that the execution of the
regicides was the accomplishment of the prophecy
as to the slaying of the witnesses; and they con-
fidently reckoned on some signal judgment taking
place in a year marked by such a portentous com-
bination of figures as the year 1666.

GOFFE, who married Whalley's daughter, and
was the affectionate companion of his exile, had
been present at the whole trial in Westminster
Hall, and generally in the Painted Chamber,

and signed the warrant of execution. He was son of a puritanical divine, rector of Stanmer in Sussex, and was apprenticed to a presbyterian drysalter in London, a great partisan of the Parliament. Disgusted with trade, he left his master and enlisted in the Parliament army, where he rose to be a Quarter-Master and Colonel of foot. He was a vehement puritan, and zealously attached to the interest of Cromwell, his wife's cousin; accompanied him to Scotland in 1651; and assisted in Colonel Pride's Purge, and in clearing out the few stubborn members who remained when Praise God Barebones Parliament was dissolved by Cromwell.

He sat for Great Yarmouth in Cromwell's Parliament in 1654, and for Hampshire in that of 1656; and, as appears by Burton's Diary, was an occasional speaker in the House. He was afterwards made one of Cromwell's " Lords" of the " other House." On his death he signed the order for proclaiming Richard Cromwell; and remained attached to this feeble Protector, and adverse alike to the royalist and the republican party. His wife's fidelity and affection to him after his expatriation were remarkably displayed in her letters.

Colonel Richard Ingoldsby (afterwards Sir Richard Ingoldsby, created Knight of the Bath by Charles II.) stands in the singular predicament of having signed the warrant for Charles's death, without having once attended the Court either at Westminster Hall or in the Painted Chamber. He was first cousin once removed to

Oliver Cromwell; his mother, the daughter of Sir
Oliver Cromwell, of Hinchinbrook House (now
the seat of the Sandwich family), having been
first cousin to Oliver; and his father, Sir Richard
Ingoldsby, having been knighted by James I.,
when that King, in one of his progresses, visited
Sir Oliver at Hinchinbrook. The Ingoldsbys
were an ancient family seated at Leathenbo-
rough, in Buckinghamshire; and Sir Richard
and his wife (Oliver's cousin) were strenuous
partisans of the Parliament from the commencement of the war. Their son, Colonel Richard,
who was educated in puritanical and antimon-
archical principles, at the commencement of the
war obtained a captain's commission in his relation
Hampden's regiment. In 1644, he was taken
prisoner by the King's officers; and on regaining
his liberty he was raised to the rank of a Colonel of foot, and then of horse. His gallant
services, and his near connection with Cromwell
and Hampden, made him the object of much
confidence by the Parliament. The important
post of commandant in the city of Oxford was
intrusted to him. He was one of the members
of the Long Parliament, but did not sit till after
the King's death, probably from being engaged
in military duties. In 1650, he was sent to Ireland by the Parliament, where he distinguished
himself in several gallant actions. In 1652, we
find him a new member added (as well as Algernon Sidney) to the Protector's Council of State
and in 1654 and 1656, he sat in Cromwell's Parliaments. He was afterwards made one of the
Lords of the " other House."

After Oliver's death he zealously adhered to his son Richard, with whom his gaiety and freedom from the prevalent fanatical austerity rendered him a favourite. Ludlow, with his usual gravity, says, "Another thing happened about the same time, that proved very disadvantageous to the interest of Mr. Richard Cromwell: for a certain inferior officer having publicly murmured at the advancement of some that had been cavaliers to commands in the army, he was carried to Whitehall to answer for the same. Mr. Richard Cromwell, besides other reproachful language, asked him in a deriding manner, whether he would have him prefer none but those that were godly? 'Here,' continued he, 'is Dick Ingoldsby, who can neither pray nor preach, and yet I will trust him before ye all.' Those imprudent as well as irreligious words, so clearly discovering the frame and temper of his mind, were soon published in the army and city of London, to his great prejudice." Ingoldsby, after the deposition of Richard Cromwell, was appointed one of the Council of Safety, where he used all his power to recommend himself to Charles II., whose restoration he saw was approaching. Monk, who knew his sentiments, intrusted him with Rich's regiment, which received their commander with great satisfaction. He was the means of crushing the last effort of republicanism, by defeating and taking prisoner General Lambert, who had escaped from the Tower, and was in negotiation with Ludlow and other officers, and at the head of a small and increasing force. These important services, as well

as the extraordinary explanation (true or false)
which he gave of his signature of the warrant of
execution, saved him from' the fate of the other
regicides, and recommended him, out of all the
number, to favour under the restored King. Ludlow says that his pardon was expressly obtained
before the King landed ; but Clarendon says that
he made no stipulations, but told Mr. Mordaunt
" that he would perform all the services he could,
without making any conditions, and be well content that the King should take off his head if he
thought fit; only desired that his Majesty might
know the truth of his case." His story was this.
— Having occasion to go to the Painted Chamber on business with an officer, on the day the
warrant was signed, he found the King's Judges
assembled. Cromwell, seeing him, immediately
laid hold of him and said, " Though you have escaped me all the while before, you shall now sign
that paper as well as they." But when he discovered what it was, he refused with vehemence ;
upon which Cromwell and others pulled him to
the table, and Oliver, putting the pen between his
fingers, guided his hand, and, laughing loudly,
wrote " Richard Ingoldsby"—he making all the
resistance he could. The handwriting, Ingoldsby
declared, would, on inspection, appear quite different from his own. The name on the warrant
is, we find, remarkably clearly and well written ;
more so than could easily have been the case, had
it been penned as Ingoldsby described. And if
this story be true, his seal must also have been
taken and used by force. For the arms of the
Ingoldsbys of Bucks (Ermine, a saltier engrailed

sable) are set opposite his name. His absence during the whole trial might, perhaps, be owing to his military duty. And the story which he told Mr. Mordaunt was the best excuse he could invent as a ground for the King's mercy. Though not very probable, it certainly was not ill adapted to the character and habits of Cromwell. Ingoldsby was made a Knight of the Bath by Charles on his coronation, and served in the Parliaments of 1661, 1679, and 1680, for Aylesbury, near which town he resided. He married the widow of Thomas Lee, Esq. of Hartwell, Bucks, daughter of Sir George Croke, Knight, one of the Justices of the King's Bench, a very learned Judge, well known for his valuable Reports of Cases in the times of Elizabeth, James, and Charles. Ingoldsby was buried in Hartwell Church, September 16. 1685.

TRIALS OF THE REGICIDES.

INTRODUCTION.— After the restoration of the monarchy under Charles II., one of the first objects which occupied that Prince and his Parliament was the judicial punishment of the murderers of his father. In a declaration addressed to his subjects from Jersey, a few months after the King's death, Charles II. declared, " that out of a bitter sense and indignation of those horrid proceedings against our dear father, we are, according to the laws of nature and justice, firmly resolved, by the assistance of Almighty God, though we perish alone in the enterprise, to be a severe avenger of his innocent blood, which was so barbarously spilt, and which calls aloud to Heaven for vengeance." In the letters to the two Houses of Parliament, and the declarations sent over from Breda in 1660, immediately before his own arrival, which are written with the conciliatory and joyful spirit natural on the occasion, this bitter topic is more delicately alluded to. After leaving it entirely to the Parliament to arrange such a security and indemnity to all persons for their past conduct as they in their wisdom shall think proper, the King says, " If there be a crying sin for which the nation may be involved in the infamy that attends it, we cannot doubt but that you will be as solicitous to redeem it, and vindicate the nation from that guilt and infamy, as we can be ;" and in the accompanying " Declaration " he offers a free pardon to all persons who shall, within forty days of that act of grace, avail themselves of it, and return to their duty and allegiance, " excepting only such persons as shall hereafter be excepted by Parliament." The House of Commons, in their zealous and ardently loyal answer to the King's letter, thus express themselves as to the death of the late King : — " Surely, Sir, as the persons of our kings have ever been dear unto parliaments, so we cannot think of that horrid act committed against the precious life of our late sovereign, but with such a detestation and abhorrency as we want words to express it ; and next to wishing it had never been, we wish it may never be remembered by your Majesty to be unto you an occasion of sorrow, as it will never be remembered by us but with that grief and trouble of mind which it deserves; being the greatest reproach that ever was incurred by any of the English nation, an offence to all the protestant churches abroad, and a scandal to the profession of the truth of religion here at home."

On the 6th of June, 1660, the King published a proclamation: — "Whereas Owen Roe, Augustine Garland, Robert Tichbourne, (and the other[1] regicides) being guilty of the most detestable and bloody treason, in sitting upon and giving judgment against the life of our royal father, and out of a sense of their own guilt, have lately fled and obscured themselves, whereby they cannot be apprehended and brought to a personal trial for their said treasons according to law, We do, therefore, by the advice of our Parliament, command, publish, and declare, that all and every the persons before named *shall, within fourteen days next* after the publishing of this our royal proclamation, *personally appear* and render themselves to our Speaker, *under pain of being excepted from any pardon* or indemnity both for their respective lives and estates."

An Act of free pardon, indemnity, and oblivion, was immediately afterwards passed by the two Houses and the King, as to all treasons and political crimes committed between the 1st of January, 1637, and the 24th of June, 1660. But it was expressly provided that *the Act should not pardon or give any benefit to* the regicides after

[1] See p. 272.

mentioned—John Lisle, William Say, Sir Hardress Waller, Valentine Wauton, Thomas Harrison, Edward Whalley, William Heveningham, Isaac Pennington, Henry Marten, John Barkstead, Gilbert Millington, Edmund Ludlow, Sir Michael Livesey, Robert Tichbourne, Owen Rowe, Robert Lilburn, Adrian Scroop, John Okey, John Hewson, William Goffe, Cornelius Holland, Thomas Challoner, John Carew, John Jones, Miles Corbet, Henry Smyth, Gregory Clement, Thomas Wogan, Edmund Harvey, Thomas Scot, William Cawley, John Downs, Nicholas Love, Vincent Potter, Augustine Garland, John Dixwell, George Fleetwood, Simon Meyn, James Temple, Peter Temple, Daniel Blagrave, Thomas Wait, John Cook, Andrew Broughton, Edward Dendy, William Hewlet, Hew Peters, Francis Hacker, Daniel Axtel, nor those two persons, who, being disguised by frocks and visors, did appear upon the scaffold before Whitehall, upon the thirtieth of January, one thousand six hundred and forty-eight: all which persons, for their execrable treason, in sentencing to death, or signing the instrument for the horrid murder, or being instrumental in taking away the precious life of our late sovereign Charles the First of glorious memory, are left to be proceeded against as traitors to his late Majesty, according to the laws of England, *and are out of this present Act wholly* [1] *excepted and foreprised.*

---

[1] The persons thus excepted, as to *life and property*, out of the Indemnity Act, were all those who were living at the Restoration (Ingoldsby excepted), who had signed the warrant for the King's execution, and also Colonel Harvey, Alder-

Nineteen of the excepted persons, viz. Owen Rowe, Augustine Garland, Edmund Harvey, Henry Smith, Henry Marten, Sir Hardress Waller, Robert Tichbourne, George Fleetwood, James Temple, Thomas Wait, Simon Meyn, William Heveningham, Isaac Pennington, Peter Temple, Robert Lilburn, Gilbert Millington, Vincent Potter, Thomas Wogan, and John Downs, personally appeared and tendered themselves, according to the King's

---

man Pennington, John Lisle, Nicholas Love, William Heveningham, and Cornelius Holland, who had not signed the warrant, but who had sat on the trial, and been present at the sentence. The exception also comprised Cook, the Counsel for the "people of England;" Broughton, the Clerk of the Court; Dendy, the Serjeant-at-Arms; Hewlet, the supposed executioner; Hugh Peters, the republican preacher; and the Colonels Hacker and Axtell who had been active in the trial and execution. Sir Harry Vane, and Lambert, though not partakers in the trial, were also wholly excepted from the Act. Vane was tried and executed, 14th June, 1662. Lambert died in prison. Twenty-two of those who signed the warrant for Charles's execution had died before the Restoration, among whom were Cromwell, Bradshaw, Ireton, Lord Grey, Sir John Bourchier, Colonel Pride, Sir John Danvers, Sir Will. Constable, &c. &c. All these were attainted by the Act, so that their estates were forfeited to the Crown. The manner in which Colonel Ingoldsby made his peace with Charles II. has been before described. Colonel Tomlinson, who had guarded the King at his execution, was allowed to have the benefit of the Act, on account of his humane and respectful behaviour towards Charles. It is said to have been through the interest of Sir William Davenant, that Milton, who had so zealously defended, in his writings, the destruction of Charles I., was not inserted in the excepting clause. Milton is said to have been the means of saving his friend Davenant's life during the rebellion. — Burnet, vol. i. 277. Speaker Onslow's note.

proclamation of the sixth day of June, one thousand six hundred and sixty, and on this ground laid ground to some favour. As to them, the Act provided, That if they should be legally attainted for the horrid treason and murther aforesaid ; then, nevertheless, their execution *should be suspended, until his Majesty, by the advice of the Lords and Commons in Parliament, should order execution by Act of Parliament.*[1]

When the trial of the Regicides was determined upon, the Judges and law officers of the Crown held

---

[1] None of these persons were executed. Colonel Adrian Scroop also surrendered; but he was proved to have said to the Lord Mayor elect (when asked if he thought it well done to murder the King), " Sir, I will not make you my confessor." — Owing to these words, which were reported in the House of Commons, his name was included in the exception. without being included in the proviso favourable to those surrendering ; and he was executed.

John Carew was, according to Ludlow, seized within the fourteen days, by a justice of the peace, under a warrant mistaking his name, and the officer refusing to detain him, Carew told him he was the person intended, and told him where he was going. The Commons voted this not to be a surrender, and Carew was accordingly excepted unconditionally, and tried and executed. Much contest took place between the two Houses as to the meaning of the King's proclamation. The Commons contended, that the fair construction was, that those who surrendered within the fourteen days were to enjoy the indemnity as to life and estate. The Lords, on the other hand, urged that such persons were only to have a legal trial, instead of being condemned for contumacy in disobeying the proclamation. Clarendon indeed affirmed, that the proclamation was only in the nature of a subpœna. In order to accommodate the difference, he suggested the expedient, which was actually adopted, viz. that those who had surrendered should not be executed, if condemned, till the Parliament should pass an Act to that effect.

a meeting in Serjeants' Inn, Fleet Street, in order to consider of various legal questions affecting the proceedings. Only four seats on the Bench were at that time filled; and these four Judges, Sir Orlando Bridgman (Chief Baron of the Exchequer), Foster and Hide (Judges of the Common Pleas), and Mallet (Judge of the King's Bench — which had been called the Upper Bench during the Commonwealth), together with Sir Geoffry Palmer and Sir Heneage Finch (the King's Attorney and Solicitor General), and Sir Edward Turner (Attorney to the Duke of York), Mr. Wadham Windham, of Lincoln's Inn, and Serjeant Keeling, specially appointed Counsel for the King (Serjeant Glanville, the King's Serjeant to Charles I., being then old and infirm), attended these meetings.

It was resolved by these eminent lawyers to be most expedient to try the prisoners at Newgate by a Commission of Gaol Delivery, and writs were accordingly ordered to be issued to the Lieutenant of the Tower, in whose custody they then were, to deliver them to the Sheriffs of London; and writs were directed to the Sheriffs to remove them to Newgate. These writs, which were accordingly issued, were ordered to be in *English*, since the use of the English language in judicial records, which had been introduced under the Commonwealth, and was now to be again replaced by the Latin, was continued by Act of Parliament till Michaelmas Term (November 6th), which was then a few months distant.[1]

[1] The technical law Latin superseded the Norman French for the enrolment and recording of legal proceedings,

It was resolved to arraign all the prisoners at once on the first day of the sessions, and then to

---

after Edward III.'s victories over the French; being introduced by the Statute 36 Edward 3. c. 15.; and it continued in use till after the destruction of Charles I. and the Monarchy, when the Records were turned into English.   The change appears to have been by no means convenient, the practisers finding it difficult to express themselves in drawing up the Records so concisely and significantly in any language as the Latin.   At the Restoration the Latin language was again introduced, and used till 1730, when it was provided by Act of Parliament, that the proceedings should be done into English, in order, as the Statute recites, that the common people might have knowledge and understanding of what was alleged or done for or against them, in the process and pleadings of a cause,— which purpose, as Blackstone truly observes, has not been answered, the people (necessarily) being as ignorant in matters of law as before.   Two serious inconveniences are mentioned by Blackstone to have resulted from the change, viz.: that many clerks and attornies are hardly able to read, much less understand, a record even of so modern a date as George I.; and Lord Ellenborough lamented that, since the change, " the literature of the inferior branches of the profession had receded."   The other objection (which has now been removed as far as relates to stamps, by the late abolition of the stamps on law proceedings) was, that the length of proceedings was considerably increased by the English language being much more verbose than the Latin. The three words, " *secundum formam statuti,*" make seven in English, "according to the form of the statute."   The four words " *contra pacem Domini Regis,*" require eight in the English translation, " against the peace of our Lord the King."   It became absolutely necessary, two years after the alteration was made, to pass an Act (6 Geo. 2. c. 14.) to allow technical phrases still to remain in the usual tongue it being utterly impossible to convert with decent gravity the terms *fieri facias, quare impedit, nisi prius, habeas corpus* into their English equivalents.

proceed, the next day, with their trials. And it was determined that, as it was usual in ordinary cases for the prosecutor to go before the Grand Jury, and to manage the evidence adduced to ground the Bill, in this case the King's Counsel might perform that office, since they were the real prosecutors, and the King could not prosecute in person.[1]

It was resolved that the indictment should be for *compassing and imagining the death of Charles*

---

[1] This improper practice (now long disused) appears to have been flagrantly abused in the trials of Fitzharris, and of College (the " Protestant joiner)," for treason, in 1681. In the latter case, the London Grand Jury disbelieved the evidence, and threw out the Bill, (the charge being a conspiracy to seize the King at Oxford,) when the King's Counsel with the witnesses proceeded immediately to the Oxford Assizes, and persuaded the Grand Jury to find the Bill, " but by what arts," says Sir John Hawkes, Solicitor-General to William III., " is not known, for he was privately shut up with them, and I should wonder if he who frequently, in the hearing of those who understood better than himself, had assurance enough to impose upon the Courts, (it was Jeffries,) should scruple in private to impose any thing on an ignorant jury." Sir John truly says, " if the Grand Jury have a doubt in point of law, they ought to have recourse to the Court, and that publicly and not privately, and not rely upon the private opinion of the Counsel, especially o₁ the King's Counsel." Such is the modern practice. On the indictment of Hardy, Horne Tooke, &c. for treason, in 1794, and also on the indictments of Watson, Thistlewood, and others, in 1817, the Solicitor for the Crown attended the Grand Jury by leave of the Court. In general cases, the prosecutor (who is always a witness) alone attends the Grand Jury with the other witnesses. In cases of treason it seems necessary that some person should attend to explain the evidence; and the real security against improper practices must be in the Jury themselves.

(which is the specific treason described by the statute 25 Edward 3.), and then that the actual murder of the King should be precisely laid in the indictment, with its special circumstances, and should be made use of as one of the overt acts to prove the compassing of his death.[1]

[1] The English law contains no express provision against killing the Sovereign; and accordingly, when this atrocity demanded punishment, the refinement was resorted to of considering his murder as an overt act proving the " compassing and imagining his death," which is the treason denounced by the statute. The absence of a direct prohibition gave rise to a serious practical anomaly; for the statute of 1 Edward 6. c. 12. requires two witnesses to support every indictment for treason, and consequently the destroyer of the King could not be convicted without two witnesses, while one was sufficient to convict an ordinary murderer. The absurdity was increased, when further protections were afforded to the prisoners tried for treason, by the statutes of William III. and Queen Anne, which required that they should be furnished with lists of the Jury and witnesses, and a copy of the indictment, before the trial, and gave them the great benefit of a Counsel empowered to address the Jury on their behalf. Accordingly, all these advantages were extended to Hadfield, when tried for shooting at his Majesty George III., in the playhouse, though, had he merely pistolled a box-keeper, he would have been tried as a common felon, and Erskine's noble oration would never have been heard. " The fault was then remedied," says a judicious writer in the *Quarterly Review*, October, 1827, " as far as the King is concerned, (by the Statute 39 and 40. Geo. 3. c. 93., passed soon after Hadfield's trial,) but traitors who may assassinate a Queen or heir apparent, or kill a Judge or Privy Counsellor in the execution of his office, or commit certain other acts of direct outrage constituting treason, are still left in possession of all their privileges."

It was resolved that when the prisoners come to the bar to be tried, their irons ought to be taken off, so that they be not in any torture while they make their defence, be their crime never so great.[1]

It not being known what hand had given the murderous blow to the King, it was resolved

[1] In Bracton, Fleta, and other ancient authorities, it is laid down, that though an indictment be of the highest nature, yet the prisoner must be brought to the bar without irons, or any manner of shackles or bonds, unless there be danger of an escape; and in Cranborne's case, 1696, (13 State Trials,) when the prisoner was brought in, being sent for to be present at a preliminary motion on his behalf, Lord Holt, the Chief Justice, seeing him in irons, said. " Look you, keeper, you should take off the prisoners' irons when they are at the bar, for they should stand at ease when they are tried." In Layer's case, in 1722, the prisoner's Counsel urged that his fetters should be taken off before he pleaded, and the resolution in the text by the Judges was cited. Pratt, Chief Justice, said, " No doubt, when he comes upon his *trial* the authority is, that he is not to be *in vinculis*, but should be so far free that he should have the use of his reason and all advantages to clear his innocence: but when he is only called upon to plead, and his Counsel by him to advise him what to plead, why are his chains to be taken off this minute and to be put on again the next? If we should order his chains to be taken off, and he escape, I do not know but we are guilty of his escape." And, accordingly, he remained in irons while some preliminary objections were taken by his Counsel, and while he pleaded. But when brought up on a following day for *trial*, the Chief Justice said, " The irons must be taken off, we will not stir till the irons are taken off." It is now accordingly held, that the Court has no authority to order the irons to be taken off till the prisoner has pleaded and the jury are charged to try him. See 4 Blackstone's Commentaries, p. 322.

that it should be laid in the indictment, that *quidam ignotus*, with a vizor on his face, did the act; and that the other persons should be alleged to be present, aiding and assisting. These niceties of the law, which may appear trifling to thoughtless persons, show the conscientious regard paid to established forms and principles by the Judges of the land, when proceeding to judgment on the most heinous criminals against the father of their Sovereign. They place the proceeding in the most striking contrast with that shameful mockery of all rules and principles which had been resorted to for the destruction of Charles I.

On the 9th of October, 1660, the proceedings commenced at Hicks's Hall, Clerkenwell, when the Commission of Oyer and Terminer was read. It was directed to the Lord Mayor (Sir Thomas Alleyn, Bart.), the Lord Chancellor (Clarendon), the Earl of Southampton (Lord Treasurer), the Duke of Somerset, the Duke of Albemarle (General Monk), the Marquis of Ormond (Steward of the Household), Earl of Lindsay (Great Chamberlain), Earl of Manchester (the Parliamentary General, Chamberlain of the King's Household), Earl of Dorset, the Earl of Berkshire, Earl of Sandwich, Viscount Say and Sele, Lords Roberts and Finch, Denzill Hollis, Esquire (afterwards Lord Hollis, the famous leader of the Presbyterians), Sir Frederick Cornwallis, Bart. (Treasurer of the Household), Sir Charles Berkley, Knt. (Comptroller), Mr. Secretary Nicholas, Mr. Secretary Morris, Sir Anthony Ashley Cooper (afterwards Lord Shaftesbury), Arthur Annesley, Esquire (afterwards

Lord Anglesey), the Lord Chief Baron (Sir O. Bridgman), Mr. Justice Foster, Mr. Justice Mallet, Mr. Justice Hide, Mr. Justice Atkins, Mr. Justice Twisden, Mr. Justice Tyrrel, Mr. Baron Turner, Sir Harbottle Grimston, Bart. (Speaker of the House of Commons), Sir William Wild, Bart. (Recorder of London), Mr. Serjeant Brown, Mr. Serjeant Hale (Sir Matthew Hale, afterwards Chief Baron, and Chief Justice of England), John Howel, Esquire, Sir Geoffrey Palmer (Attorney-General), and Sir Heneage Finch (Solicitor-General, afterwards Lord Nottingham), Sir Edward Turner (Attorney-General to the Duke of York), Wadham Windham, and Edward Shelton, Esquires (Clerk of the Crown). The Grand Jury, of which Sir William Darcey, Bart., was foreman, was composed of five Baronets, four Knights, seven Esquires, and three Gentlemen. They were sworn in the usual manner.

After proclamation for silence was made, Sir Orlando Bridgman, Lord Chief Baron of the Exchequer, spoke to the Jury as followeth :—

The Lord Chief Baron's speech. — Gentlemen, — You are the Grand Inquest for the body of this county of Middlesex. You may perceive by this Commission that hath been read, that we are authorised by the King's Majesty to hear and determine all treasons, felonies, and other offences within this county : but because this Commission is upon a special occasion, the execrable murder of the blessed King, that is now a saint in Heaven, King Charles the First, we shall not trouble you with the heads of a long charge. The ground of this Commission was, and is, from the Act of Oblivion and Indemnity.   You shall find in that act there is an exception of several persons, who (for their execrable treasons, in sentencing to death and signing the warrant for the taking away the life of our said Sovereign) are left to be proceeded against as traitors, according to the laws of England, and are out of that act wholly excepted and foreprised.

Gentlemen, — You see these persons are to be proceeded with according to the laws of the land ; and I shall speak nothing to you but what are the words of the laws. By the statute of the 25th of Edward the Third (a Statute or Declaration of Treason), it is made high treason to compass and imagine the death of the King. · It was the ancient law of the nation.   This compassing and imagining the cutting off the head of the King is known by some overt act.

Then what is an overt act of an imagination or compassing of the King's death? Truly, it is any thing which shows what the imagination is. Words, in many cases, are evidence of this imagination ; they are evidences of the heart.   But if men shall go and consult together to kill the King, to put him to death, this consultation is clearly an overt act to prove this imagination, or compassing of the King's death.

But what will you say, then, if men do not only go about to conspire and consult, but take upon them to judge, condemn, nay put to death, the King? Certainly, this is so much beyond the imagination and compassing, as. it is not only laying the cockatrice's egg, but brooding upon it till it hath brought forth a serpent. I must deliver to you for plain and true law, that no authority, no single person, no community or persons, not the people collectively, or representatively, have any coercive power over the King of England.

Gentlemen,—Let me tell you what our lawbooks say. How do they style the King? They call him, " the Lieutenant of God;" and the book of 1 Henry VII., says "the King is immediate from God, and hath no superior." The statutes say, that the Crown of England is immediately subject to God, and to no other power. Common experience tells you, when we speak of the King, and so the statutes of Edward the Third, we call the King, " Our sovereign Lord the King :" " Sovereign," that is, " Supreme." Look upon the statute 1 James; there is a recognition, that the crown of England was lawfully descended on the King and his progeny. [The statute itself was read, to which the reader is referred.]

These are the words of the act. And this is not the first precedent; for you shall find it 1 Eliz. c. 3. They do acknowledge the Imperial Crown lawfully descended on the Queen, the same recognition with this.

Gentlemen, —This is no new thing to talk of an Emperor, or an Imperial Crown. Do not mistake me all this while : it is one thing to have an Imperial Crown, and another thing to govern absolutely.

God forbid I should intend any absolute government by this. It is one thing to have an

Absolute Monarchy, another thing to have that government absolutely without laws, as to any coercive power over the person of the King; for as to things or actions, they will fall under another consideration, as I will tell you by and by.

Gentlemen,—Since this is so, consider the Oath of Supremacy which most men have taken or should take. All men that enter into the Parliament House, they are expressly enjoined by statute to take the Oath of Supremacy. What says that oath? We swear that "the King is the only supreme governor within this realm and dominions." I do set forth this, and declare this to you, to let you know that the King was immediately subject to God, and so was not punishable by any person; yet let me tell you there is that excellent temperament in our laws, that for all this the King cannot rule but by his laws. It preserves the King, and his person, and the people's rights.

There are three things touching which the law is conversant, *personæ, res, et actiones;* persons, things, and actions. For the person of the King, he is the supreme head, he is not punishable by any coercive power: the laws provide for that. Now the law, though it provide for the King, yet if any of his ministers do wrong, though by his command, they are punishable. The King cannot arrest a man, as he cannot be arrested himself; but if he arrest me by another man, I have remedy against this man, though not against the King; and so he cannot take away my estate. This as to the person of the King: he is not to be touched. "Touch not mine Anointed."

I come to things. If the King claim a right,

the King must sue according to his laws; the King is subject to the laws in that case, his possessions shall be tried by juries. If he will try a man for his father's death, you see he will try them by the laws.

Then for actions, that is, such actions whereby rights and titles are prosecuted or recovered; the King cannot judge in person betwixt man and man, he does it by his Judges, and upon oath; and so in all cases whatsoever, if the King will have his right, it must be brought before his Judges. Though this is an Absolute Monarchy, yet this is so far from infringing the people's rights, that the people, as to their properties, liberties, and lives, have as great a privilege as the King. It is not the sharing of government that is for the liberty and benefit of the people; but it is how they may have their lives, and liberties, and estates, safely secured under government. And you know, when the fatness of the olive was laid aside, and we were governed by brambles, these brambles they did not only tear the skin, but tore the flesh to the very bone.

Gentlemen, — To come a little nearer: suppose there were the highest authority, what then? but when we shall consider this horrid murder (truly I cannot almost speak of it, but " Vox faucibus hæret "), when we consider, that a few members of the House of Commons, those that had taken the Oath of Supremacy, and the Oath of Allegiance, that was to defend the King, and his heirs, against all conspiracies and attempts whatsoever, against his person, crown, and dignity, by any power, authority, or pretence what-

soever : I say, when a few members of the House
of Commons,—not an eighth part of them,—
having taken these oaths, shall assume upon themselves an authority ;—an authority, what to do ?
Shall assume an authority to make laws, which
was never heard before ; authority to make what
laws ? A law for an High Court of Justice, a
law for lives, to sentence men's lives ;—and whose
life ? The life of their Sovereign : upon such a
King, who, as to them, had not only redressed
long before, at the beginning of the Parliament,
all grievances that were, and were imaginable,
taken away the Star Chamber, High Commission
Court, and Ship Money ; such a King, and after
such concessions that he had made in the Isle
of Wight ; more than the people would have desired : when these few Commons, not only without, but excluding the rest of the Commons ; not
only excluding the rest, but rejecting the Lords
too : when these few Commons shall take upon
them this authority, and by colour of this, their
King, sovereign liege Lord, shall be sentenced,
put to death ; put to death as their King, and this
before his own door, even before that place where
he used in Royal Majesty to hear ambassadors,
to have his honourable entertainments ; it is such
an aggravation of villany, that truly I cannot tell
what to say. No story, I do not think any ro-
mance, any fabulous tragedy, can produce the like.
Gentlemen,—If any person shall now come, and
shroud himself under this pretended authority,
this is so far from an excuse, that it is an height
of aggravation. I have no more to add, but one
particular.

As you will have Bills presented against those for compassing, imagining the death of the King, so possibly you may have Bills presented against some of those for levying war against the King. Levying of war is another branch of the statute of the 25th Edward III. It was but declarative of the common law. By that law it was treason to levy war against the King. But to levy war against the King's authority, you must know, is treason too. If men will take up arms upon any public pretence; if it be to expulse aliens; if but to pull out privy counsellors; if it be but against any particular laws, to reform religion, to pull down inclosures. In all these cases, if persons have assembled themselves in a warlike manner to do any of these acts, this is treason, and within that branch of levying war against the King (Croke Car. 583.). This was adjudged in the late King's time, in Queen Elizabeth's, in Henry VIII.'s, in King James's time; much more, if men will go not only to levy war against the King, but against all the laws, to subvert all the laws, to set up new laws, models of their own. If any of these cases come to be presented to you, you know what the laws are. To conclude; you are now to enquire of blood, of royal blood, of sacred blood, blood like that of the Saints under the altar, crying, *Quousque, Domine*, &c. This blood cries for vengeance, and it will not be appeased without a bloody sacrifice.

God save the King. Amen.

His Lordship's speech being ended, there was presented to the Grand Jury a Bill of Indictment of High Treason against the following persons[1] :—

1. Sir Hardr. Waller.	17. Gilbert Millington.
2. Geo. Fleetwood.	18. Robert Tichburne.
3. Thomas Harrison.	19. Owen Rowe.
4. Adrian Scroop.	20. Robert Lilburne.
5. John Carew.	21. Henry Smith.
6. Thomas Scot.	22. John Downes.
7. Gregory Clement.	23. Vincent Potter.
8. John Jones.	24. Augustine Garland.
9. John Cook.	25. Simon Meyn.
10. Hugh Peters.	26. James Temple.
11. Daniel Axtell.	27. Peter Temple.
12. Francis Hacker.	28. Thomas Waite.
13. William Hulet.	29. W. Heveningham.
14. Edmund Harvey.	30. John Barkstead.
15. Isaac Pennington.	31. John Okey.
16. Henry Martin.	32. Miles Corbet.

[1] Of the fifty-one persons wholly excepted from the Indemnity Act, nineteen had fled beyond sea. Generals Whalley and Goffe, and Mr. Dixwell, M.P. for Dover, to America; Colonel Okey, Sir John Barkstead, Colonel Wauton, and Mr. Corbet, to Germany; Sir Michael Livesey, Cawley, M.P. for Chichester, Thomas Wogan, Blagrave, M.P. for Reading, to other parts of the Continent; General Ludlow, and John Lisle, one of Bradshaw's assistants, and Nicholas Love, escaped to Switzerland; Ludlow was buried at Vevai, aged 73, in 1693. His wife erected a monument to his memory in the church of Vevai, with a very laudatory inscription. He appears to have escaped several plots of assassination, and was warmly protected by the Council of Berne, to whom he dedicates his curious and interesting Memoirs. The Council of Berne received Ludlow, Love, and Broughton with honour;—the Treasurer and some of the Council dined with them, accompanied them to church, and made them a present of wine. John Lisle was assassinated at Lausanne, it is said by the instigation of Charles's Queen, Henrietta Maria. His widow, the Lady Alicia Lisle, was arbitrarily tried in 1685, by the ferocious Jeffries,

The Grand Jury, the same day, returned into Court, and presented a " True Bill" against all the prisoners ; and the Court then adjourned till the next morning. On the 10th of October, at an early hour, the prisoners were conveyed in several coaches, with a strong guard of horse and foot, from the Tower to Newgate, where they were delivered by Sir John Robinson, Lieutenant of the Tower, to the Sheriffs of London, and were afterwards, on the same morning, brought before the assembled Court at the Sessions House in the Old Bailey. Silence being commanded, the Commission of Oyer and Terminer was again read ; — after which, Sir Hardress Waller [1], Major-General

---

for concealing a dissenting minister in Monmouth's rebellion ; and she was executed at Winchester. Cornelius Holland, originally a servant of Sir Harry Vane, and who had acquired in the rebellion large estates, a residence in Somerset Palace, and the Keepership of Richmond Park, also escaped to Lausanne, and died there in 1661. Thomas Chaloner fled to Zealand, where he died in the same year.

[1] Waller was of a gentleman's family in Kent, and entered early into the King's army before the rebellion, and served in Ireland. At the commencement of the civil war he joined the army of the Parliament, was distinguished in many engagements, and rose rapidly to the rank of Colonel, and afterwards to that of Major-General under Cromwell. At the Restoration, he at first fled to France, but came to England in hopes of saving the considerable estates he had acquired, and surrendered under the proclamation. After his sentence he was sent back to the Tower, where he appears to have died. Ludlow (who, however, is extremely partial,) says that it was contrived Waller should be tried first, he being a man who would say any thing to save his life, and would therefore plead Guilty. But if the Government were afraid of the effect of a vigorous defence, why did they try the determined Harrison second?

Thomas Harrison, and Mr. William Heveningham, were brought to the bar and commanded to hold up their hands.

The indictment was then read, charging that the prisoners, instigated by the devil, traitorously compassed and imagined to take away the life of Charles Stuart, late King of England; and in pursuance of that intent and design, assembled and sat upon, judged, tried, and condemned, his said late Majesty of blessed memory, and also signed a warrant for killing and executing him, &c.

Clerk of the Crown. How sayest thou, Sir Hardress Waller; art thou Guilty of the treason whereof thou standest indicted, or Not Guilty?

Sir H. Waller (after considerable hesitation and debate). Insomuch as I said I dare not say Not Guilty, I must say Guilty.

Clerk. Thomas Harrison, how sayest thou? Art thou Guilty of the treason whereof thou standest indicted, and are now arraigned? or Not Guilty?

Harrison. My Lords, have I liberty to speak?

Court. No more (at this time) than Guilty, or Not Guilty. Mr. Harrison, you have heard the direction before.—We can give you but the same rule. If you plead Not Guilty, you shall be heard at large; if Guilty, you know what remains.

Harrison. Will you give me leave to give you my answer in my own words?

L. C. Bar. There is no answer but what the law directs; it is the same with you as with all others, or as I would desire, if I were in your condition.

Clerk. Thomas Harrison — Are you Guilty, or Not Guilty?

After considerable demur, Harrison pleaded not Guilty.

Clerk. How will you be tried?

Harrison. I will be tried according to the laws of the Lord.

L. C. Bar. Now I must tell you, if you do not put yourself upon your country, you have said nothing.

Harrison. I will be tried according to the ordinary course.

Clerk. Whether by God and the country? you must speak the words.

Harrison. They are vain words ——

Court. We have given you a great deal of liberty and scope, which is not usual. You must put yourself upon God and the country.

Harrison. I do offer myself to be tried in your own way, by God and my country.

Clerk. God send you a good deliverance.

The other prisoners were then severally arraigned in the same form. All of them, after some little hesitation and argument, pleaded Not Guilty, except George Fleetwood, who said, — " I must confess I am Guilty;" and presented a petition to the Court addressed to the King. Henry Marten (the facetious and learned republican) claimed the benefit of the Act of Indemnity; and, on being told he was excepted out of it by name, he alleged his name was not in the Act, for his name was Harry Marten, and not Henry Martin, as in the Act. The Court said, " The difference of the sound is very little; you are known as

Henry Martin ;" and over-ruled the objection. The fanatical John Carew said he was Not Guilty, " saving to our Lord Jesus Christ his right to the government of these Kingdoms." Hugh Peters, the extravagant Commonwealth preacher, when called upon for his plea, said, " I would not, for ten thousand worlds, say I am Guilty,—I am not Guilty :" and when asked how he would be tried, said, " By the word of God ;" which occasioned some laughter in the crowded audience. Colonel Axtell, when asked how he would be tried, re- plied, " By twelve lawful men, according to the constitutions of the law."

Court. That is by God and the country.

Axtell. That is not lawful, — God is not locally here. He presently, however, submitted, and gave the usual answer. The Court then ad- journed.

On the 11th of October, the Court assembled in the morning, and the trials of the prisoners commenced. The body of the Court and the galleries were crowded with spectators. Harrison, Scroop, Carew, Jones, Clement, and Scot, were brought to the bar.

Court. You that are the prisoners at the bar, if you, or any of you, desire pen, ink, and paper, you shall have it : and if you, or any of you, will challenge any of the jury, you may when they come to be sworn, and that before they are sworn.

Sir Thomas Allen, the first juror, was then called and sworn. Sir Joshua Ash, who was next called, was excepted to by Mr. Scroop, as was Sir Jeremy Whichcote by Harrison.

The Court (speaking to the prisoners). If you will not agree in your challenges, we must be forced to try you severally :" and on Henry Mildmay, Esquire, being excepted to by Scroop, the Court said, " We must needs try them severally, — therefore set them all aside but Harrison." The swearing of the jury for the trial of Harrison alone accordingly proceeded. Sir Jeremy Whichcote, Bart., James Halley, Henry Mildmay, and Christopher Abdy, Esquires, were excepted to by Harrison as they were called.

Court. Mr. Harrison, you know how many to challenge, — if you go beyond the number, at your peril be it.

Harrison. My Lord, pray tell me what it is.

Court. You say very well; God forbid but you should know, — you may challenge five and thirty *peremptorily;* if you go beyond, you know the danger.[1]

---

[1] In addition to the ordinary challenges or objections to jurors which may be made in all suits on the ground of the juror's interest in the cause, relationship to one of the parties, conviction of a crime, alienage, &c., every person tried for felony or treason is allowed to make a certain number of *peremptory* or capricious challenges, without assigning any ground for his objection; " a provision," as Blackstone says, " full of tenderness and humanity to prisoners," and which is not allowed to the Crown, at least unless the person challenged is not wanted to fill the jury. Two reasons are assigned for this privilege: First, that the law will not have a man tried for his life by a juror against whom he may have conceived a suspicion and prejudice, even though unable to assign a cause; and, secondly, that if the prisoner were confined to his challenge for some definite cause which should be adjudged insufficient by the Court, the very circumstance of having objected to the juror might provoke

When he had challenged thirty-five, the names were, at his request, read to him; and the other jurors not excepted to were then called on, and sworn as the jury to try him.

The Court. Gentlemen, that are not of the Jury, pray clear the passage. The prisoner is here for life and death; let him have liberty to see the Jury.

The Clerk. Thomas Harrison, hold up thy hand.

The Clerk. Look upon the prisoner, you that are sworn. You shall understand that the prisoner at the bar stands indicted by the name of Thomas Harrison, late of Westminster, in the county of Middlesex, gentleman, for that he, together with John Lisle, &c. [here the indictment was read] upon which indictment he hath been arraigned, and thereunto hath pleaded Not Guilty, and for his trial hath put himself upon God and the country, which country you are. Now your charge is to enquire, whether he be guilty of the high treason in manner and form as he stands indicted, or not guilty. If you find that he is guilty, you shall enquire what goods and

---

him to resentment. The prisoner may, therefore, peremptorily set him aside. In treason the prisoner is limited to thirty-five peremptory challenges, being the number of three full juries save one. In felony the number is reduced to twenty. The law considered that a traitor who challenged three full juries had no intention to be tried at all; and, therefore, if he peremptorily challenges more than thirty-five, and will not retract his challenge, the law at this day regards him as standing mute and refusing trial, and he will be attainted of the treason.

chattels he had at the time of committing the said treason, or any time sithence. If you find that he is not guilty, you shall enquire whether he did fly for it; and if you find that he fled for it, you shall enquire of his goods and chattels, as if you had found him Guilty. If you find that he is Not Guilty, nor that he did fly, you shall say so, and no more. And take heed to your evidence.

Mr. Keeling, one of the Counsel for the Crown, then enforced the charge at large: after whom Sir Heneage Finch, his Majesty's Solicitor-General, spoke:—

May it please your Lordships,—We bring before your Lordships into judgment this day the murderers of a King. A man would think the laws of God and men had so fully secured these sacred persons, that the sons of violence should never approach to hurt them. For, my Lord, the very thought of such an attempt hath ever been presented by all laws, in all ages, in all nations, as a most unpardonable treason.

The scope of this indictment is for the compassing the death of the King. The rest of the indictment, as the usurping authority over the King's person, the assembling, sitting, judging, and killing of the King, are but so many several *overt acts* to prove the intention of the heart. We are not bound, under favour, to prove every one of these against every particular person that is indicted; for he that is in at one, is guilty in law of all the rest, as much as if he had struck the fatal stroke itself. Nay, under favour, if we can prove any other overt act besides what is

laid in the indictment, as the encouraging of the
soldiers to cry out, " Justice, Justice," or preaching to them to go on in this work, as godly and
religious; or any other act of all that catalogue
of villanies, for which the story will be for ever
infamous; this may be given in evidence to prove
the compassing and imagining the King's death.[1]

As for the fact itself, I shall not need to open
it at large, for these things were not done in a
corner; every true English heart still keeps
within itself a bleeding register of this story.

They seize upon the blessed person of our
sacred King by force, and bring him to London;
and here they force the Parliament, shut out
some members, imprison others, and then called
this wretched little company which was left, a
Parliament. By this, and before they had taken
upon them the boldness to dissolve the House of
Peers, they pass a law, and erect, forsooth! an
High Court of Justice, as they call it, — a
shambles of justice, — appoint judges, advocates,
officers, and ministers, sit upon the life of the
King.

My Lords, when they had thus proceeded to
appoint their judges, officers, and court, then
they call their only liege Lord and Sovereign
to the bar, and by a formal pageantry of justice
proceed to sit upon him, arraign, try, sentence,
condemn, and kill, I had almost said crucify, him,
whom they could not but know to be their King;

---

[1] Such was the law at this period; but the 7 William 3.
c. 3. s. 8. expressly provides that no evidence shall be given
of any overt act not laid in the indictment.

and all this against the clearest light, the sharpest checks, and most thorough convictions of conscience that ever men resisted. And yet in this moment of time, such was the majesty and innocence of our gracious Sovereign, that the people followed him with tears in their eyes, and acclamations in their mouths, "God save the King!" even then, when the soldiers were ready to fire upon all those who did either look sadly, or speak affectionately. So few of the very common soldiers could be brought to approve these proceedings, or to cry out "Justice!" that their officers were fain, by money or blows, or both, to bring a great many to it.

The judges, officers, and other immediate actors in this pretended court, were about fourscore: of these some four or five and twenty are dead, and gone to their own place. Some six or seven of them, who were thought to have sinned with less malice, have their lives spared indeed, but are like to be brought to a severe repentance by future penalties. Some eighteen or nineteen have fled from justice, and wander to and fro about the world with the mark of Cain upon them, and perpetual trembling, lest every eye that sees, and every hand that meets them, should fall upon them. Twenty-nine persons do now expect your justice. Amongst them the first that is brought is the prisoner at the bar, and he deserves to be the first; for if any person now left alive ought to be styled the conductor, leader, and captain of this work, that is the man. He, my Lord, brought the King up a prisoner from Windsor. He sat upon him, sentenced him,

he signed the warrant first to call that court together, then the bloody warrant to cut off his sacred
head.   But now we shall proceed to our evidence.

Proclamation was made for silence.

Sir Edward Turner.[1]   My Lords, the service
of this day doth call to my memory the story of
good king Amaziah.   We read in Holy Writ, that
his father, King Joash, was murdered, and murdered by his own subjects; but we read further,
that when Amaziah had regained the crown, was
settled in the government, he slew those who
slew his father.   He did go down into Edom,
the valley of Salt, and there he did slay 10,000.
The work of this day doth very much resemble
that action.   Our good and gracious King, his
father of blessed memory, and our father, his
natural and our politic father, to whom our natural allegiance was due, was murdered, and by
his own subjects.   But, my Lords, this was not
a national crime; and our good and gracious
Sovereign hath done us that honour and right to
vindicate us in foreign nations.

My Lords, I do read in the Roman story, that
both amongst them and other nations, there was
no law against parricide.   It was not thought
that any man was so unnatural and devilish to
destroy his father.   But we do find among the

[1] This speech of a *second* counsel for the prosecution
was one of the practices bearing hard on the prisoner, at
this period not unfrequent.   In the present day the single
speech of the prosecuting counsel is confined to a very
short statement of the facts, free from general observations,
or aggravating remarks.   But in cases of treason, and all
cases where the Crown prosecutes *for itself*, the Crown
Counsel has the privilege of a reply.

Romans such a fact was committed, and then they were at a loss to punish it. The way was this that was found out; the offender they sewed into a mail of leather, so close that no water could get in; when they had done, they threw him into the sea: by this denoting the offender was not worthy to tread upon the ground, nor to breathe in the air, nor to have the benefit of any of the four elements, nor the use of any of God's creatures.

Gentlemen, parricide and regicide differ not in nature, but in degree. I am not willing to hold your Lordships too long in the porch, but desire to descend into the body of the business; and so we shall call our witnesses, and prove, that this man was the first, and not the least, of these offenders.

Mr. George Masterson was called.

Harrison. When I was before your Lordships yesterday, I offered something very material, in reference to the jurisdiction of the Court; but you told me, according to the rule, I must plead Guilty, or Not Guilty, and what I had to offer should be heard in its proper place. I now desire to know, whether it be proper now to deliver myself, before you proceed to the calling of witnesses; for I would go the best way, and would not willingly displease you.

L. C. Baron. What was promised you yesterday, God forbid but you should have it! But I think it will be best for you to hear the evidence, and then what you have to say shall be fully heard.

Harrison. 1 am content.

Whereupon George Masterson, Stephen Kirk, Francis Hearn, William Clark, Robert Coytmore, and James Nutley, were called, and sworn.

Counsel. Mr. Masterson, whether did the prisoner at the bar sit in that which they called the High Court of Justice, to sentence the King, or no? Pray tell my Lords and the Jury thereof, and what else you know of the matter.

Masterson. Upon the oath I have taken, my Lords and Gentlemen of the Jury, I saw the prisoner, Thomas Harrison, sit in that which they called the High Court of Justice, upon the 27th day of January, in the year 1649, to sentence the King.

Counsel. Was it the day the sentence was passed against the King?

Masterson. It was the day of the sentence. I saw the prisoner at the bar, together with others, stand up, to my apprehension, as assenting to it.

Counsel. Was there not direction that all should stand up as assenting?

Masterson. I do not know that; but when the sentence was read, several of them did stand up, and he among the rest, as assenting to the sentence, as the spectators understood.

William Clark and Stephen Kirk then gave evidence to the same effect; and then James Nutley was examined.

The Court. Mr. Nutley, did you know the prisoner at the bar? Have you seen him sit in Westminster Hall at any time upon the bench when the King was brought as a prisoner to the bar?

Nutley. I saw the prisoner at the bar several days sit there, amongst the rest of the judges. To the best of my remembrance, he sat there four days together.

The Court. Was he there upon the day of the sentence?

Nutley. I did take notes, and I find he did sit that day.

The Court. Do you know any thing more of the prisoner at the bar?

Nutley. The first day they sat in public was the 20th of January, 1649; some few days afore that, there was a committee that sat in the Exchequer Chamber, and of that committee the prisoner at the bar was one of the members. I do remember well it was in the evening; they were lighting of candles. This gentleman was there, I saw him; for through the kindness of Mr. Phelps, who was then clerk to that committee, I was admitted, pretending first to speak with the said Mr. Phelps, and so I was admitted into the committee chamber; being there, I did observe some passages fall from the prisoner; he was making a narrative of some discourses that passed between his late Majesty and himself in coming between Windsor and London or Hurst Castle, I know not well whether. My Lord, he said that the King, as he sat in the coach with him, was importunate to know what they intended to do with him.

Harrison. In the coach was it?

Nutley. Yea, Sir, it was in the coach. He told the rest of the company that the King asked, " What do they intend to do with me? Whether to murder me or no?" And I said to him, "There was no such intention as to kill him; we have no such thoughts. But," (said he,) " the Lord hath reserved you for a public example of justice." There is one word more, my Lords, I observed that some found fault with the length of the charge as it was drawn. I heard this prisoner at the bar vent this expression :—"Gentlemen, it will be good for us to blacken him what we can : pray let us blacken him;" or words to that purpose.

Counsel. It was to draw up that impeachment so as to blacken him? Was it so?

Nutley. Yes, Sir.

Mr. Coytmore sworn,—proved Harrison's presence in the Court for trial of the King.

The Lord Newburgh sworn.

Counsel. Pray, my Lord, raise your voice, and tell my Lords and the Jury what you know of the prisoner at the bar; the part that he acted in bringing up the King.

Lord Newburgh. I was then living at his Majesty's lodge at Bagshot, when the prisoner at the bar brought the King from Hurst Castle to London. He was the person that commanded the whole party; and when the King by the way went to dinner, by his orders there were sentries set at every door where he was. When the King had dined he carried him to Windsor, and appointed several of his officers to ride close to the King, as he was riding, lest he should make his escape from them.

Counsel. That was an imprisonment itself, and so a treason.

Mr. Windham. My Lords, we shall now produce to you two instruments which were made, the one for convening and summoning the assembling of that which they called the High Court of Justice, and show this prisoner's hand and seal to that; and then show you likewise that which was the consummating of all, that bloody warrant for execution of his late Majesty of blessed memory, with the hand and seal of the prisoner at the bar unto it amongst others.

Mr. Jessop called, and sworn.

Solicitor. Mr. Jessop, pray tell my Lords and the Jury how you came by that instrument you have in your hand.

Mr. Jessop. May it please your Lordships,—I having the honour to attend the House of Commons, the House was pleased to make an order that Mr. Scobell should deliver into my hands all such books and records, papers, and other things, as did belong to the House of Commons; and in pursuance of that order I did receive amongst other things this instrument, as a thing that had been formerly in his hands, as clerk of the House of Commons.

Solicitor. We desire it may be read, my Lords.

The Court. Pray first prove his hand.

Mr. Kirk then proved his hand to the warrant for summoning the Court for the trial of the King, and he was confirmed by another witness.

Harrison. I desire to see the instrument.—

Which being showed to him, he said, " I believe it is my own hand."

Counsel. That's the warrant for summoning that Court that he owns his hand to.

The Court. Show him the other instrument.

Harrison. I do think this is my hand too.

Counsel. If you think it, the jury will not doubt it.

Harrison. My Lords, do these learned gentlemen offer these as being any records?

Counsel. No, but as your own hand-writing.

Harrison. If you do not read it as a record, I hope your Lordships will not admit of any thing of that kind against me.

The Court. You have confessed these to be your hands. Whether they are records, or no; whether papers, or letters, they may be read against you : you signed the warrant for convening together those which you called the High Court of Justice, and you signed the other warrant for putting the King to death. You do confess these two things.

Harrison. I do not come to be denying any thing that in my own judgment and conscience I have done or committed, but rather to be bringing it forth to the light.

[The two warrants for trial, and for execution of his Majesty, were here read.]

Mr. Windham.[1] Gentlemen of the Jury, we have done our evidence. Taking of him, impri-

---

[1] This sort of summing up and comment by the Counsel on the evidence for the prosecution, which was in use for a considerable period after these trials, has been now long disused. The same observation applies to the occasional remarks thrown in by the Counsel in the course of the trial.

soning of him, bringing him to London, and setting guards on him. You see also his malice, " Let
us blacken him;" for they knew his innocency
would shine forth, unless it was blackened by
their imputations. He sate many times, as you
hear, and sentenced him, and assented to that
sentence by standing up; and likewise by concluding the catastrophe of that sad beginning of
sufferings, his making a warrant for his execution; and accordingly you know what did follow :
I think a clearer evidence of a fact can never be
given than is for these things.

[Here the spectators hummed.]

Lord Chief Baron. Gentlemen,——This hum-
ming is not at all becoming the gravity of this
Court. It is more fitting for a stage-play than
for a Court of Justice.

Harrison. It is now time, my Lords, to offer
what I have to say. My Lords,——The matter that
hath been offered to you, as it was touched, was
not a thing done in a corner. I believe the sound
of it hath been in most nations. I believe the
hearts of some have felt the terrors of that presence of God that was with his servants in those
days, (however it seemeth good to him to suffer
this turn to come on us,) and are witnesses that
the things were not done in a corner. I have
desired, as in the sight of Him that searcheth all
hearts, whilst this hath been done, to wait, and
receive from him convictions upon my own conscience, though I have sought it with tears many
a time, and prayers over and over, to that God to
whom you and all nations are less than a drop of

U

water of the bucket; and to this moment I have
received rather assurance of it, and that the things
that have been done as astonishing on one hand,
I do believe ere it be long it will be made known
from Heaven, there was more from God than
men are aware of.   I do profess that I would not
offer of myself the least injury to the poorest
man or woman that goes upon the earth.   That I
have humbly to offer is this to your Lordships;
you know what a contest hath been in these
nations for many years.   Divers of those that sit
upon the bench were formerly as active——[1]

[1] Harrison alludes to the leaders of the Presbyterian
party, who had so vehemently spoken and fought against
the King at the commencement of the rebellion, and who
now, with little decency, sat as judges on the men who had
followed in their steps, and pursued their projects to their
natural termination.   The Earl of Manchester was long
commander of the parliamentary forces against the King,
and, as Lord Kimbolton, had been included with the five
Commoners in an accusation of treason by Charles.   Denzil
Hollis was one of these five accused members whom
Charles imprudently went to the House to demand, and
a violent leader of the opposition against the King.   Lord
Roberts and Lord Say both commanded in the parliamentary army in the civil wars.   Monk and Lord Sandwich were privy counsellors under Cromwell's reign, and
" Lords " of his " other House."   The unprincipled Shaftesbury had sat in the republican Councils of State, together
with Harrison and other of the regicides; and had been,
as well as Harrison, the adviser and friend of Cromwell.
Atkyns and Tyrrell were Judges, appointed by the Rump
Parliament which ordered and confirmed the proceedings
against the King.   Serjeant Wild (now Recorder of London) had been the most unhesitating tool of the republicans, and had actually gone down to the Isle of Wight
when Charles was at Carisbrook, and tried and sentenced

Court. Pray, Mr. Harrison, do not thus reflect on the Court. This is not the business.

Harrison. I followed not my own judgment; I did what I did, as out of conscience to the Lord; for when I found those that were as the apple of mine eye to turn aside, I did loath them, and suffered imprisonment many years. Rather than to turn as many did, that did put their hands to this plough, I chose rather to be separated from wife and family than to have compliance with them, though it was said, " Sit at my right hand," and such kind expressions. Thus I have given a little poor testimony that I have not been doing things in a corner, or from myself. May be I might be a little mistaken; but I did it all according to the best of my understanding, desiring to make the revealed will of God in his Holy Scriptures as a guide to me. I humbly conceive that what was done, was done in the name of the Parliament of England, by their power and authority. Those Commissions were issued forth, and what was done was done by their power; and whereas it hath been said we did assume and usurp an authority, I say this was done rather in the fear of the Lord.

Court. Away with him. Know where you are, Sir; you are in the assembly of Christians;

---

to death Captain Burley, for *treason !* in endeavouring to excite the islanders to rise and liberate their Sovereign. These men, especially Monk, Sandwich, Manchester, Shaftesbury, Hollis, and Roberts, were the main authors of the Restoration, and acquired from Charles II. titles and offices at Court, which accounts for their being inserted in the Commission.

will you make God the author of your treasons
and murders? Take heed where you are. Christians must not hear this. For your having of
Counsel [1], this is the reason for allowing of Counsel:

[1] The established rule of law, that a prisoner on his trial
for a capital offence is not to be allowed a Counsel as to
matters of *fact*, but only in case a question of *law* arises,
appears to have had its rise in the sort of interest which
the Crown was considered to have in the conviction of
the accused, which led also to refusing him the benefit
of witnesses on oath, and to an extraordinary leaning and
deference, by the Judges, for the " King's evidence."
It is singularly at variance with the humanity of the
common law, in allowing a prisoner thirty-five peremptory
challenges, and in requiring him to be free from fetters on
his trial: and its hardship in former days certainly was
seldom, in practice, mitigated by the rule which is put forward to excuse it, viz. that the Judge is the prisoner's Counsel. In modern times the case is different; and the prisoner can seldom be left in equally safe, or more humane
hands, than those of the Judge. Nor was the privilege
of having Counsel's assistance as to matters of law in
early times, and up to the Revolution, of much value to
a prisoner; since, in order to obtain Counsel, he was
compelled, by his own ingenuity and skill, to start some
legal objection, and to lay it properly before the Court, who
were then to determine, at their own discretion, whether the
suggestion was or was not such matter of law as required
argument by Counsel. The Judges, in considering these
applications of prisoners, often (not unnaturally) took into
consideration whether the objection made was a *sufficient*
matter of law to be of *avail* to the prisoner, rather than
whether it was matter of law at all; though the last was the
only question properly to be determined before allowing
counsel to be heard. The point started by Harrison, in the
text, and by many of the other regicides, viz. that they acted,
in destroying Charles I., under the authority of the House
of Commons, was, perhaps, one which the Court might fairly
over-rule as not being matter of law arguable by a lawyer;

When a man would plead any thing, because he would plead it in formality, Counsel is allowed. But you must first say in what the matter shall be, and then you shall have the Court's answer.

---

since it was contrary to first principles to set up an authority from the House of Commons alone to justify the acts committed; besides, that the fact was not as alleged; the House had never given any such authority, since the majority of the members were excluded by armed force before the ordinance for trying the King was passed. In modern days, however, when the leaning towards prisoners is carried almost to an extreme, points even less arguable than the regicides' justification, are, in favour of life, allowed to be discussed at length by Counsel. In the present day, Counsel have in all cases the utmost liberty, not only of finding out and arguing legal objections, but also of cross-examining witnesses for the prosecution, and of examining witnesses for the prisoner, who, by a most proper provision of 1 Ann. stat. 2. c. 9. § 3., are sworn to speak the truth. And in cases of treason, the prisoner, by the statute of William, is allowed to make a *full defence* by Counsel; a provision which has called forth many noble efforts of forensic eloquence from Erskine, Law, Copley, Wetherell, Denman, and other distinguished English lawyers. The existing authority of Counsel to cross-examine the opposite witnesses, object to evidence, and assist prisoners as to the facts of the case, has grown up without any statutory provision, and by such insensible gradations, that it is not easy to assign a date to the change. Some symptoms of it appear in the case of Arnold, for shooting at Lord Onslow, in 1724; and on the trial of the gaolers, Acton and others, in 1729, the change is more visible. " In the proceedings against Mr. Chetwynd for murder, in 1743," says the sensible writer in the Quarterly Review for October, 1827, before quoted, " the liberty of cross-examining for the prisoner appears fully recognised, and his defence is conducted according to the usage now prevailing, which, although it may continue open to speculative objections, could hardly, we believe, be placed upon a footing more substantially favourable to the accused."

Lord Finch. **Though my Lords here have** been pleased to give you a great latitude, this must not be suffered, that you should run into these damnable excursions, to make God the author of this damnable treason.

Harrison.   I have two things to offer to you, for my defence in matter of law.   One is, That this that hath been done was done by a Parliament of England, by the Commons of England assembled in Parliament; and that being so, whatever was done by their commands or their authority, is not questionable by your Lordships, as being (as I humbly conceive) a power inferior to that of the High Court of Parliament; that is one. A second is this, That what, therefore, any did in obedience to that power and authority, they are not to be questioned for it; otherwise we are in a most miserable condition, bound to obey them that are in authority, and yet to be punished if we obey.   My Lords,—Upon these two points I do desire that those that are learned in the laws may speak on my behalf.   I hope it will seem good to you that Counsel may be assigned, for it concerns all my countrymen.

Counsel.   You are mistaken, if you appeal to your countrymen; they will cry you out, and shame you.

Harrison.   May be so, my Lords; some will, but I am sure others will not.

Mr. Solicitor General.[1]   These two points, my

[1] Nothing can be more opposite to the spirit in which prosecutions are now generally conducted, than this speech of the Crown advocate against the prisoner being allowed the assistance of Counsel.

Lords, are but one, and they are a new treason, at the bar, for which he deserves to die. It is the malice of his heart to the dignity and Crown of England. I say, this is not matter for which Counsel can be assigned. It is so far from being true, that it was the act of the Supreme Parliament of the people of England, that there was nothing received with more heart-bleeding than this bloody business. Shall he pretend that one House, nay, the eighth part of a House (for so it was), can condemn a King, when both Houses cannot condemn one man in spite of the King?

L. C. Baron. It is true, your questions are but one point. You pretend the Parliament's authority, and when you come to speak of it, you say the Commons of England. They were but one House of Parliament. The Parliament, what is that? It is the King, the Lords, and the Commons. I would fain know of you where ever you read, by the light you say you have in your conscience, that the Commons of England were a Parliament of England, that the Commons in Parliament used a legislative power alone? Do you call that a Parliament that sat when the House was *purged*[1], as they call it, and was so much under the awe of the army, who were then but forty, or forty-five at most? Then you say it was done by authority of them. You must know, he that confirms such an authority, he commits a double offence; therefore consider what your plea is. If your plea were doubtful[2], we should,

---

[1] See 3 Cobb. Parl. Hist. p. 1240.
[2] If his plea was doubtful, he was, according to principle, entitled to have Counsel assigned to him.

and ought, and would, *ourselves* be of Counsel for you. You make yourself a Solicitor in the business. "Let us blacken him as much as we can." I have not touched at all upon the evidence, I will not urge it now. I say you justify it upon "convictions of conscience," and pretend it upon authority; a thing never known or seen under the sun, that the Commons, nay, a few Commons alone, should take upon them, and call themselves the Parliament of England. For you to speak of this power, and justify this power, is an aggravation, adding one sin and treason to another. We shall tell you, that neither both Houses of Parliament, if they had been there, not any single person, community, not the people, either collectively or representatively, had any colour to have any coercive power over their King.[1] And this plea which you have spoken of, it ought to be overruled, and not to stand good.

Mr. Annesley. I do the more willingly speak to this business, because I was one of those that should have made up that Parliament that this prisoner pretends to. I was one of that "corrupt majority" (as they called it) that were put out of the House. He cannot forget, that the Lords and Commons of England in Parliament assembled, a full House of Commons, did resolve, notwithstanding what was aforesaid, that the treaty in the Isle of Wight "was a ground for Peace." Afterwards the major part of the House of Com-

---

[1] This sentence of the Chief Baron has been vehemently attacked by Ludlow and the republicans. But, as a statement of the law of England, it is undeniably sound.

mons, having resolved on this, sent it up to the
Lords ; that very day when they were adjourned,
there were forces drawn down to the House of
Commons' door, and none suffered to come into
the House but those that they pleased: and then
to call this a House of Commons, nay, the Supreme Authority of the Nation, he knows is
against the laws of the land. I shall only say,
that he knowing the laws so well, I hope he shall
suffer for transgression thereof.

Mr. Hollis.   You do very well know that this
horrid, detestable act which you committed,
could never be perfected by you till you had
broken the Parliament.   That House of Commons, which you say gave you authority, you
know what yourself made of it when you pulled
out the Speaker [1], therefore do not make the
Parliament to be the author of your black crimes.
It was innocent of it. You know yourself what
esteem you had of it, when you broke and tore
it in sunder, when you scattered, and made them
hide themselves, to preserve them from your
fury and violence: do not make the Parliament
to be the author of your crimes.   You know that
no act of Parliament is binding but what is acted
by King, Lords, and Commons : and now, as you
would make God the author of your offences, so
likewise you would make the people guilty of
your opinion ; but your plea is over-ruled. [2]

---

[1] See *antè*, in the Memoirs of Harrison.

[2] Hollis, who was a vehement man and a sturdy Presbyterian, and who had been excluded from the House and
obliged to fly to the Continent by the independent party
and the army, could not be in a very impartial frame of

To which the Court assented.

Counsel. My Lords, — If it were a House oɪ Commons, neither House of Commons nor House of Lords, nor House of Lords and Commons together; no authority upon earth can give authority for murdering the King; this that he allegeth is treason.

L. C. Bar. It is clear as the noon-day, that this was not the House of Commons. Suppose it had been a House of Commons, and full; and suppose (which far be it from me to suppose) they should have agreed upon such a murderous act; for the House of Commons to do such an act, it was void in itself: nay, any authority without the House of Lords and King is void. — What you have said doth aggravate your crimes.

Justice Mallet. · I have been a Parliament-man as long as any man here present, and I did never know or hear that the House of Commons had jurisdiction over any, saving their own members, which is as much as I will say concerning the Parliament. I do hold the prisoner's plea vain and unreasonable, and to be rejected.

---

mind towards his personal and political enemies, whom he was now trying. His Memoirs are written with the bitterest rancour against the independents, and are dedicated thus:— " To that unparalleled couple, Mr. Oliver St. John, His Majesty's Solicitor-General, and Mr. Oliver Cromwell, the Parliament's Lieutenant-General, the two grand designers of the ruin of three kingdoms."

1 This Judge Mallet had been imprisoned in the Tower by the Parliament, for an offence in the matter of the Kentish Petition, in 1642.

Mr. Justice Hyde and *Mr. Justice Twisden* concurred in over-ruling the plea.

Earl of Manchester. I beseech you, my Lords,
let us go some other way to work ——

Sir William Wild. I beseech you, my Lord,
direct the Jury for their verdict. This gentleman hath forgot their own barbarousness; they
would not hear their King.

Court. No Counsel can be allowed to justify a
treason; that this is a treason, appears by an
act of the 25th of Edw. III.; and therefore your
plea is naught, and all the Court here is of the
same opinion. Have you any thing else to offer?

Harrison. Notwithstanding the judgment of
so many learned ones, that the Kings of England
are no ways accountable to the Parliament, the
Lords and Commons, in the beginning of this war,
having declared the King's beginning war upon
them; the God of Gods ——

Court. Do you render yourself so desperate,
that you care not what language you let fall? It
must not be suffered.

Harrison. I would not willingly speak to offend
any man; but I know God is no respecter of
persons. His setting up his standard against the
people ——

Court. Truly, Mr. Harrison, this must not be
suffered: this doth not at all belong to you.

Harrison. Under favour this doth belong to
me. I would have abhorred to have brought him
to account, had not the blood of Englishmen, that
had been shed ——

Counsel. Methinks he should be sent to Bedlam till he comes to the gallows to render an account of this.

Solicitor-General. My Lords, I pray that the Jury may go together upon the evidence.

Sir Edward Turner. My Lords, — This man hath the plague all over him; it is pity any should stand near him, for he will infect them.

Harrison. I must not speak so as to be pleasing to men; but if I must not have liberty as an Englishman——

Court. Pray do not reflect thus; you have had liberty, and more than any prisoner can expect; I wish you had made a good use of it. Keep to the business, say what you will.

Harrison. My Lords, thus: There was a discourse by one of the witnesses, that I was at the committee preparing the Charge, and that I should say, "Let us blacken him." This thing is utterly untrue; I abhorred the doing of any thing touching the blackening of the King.

Court. Mr. Harrison, you have said that you deny that of "blackening," which the witness hath sworn; and somewhat else touching the King in his way to London, that the witness hath sworn to also. The Jury must consider of it, both of their oaths and your contradictions. If you have nothing more to say, which tends to your justification, we must direct the Jury. The end of your speech is nothing but to infect the people.

Harrison. You are uncharitable in that.

Justice Foster. My Lords, — This ought not to come from the Bar to the Bench; — if your conscience should be a darkened conscience, that must not be the rule of other men's actions.

Harrison. The things that have been done, have been done upon the stage, in the sight of the sun ——

Court. All this is a continuance of the justification and confession of the fact. We need no other evidence.

Gentlemen of the Jury,—You see that this prisoner at the bar is indicted for compassing, imagining, and contriving the death of our late sovereign Lord, King Charles the First, of blessed memory. In this indictment there are several things given but as evidences of it; they are but the overt acts of it. The one is first, that they did meet and consult together about the putting the King to death; and that alone, if nothing else had been proved, was enough for you to find the indictment; for the imagination is treason by the law. The second is more open; namely, their sitting together, and assuming an authority to put the King to death. The third is sentencing the King. And I must tell you, that any one of these acts prove the indictment. If you find him guilty but of any one of them, either consulting, proposing, sitting, or sentencing (though there is full proof of all), yet notwithstanding you ought to find the indictment. You have heard what the witnesses have said, and the prisoner's own confession. He hath been so far from denying, that he hath justified these actions. The evidence is so clear and pregnant as nothing more is necessary. I think you need not go out.

The Jury went together to the bar, and presently unanimously agreed on their verdict.

Clerk. Thomas Harrison, hold up thy hand.

Gentlemen of the Jury, look upon the prisoner. How say ye ? Is he Guilty of the treason whereof he stands indicted, and hath been arraigned, or Not Guilty ?

Foreman. Guilty.

Solicitor-Gen. My Lords, — Upon this verdict against the prisoner I humbly move, that we may have judgment given.

Court. Mr. Harrison, what do you say for yourself why judgment should not pass against you ?

Harrison. I have nothing further to say, because the Court have not seen meet to hear what was in my heart to speak. I submit to it.

L. C. Baron. You that are the prisoner at the bar, you are to receive the sentence of death, which sentence is this : The judgment of this Court is, and the Court doth award, That you be led back to the place from whence you came, and from thence be drawn upon an hurdle to the place of execution; and there you shall be hanged by the neck, and being alive shall be cut down [1], and your head to be cut off, your body to be divided into four quarters, and head and quarters to be disposed of at the pleasure of the King's Majesty; and the Lord have mercy upon your soul!

[1] The more revolting parts of this old sentence against traitors are here omitted. The sentence is abolished by 54 Geo. 3. c. 146.; and the sentence now is, that the culprit shall be drawn upon a hurdle to the place of execution, and hanged by the neck till he is dead, and afterwards the head shall be severed from the body, and the body divided into four quarters, to be disposed of as the King shall think fit. His Majesty has power to dispense with the drawing on a hurdle, and to order the convict to be decapitated instead of hanged.

THE TRIAL OF HUGH PETERS.

October 13. at the same Bar.

Clerk of the Crown. Set Hugh Peters to the bar. [Which was done accordingly.]

Clerk. Hugh Peters, hold up thy hand; thou standest indicted, &c. If you will challenge any of the Jury, you must challenge them when they come to the book, before they are sworn.

L. C. Baron. Mr. Peters, you may challenge to the number of thirty-five peremptorily, but beyond that you cannot, without good cause shown; and you may have pen, ink, and paper.

Peters. My Lord, I shall challenge none.

The Jury were then sworn.

Sir Edward Turner.[1] Gentlemen, — You have often heard repeated to you, that the substantial part of the charge is the compassing and imagining the death of the King, and all the rest will be but evidence to prove that imagination against the prisoner at the bar, whom we will prove to be a principal actor in this sad tragedy, and next to him whom God hath taken away, and reserved to his own judgment; and we shall endeavour to prove, that he was a chief conspirator with Cromwell at several times, and in several places; and that it was designed by them: we shall prove that he was the principal person to procure the soldiery to cry out, "Justice, justice!" or assist or

---

[1] Several others of the prisoners were tried before Peters.

desire those for the taking away the life of the
King. He did make use of his profession, wherein
he should have been the minister of peace, to
make himself a trumpeter of war, of treason, and
sedition, in the kingdom: he preached many sermons to the soldiery, in direct terms for taking
away the King, comparing the King to Barabbas:
he was instrumental when the proclamation for
the High Court of Justice (as they called it) was
proclaimed, directing where it should be proclaimed, and in what place. The next day after
the King was brought to trial he commends it:
you shall hear all out of the mouth of the prisoner,
therefore I say no more; call the witnesses.

Dr. William Young sworn.

Counsel. Tell my Lords and the Jury what the
prisoner at the bar has declared to you concerning
the contrivance of bringing the King to trial.

Dr. Young. My Lords, and Gentlemen of the
Jury, — It was near about the month of July, 1648,
since we came first acquainted, when he went over
to Ireland; it was about the siege of Pembroke
Castle; but afterwards, in the year 1649, we renewed our acquaintance; he went over to Ireland,
with that usurper, the late Protector, as he was
called, after the town of Wexford was taken.
Coming over he fell sick of the flux, and said he
received it by infection, praying over Captain
Horton. Coming into Milford, that captain sends
a summons to me to come on board; that was to
fetch this prisoner at the bar, who was sick. I
found him there grovelling upon the deck, and
sick he was indeed; with much difficulty we got

him on shore; within a very few days, to the best of my remembrance five days, I perfected his cure : we became very familiar; I observed to him that he had some secret thoughts that I could not well discover, neither well understand; whereupon I thought it might tend to my security that I should so much sympathise with him, to get within him to know his intentions. After some weeks. (for he continued with me ten weeks, or thereabouts), he began to enlarge his heart to me. Many times I should hear him rail most insufferably against the Blood Royal; not only against our martyred King, but against his offspring : we would sit up discoursing till about twelve or one of the clock at night very often, about these unhappy wars late in England. At last, he began to tell me how he came into England, and upon what account he came out of New England. First, he told me, (discoursing of New England and the clergy there, and much of the clergy here in England,) that for the driving on of this interest of this Reformation, he was employed out of New England for the stirring up of this war, and driving of it on : and, secondly, that some time after he was come into England he was sent over into Ireland by the Parliament to drive on the design, to extirpate monarchy : saith he, I did dispend a great deal of my own money, yet never had that satisfaction from them which they promised me ; they promised 2000l. or 3000l. for my journey, and yet they have given me no more but only a small pittance of land out of my Lord of Worcester's estate in Worcestershire. I have seen his letters directed to his

x

kinsman here in London, — his name was Parker, — advising him for the settling of his land, and selling it. Thirdly, my Lord, by way of vilification of the monarchical government, I have found him jocundarily scoffing at it: he would ordinarily quibble in this manner, " this Commonwealth will never be at peace till 150 be put down." I asked him what this 150 was; he told me three L's, and afterwards interpreted the meaning to be the Lords, the Levites, and the Lawyers: with that, said I, we shall be like Switzers, Tinkers, and Traitors. Now, my Lord, we are come to the last particular: we discoursing thus frequently, and withal he was then a Colonel, and had a commission under that usurper Oliver, and brought over his commission for raising of soldiers to foment that war in Ireland; that it was so I appeal to his own conscience, and whether he did not press me very importunately to accept of a commission of Major, or a Captain; he did issue forth two commissions under his own hand — one of them to bring over from Devonshire two foot companies unto Cork. My Lord, because we were militarily affected, amongst the discourses of our unhappy wars, we were discoursing concerning our martyred King, as then we called him, and of his imprisonment in Holmby House, which I wondered at; he told me the story how they had used him at Holmby; and at last came up to this, when he was taken away from Holmby House[1], the Parliament had then a design to have

[1] It appears from Whitlock, that shortly after King Charles I. was removed by Joyce from Holmby to New-

secured Oliver Cromwell, and himself, being then in London; saith he, we, having intelligence of it, escaped out of London, and rode hard for it, and as we rode to Ware, we made a halt, and advised how we should settle this kingdom in peace, and dispose of the King; the result was this, they should bring him to justice, try him for his life, and cut off his head: whether this was the expression of Cromwell I cannot tell; but to the utmost of my remembrance, it was the advice of Mr. Peters to Cromwell; and I believe it, because his former relations of his instructions out of Ireland did tend to that effect.

Peters. My Lord, I desire to speak a word. [His voice being low, he was brought to the second bar.] This gentleman I do know ——

Counsel. What say you to him?

Peters. That which I have to say is this, that in his story he hath told that which is not true; but I will not find fault with him, because he was my host, I will not reflect and recriminate: my trouble at this discourse is this, — I do not know, my Lord, that I found a more violent man for the Parliament than himself; so far he undertook to be a spy on one side; he will not deny it; he was very fierce in that way; I think words of such a man ought to be little attended to. The second is, this gentleman is not a competent witness

---

market, " Mr. Peters went to the King to Newmarket, and had much discourse with him." Mr. Peters moved his Majesty to hear him preach, but his Majesty refused. Whitlock's Mem. 257. 6 Rushw. Coll. 578. This refusal appears to have greatly offended this vain turbulent declaimer.

x 2

upon a twofold ground. First, because 'I know he is under a very great temptation and trouble in this very thing, and it is upon this account he was put out of his living in the country, and here he came to me to help him in again, and was very highly offended because I did not do it. Secondly, give me leave to tell you, it is his way to snap and catch at every man, which is the complaint of the people in his own country. I know that same which is spoken is false; I speak it in the presence of God; I profess, I never had any near converse with Oliver Cromwell about such things; I was in sickness then; and to take words that are spoken in a sick condition, he ought not to do it; for the words themselves I do here profess against them, for the generality of them; and that he hath been freer in my judgment in any communication in this way than I have been; I profess the things untruths, I call God and angels to witness they are not true.

The Court. You shall be heard at large; that which you have been heard now is concerning the competency or incompetency of the witness: the incompetency against him is this, that when you came thither none more violent for the Parliament than himself, and that he was a great spy, and you say it was usual with him to take such courses; these are but words; if you have any witnesses we will hear them; the man may be traduced and slandered, and so all witnesses may be taken away.—Mr. Peters, if you take this course, God knows when this business will end; if you have a mind, take pen, ink, and paper, and take notes of the witnesses, and make exceptions to them one after another; but interrupting one, and so another, we shall never have done.

Young. I do recollect myself of some other conferences between us; but, my Lord, that which I would inform your Lordship is this, he told me he took Duke Hamilton a prisoner himself in his own chamber, seized on his goods, and took his George and blue ribbon off his shoulder, and the George he showed me.

Wybert Gunter sworn.

Counsel. Mr. Gunter, what can you say concerning a meeting and consultation at the Star in Coleman-street?

Gunter. My Lord, I was a servant at the Star in Coleman-street, with one Mr. Hildesley. That house was a house where Oliver Cromwell and several of that party did use to meet in consultation; they had several meetings; I do remember very well one among the rest, in particular that Mr. Peters was there; he came in the afternoon about four o'clock, and was there till ten or eleven at night; I being but a drawer could not hear much of their discourse; but the subject was tending towards the King, after he was a prisoner, for they called him by the name of Charles Stuart: I heard not much of the discourse; they were writing, but what I know not; but I guessed it to be something drawn up against the King; I perceived that Mr. Peters was privy to it, and pleasant in the company.

The Court. How old were you at that time?

Gunter. I am now thirty years the last Bartholomew-day, and this was in 1648.

x 3

The Court. How long before the King was put to death?

Gunter. A good while; it was suddenly, as I remember, three days before Oliver Cromwell went out of town.

Peters. I was never there but once with Mr. Nathaniel Fines. [1]

Counsel. Was Cromwell there?

Gunter. Yes.

Counsel. Was Mr. Peters there any oftener than once?

Gunter. I know not, but once I am certain of it; this is the gentleman; for then he wore a great sword.

Peters. I never wore a great sword in my life.

Mr. Starkey sworn.

Starkey. My Lords,—In the month of December, before the King died, in the beginning of that month, and so towards the 12th of January following, the head-quarters of the army were at Windsor, and Mr. Ireton, that is dead, (who was a general officer of the army,) was quartered in my father's house there, and by reason of his long residence there, being about two months, I knew him very well. My Lords,—This gentleman, Mr. Peters, he likewise quartered in another place in that town, and Cromwell himself was quartered at one Mr. Baker's, that lay low in the town; so that, in truth, my father's house being near the Castle, and there being in it a large room, and in respect that Mr. Ireton was quartered there,

---

1 Probably Fiennes.

usually the Council of War sat there. My Lords,
—I was then in the house constantly: besides this
Council of War, which did commonly sit there, I
did observe that Cromwell, Ireton, and this gentleman, Mr. Peters, and one Colonel Rich, and a
fifth person, whose name I have forgot, did usually
meet and consult together, and would sit up till
two or three o'clock in the morning very privately
together: this was their usual course when their
Council of War sat; Mr. Ireton came in to supper,
but went out again; there were guards upon
them: after this time it happened that I was
often in Mr. Ireton's company; Mr. Peters
coming to him, was very often at meals there, but
especially at nights. Mr. Ireton being civil in
carriage, would usually entertain discourses with
Mr. Peters, likewise would favour me sometimes
with discourse; and in that discourse I did many
times take occasion to assert the laws in point of
the King; and discoursing about the King as being
a capital instrument in the late inconveniences,
as they called it, in the times of the war, Mr.
Ireton would discourse this ordinarily; I was bold
to tell them that the person of the King was
solutus legibus. This gentleman, the prisoner at
the bar, told me it was an unequal law. I did
observe Mr. Peters did bend his discourse, not by
way of argument only, but in point of resolution
of judgment, fully against the person and government of the King. I remember some of his expressions were these, That he was a tyrant, that
he was a fool, that he was not fit to be a King, or
bear that office; I have heard him say, that for
the office itself, (in those very words which shortly

after came into print,) that it was a dangerous, chargeable, and useless office. My Lords, — The constant discourse of this gentleman at that time was such as he did believe would never be called in question, so it was not a thing that a man was necessitated to observe by an accident, but it was their whole discourse. I will put you in mind of a particular passage. When the news came to Windsor that the King was in prison at the Isle of Wight, my father was very much troubled at it; and being an ancient man, was not able to control his passions with reason. He told my mother that they (meaning Mr. Ireton, &c.) should have no entertainment there, and took the key of the cellar and put it in his pocket. His passions being lessened, Mr. Ireton, his wife, and another officer were at supper with him, and afterwards my father said grace, and, as he usually did, though they were there, he said that usual and honest expression, praying for the King, " God save the King, Prince, and realm." Sometimes they did laugh at it, but never did reflect upon him; but this night he made this expression, " God save the King's most excellent Majesty, and preserve him out of the hands of all his enemies." Peters, who was then at the table, turns about to him, and said, " Old gentleman, your idol will not stand long;" I do conceive he meant it of the King For a matter of two months of the constant residence and being of the army there, I did observe that in the General Council there, and in this private cabal, (after the business was broke out, and when the King was taken prisoner, and carried to Windsor,) Mr. Peters was the constant man. When the business broke out, I looked upon it in reason that Cromwell, Ireton, and this gentleman at the bar, and Rich, and that other gentleman, whose name I have forgot, that they were the persons that did the business. My Lords,—Mr. Peters he continued at Windsor: I remember very well that after the body of the army, the General, and the officers of the army were gone to London, he continued in Windsor: I remember a passage of one Bacon, who was a sectary: Mr. Peters being in discourse of the King, Mr. Bacon took great distaste at Mr. Peters for some affront put upon the King; Mr. Peters falls upon him, and rails at him, and was ready to beat him; we understood it so, because he did tell him of his affronting the King.

Counsel. Mr. Peters, if you have any thing to ask this witness, you may.

Peters. I have many things to ask him. Did I ever lie there?

Starkey. No.

Peters. Did you see me there at three o'clock in the morning?

Starkey. I have seen you go up at ten o'clock at night to Mr. Ireton's chamber, and sometimes I understood you did not go away till four o'clock in the morning; I went to bed, it is true, but I understood it so.

Thomas Walkely sworn.

Counsel. Give your testimony what consultation you have had with the prisoner at the bar.

Walkely. I came out of Essex in at Aldgate;

just as I came in a proclamation was read for trial
of his late Majesty; I went down the next day
to the Painted Chamber at Westminster, where I
saw Oliver Cromwell, John Goodwin, and Peters,
and others; John Goodwin sat in the middle of
the table, and he made a long speech or prayer,
I know not whether, but Mr. Peters stood there.
After John Goodwin had done his prayer, it was
desired that all strangers might avoid the room;
then came up Cook, and Dorislaus, and Humphreys, and Ask, and Dendy, and several others,
and stood by Bradshaw at the upper end of the
table; but Cromwell stood up and told them it
was not necessary that the people should go out;
but that was over ruled: and so I went out and
staid their rising, and saw this gentleman, Mr.
Peters, come out with them. After that, when the
King was brought to town a prisoner, the Lord
Carew, a very honourable person, meeting with
me, saith he, " Walkely, if you will ever see your
old master, go now, or else it may be you will
never see him."—" Where is he, my Lord?" said I.
Saith he, " He is coming on this side Brainford."[1]
I went to the further end of St. James's Corner,
and there I met some of the army coming, and
then I saw his Majesty in his coach with six
horses, and Peters, like Bishop almoner, riding
before the King triumphing; then, after that, in
St. James's Park, I saw Peters marshalling the
soldiers, and I was forced to go about. My Lord,
this is all I can say concerning that. I remember
one thing further of him; I heard him in West-

[1] Brentford.

minster Hall say, within a year or two after the army was raised, "If we can keep up our army but seven years longer, we need not care for the King and all his posterity."

Holland Simpson sworn.

Counsel. What do you know concerning the prisoner at the bar ?

Simpson. I do know Mr. Peters very well; I have known him these eleven or twelve years: when the High Court of Justice was sitting, both in the Court and Painted Chamber, I saw this gentleman in consultation there, and at Sir William Brereton's and other where.

Counsel. Did you see him at the trial ?

Simpson. I saw him, but not as a Judge.[1] There was one day in the Hall Colonel Stubbards, who was Adjutant-General, (he was a very busy man,) and Colonel Axtell ; Mr. Peters going down the stairs, comes to him, and bids Stubbards to command the soldiers to cry out " Justice, justice, against the traitor at the bar !"

Counsel. Who did he mean ?

Simpson. The King was at the bar at the same time; whereupon, my Lord, the soldiers did cry out upon the same; and as the King was taken away to Sir Robert Cotton's, some of them spit in the King's face, but he took his handkerchief, wiped it off, and smiled.

Peters. I do not know this gentleman; did he ever see me ?

---

[1] Peters was not one of the Commissioners, probably owing to his being a preacher.

Simpson. Yes, divers times in the Painted Chamber, at Sir William Brereton's at the Deanery, in consultation with Bradshaw, and you were admitted, and no man else, as I know, unless Sir William Brereton, who came along with you.[1]

Thomas Richardson sworn.

Richardson. My Lords, — The first day that this Court of Justice (as they called it) did adjourn, I saw the prisoner at the bar with some more standing in the Court, and I came and stood close by him; I heard him commend Bradshaw, the carriage of him in the trial of the King. To be short, Mr. Peters, holding up his hands, said, "This is a most glorious beginning of the work."

Sir Jeremy Whichcot sworn.

Whichcot. My Lords, — I have, by accident, not by choice, been several times in Mr. Peters's company; truly I have heard him speak very scurrilously of the King; amongst the rest he said there was a meeting of the officers of the army, where he used this expression, "And there

---

[1] Sir William Brereton, Bart., was of an ancient Cheshire family, a member of the Long Parliament, and one of the most active of the parliamentary Generals. He was a staunch Presbyterian, and rather an enemy to the Church than the King. His name was inserted in the ordinance for the King's trial; but he never took any part in the proceeding. It would rather seem that the Deanery at Westminster, which was voted for Bradshaw's residence, had been before occupied by Sir William Brereton.

we did resolve to set aside the King." My Lord, at another time he was speaking of that which they called the High Court of Justice, and I do very well remember this was his expression — " I cannot but look upon this Court with a great reverence, for it doth resemble in some measure the trial that shall be at the end ot the world by the Saints." I remember one time he was saying he would have preached before the King, but, said he, " the poor wretch would not hear me."

Richard Nunnelly sworn.

Counsel. Was Peters upon the scaffold at the time of execution, or before ?

Nunnelly. On that unhappy day, 30th of January, 1649, this Hugh Peters came an hour before the King came to Whitehall; I came to bring a warrant of 40,000*l.* or 50,000*l.* to Oliver Cromwell, being door-keeper to the Committee of the Army; " Nunnelly," says Oliver Cromwell, " will you go to Whitehall? Surely you will see the beheading of the King?" and he let me into Whitehall. Coming into the boarded gallery I met Hugh Peters, and then I got with Hugh Peters into the Banqueting House. Being there, Hugh Peters met one Tench of Houndsditch, that was a joiner; he speaks to him, and whispers in his ear, and told him somewhat, I do not know what it was; but Tench presently went and knocked four staples upon the scaffold; I meeting Tench again, " What art thou doing?" said I; "what, will you turn hangman?" Says he, " This day will be a happy day" Said I, " Pray God send it be not a bloody day;" upon that Hugh Peters went upon the scaffold just an hour before the King came, and then he went off again. I watched at the window when the King's head was cut off, and afterwards I saw the vizards going into a chamber there; about an hour afterwards (I staying there at the door) there comes Hugh Peters in his black cloak and broad hat out of that chamber (as I take it) with the hangman; I am sure I did see him go along with the hangman to take water.

Peters. I have here a witness: I here call God to witness I was not out of my chamber that day; I was sick.

The Court. If your witness will stay he shall be heard; there are more witnesses to the same thing, and so he may speak to all together.

Stephen Clough sworn.

Counsel. What do you know of Hugh Peters?

Clough. My Lords, and Gentlemen of the Jury, — In 1648 I heard of a meeting of the Council of Officers at Westminster, I think in the Painted Chamber, and I being willing to hear what their consultations were, I went thither, and was there as one of them, (but I was not one,) amongst the rest Hugh Peters was one. When the room was pretty full the door was shut. Mr. Peters desired to call for a blessing upon their business, and in his prayer he uttered these words, " O Lord, what a mercy is it to see this great city fall down before us! And what a stir is there to bring this great man to trial, without whose blood he will turn us all into blood if he reign again!"[1]

Peters. What day was this?

Clough. It was about three weeks or a month before the King died.

Peters. Where was this?

Clough. In the Painted Chamber.

Peters. How long was this ago?

Clough. In 1648.

Peters. How long before the King died, do you say?

Clough. About three weeks or a month before the King was murdered.

Mr. Beaver sworn.

Counsel. What do you know of Peters?

Beaver. My Lord, and Gentlemen of the Jury,— Upon a day that was appointed for a fast for those that sat then as a Parliament, I went to Westminster to find out some company to dine with me, and having walked about an hour in Westminster Hall, and finding none of my friends to dine with me, I went to that place called Heaven[2], and dined there; after I had dined I passed through St. Margaret's Churchyard to go home again (I lay in the Strand), I perceived all the churchyard full of muskets and pikes upon the

---

[1] Evelyn, in his Diary of January 17. 1648, says, — " I heard the rebell Peters incite the rebell powers, met in the Painted Chamber, to destroy his Majesty."

[2] " False Heav'n, at the end of the Hall." — Hudibras.

Pepys speaks of dining at this tavern; and at its rival, denominated Hell. It was on the site of the present Committee-rooms of the House of Commons.

ground, and asked some soldiers that were there what was the business. They told me they were guarding the Parliament that were keeping a fast at St. Margaret's. "Who preaches?" said I. They told me Mr. Peters is just now gone up into the pulpit. Said I, " I must needs have the curiosity to hear that man, having heard many stories of the manner of his preaching (God knows I did not do it out of any manner of devotion)," I crowded near the pulpit, and came near the Speaker's pew; and I saw a great many members there, whom I knew well. I could not guess what his text might be, but hearing him talk much of Barabbas and our Saviour, and insisting altogether upon that, I guessed his text was that passage wherein the Jews did desire the release of Barabbas and crucifying of Christ; and so it proved; the first thing I heard him say was, " It was a very sad thing that this should be a question amongst us, as among the old Jews, whether our Saviour Jesus Christ must be crucified, or that Barabbas should be released, the oppressor of the people: O Jesus," saith he, " where are we, that that should be a question amongst us?" says he; " and because that you should think, my Lords and Gentlemen, that it is a question, I tell you it is a question; I have been in the city, which may very well be compared to Hierusalem in this conjuncture of time, and I profess those foolish citizens for a little trading and profit they will have Christ" (pointing to the red-coats on the pulpit-stairs) "crucified, and the great Barabbas at Windsor released." Says he, " But I do not much heed what the rabble say: I hope," says he, " that my brethren of the clergy will be wiser, the lips of the priests do use to preserve knowledge; I have been with them, too, in the assembly, and having seen and heard what they said, I perceive they are for crucifying of Christ, and releasing of Barabbas; O, Jesus, what shall we do now?" With such like strange expressions, and shrugging of his shoulders in the pulpit.[1]

Counsel. How long was this before the King was murdered?

Beaver. It was a few days before the House of Commons made that thing called an Act for his trial.

Counsel. What did he say to the members?

Beaver. I am coming to it. Says he, " My Lords, and you, noble Gentlemen of the House of Commons, you are the Sanhedrim, and the great Council of the nation, therefore you must be sure to do justice, and it is from you we expect it : you must not only be inheritors of your ancestors, but you must do as they did; they have opposed tyrannical kings, they have destroyed them; it is you chiefly that we look for justice from. Do not prefer the great Barabbas, Murderer, Tyrant, and Traitor, before these poor hearts (pointing to the red-coats), and the army, who are our saviours:" and thus for two or three hours' time that he spent, he nothing but raked up all the reasons, arguments, and examples he

[1] Pepys says in his Diary, March 1. 1661, he went to hear Creeton, the Scotch chaplain, preach at Whitehall " on the words in Micah, ' Roule yourselves in the dust.' He made a most learned sermon upon the words, but in his application the most comical man I ever heard in my life — *just such a man as Hugh Peters.*"

Y

could, to persuade them to bring the King to condign, speedy, and capital punishment.

Peters.   I did not preach there at that time.

Counsel.   Pray, my Lord, will you call Mr. Jessop, who hath the records of the Parliament, and can produce the Order, whereby he was appointed to carry on the work of that fast; there was the Order for his preaching, and Order of thanks for his work.

[Mr. Jessop produced the Journal, wherein was the order following, which was read.]

[Clerk reads.] " 20 December, 1648. Ordered, That Mr. Peters be desired to preach on Friday next, the day of public humiliation, at Margaret's, Westminster, in the place of——"

Counsel.   Call Mr. Chace.   After this the work went on, and the High Court of Justice sat; and the first day they sat was Saturday, January 20th, in Westminster Hall, the 21st being the Sunday following; I think Mr. Chace was at Whitehall; he will tell you what he preached.

Mr. Chace sworn.

Chace.   My Lord, I heard the prisoner at the bar preaching before Oliver Cromwell and Bradshaw, who was called the Lord President of the High Court of Justice, and he took his text out of the Psalms, in these words: " Bind your kings with chains, and your nobles with fetters of iron;" that was part of the text: but says he in his sermon, " Beloved, it is the last Psalm but one, and the next Psalm hath six verses, and twelve Hallelujahs, praise ye the Lord, praise God in his Sanctuary, and so on.   For what?" says he; " Look into my text, there is the reason of it; that kings were bound in chains, and nobles with links of iron." He went on with a story of a Mayor, a Bishop, and his man; " The Bishop's man," saith he, " being drunk, the Mayor laid him by the heels; the Bishop sends to the Mayor, to know by what authority he imprisoned his servant; the Mayor's answer was, there is an Act of Parliament for it, and neither the Bishop nor his man is excepted out of it;" and applied it thus: " Here is," saith he, " a great discourse and talk in the world, what, will ye cut off the King's head? The head of a protestant Prince and King? Turn to your Bibles, and you shall find it there, ' Whosoever sheds man's blood, by man shall his blood be shed.'" Says he, " I will even answer them as the Mayor did the Bishop, here is an act of God, ' Whosoever sheds man's blood, by man shall his blood be shed; and I see neither King Charles, nor Prince Charles, nor Prince Rupert, nor Prince Maurice, nor any of that rabble, excepted out of it." And further he said, " This is the day that I, and many saints of God besides, have been praying for these many years."

Peters. Ask him whether he took notes.

Chace. No, Sir, but it being so memorable a sermon I took special notice of it. I observed that Oliver Cromwell did laugh at that time when you were preaching.

Thomas Tongue sworn.

Counsel. What do you know of the prisoner's preaching?

Tongue. Upon January 21. 1649, I was at Whitehall, where this gentleman preached, and he preached upon this text, Psalm cxlix. v. 8., " To bind their kings in chains, and their nobles in links of iron;" in which text this Peters did much applaud the soldiers there; he said he hoped to see such another day following as the day before, and that, " Blessed be God (says this Parson Peters) the *House, the lower House, is purged, and the House of Lords themselves they will down suddenly;*" this is all that I well remember at that time. Upon the 28th of January, 1649, next day after sentence of the King, I heard Peters preach upon this text, in St. James's Chapel, Psalm cxlix. 6, 7, 8, 9. " Let the high praises of God be in their mouth, and a two-edged sword in their hands, to execute vengeance on the heathen, and punishment upon the people; to bind their kings with chains, and their nobles with fetters of iron; to execute upon them the judgment written, this honour have all his Saints ; praise ye the Lord :" and there he did so saint the red-coats, and so reprobate the poor King's friends ! Says he, " This I did intend to insist and preach upon before the *poor wretch,* and the *poor wretch* would not hear me."

William Rider sworn.

Rider. I was at the same time at church in St. Sepulchre's. My Lord, as soon as ever he had read the words of his text, which was, " He shall call his name Emmanuel," he presently shook hands with his text, and fell (as he was wont) to news, and there he said, " The great enquiry now is, to know what should become of the King? Let that alone," saith he; and presently he falls to it again, and was pleased to style the King Barabbas; saith he, " There is a great many of the people had rather Christ should be crucified than Barabbas;" and here he was applauding the soldiers; and said that " Emmanuel" was. written upon the bridles of their horses; and he was speaking of the King's soldiers; saith he, " I have known eighty thousand of them, and not one of them a gracious person."

Counsel. Now we expect the answer of the prisoner at the bar, the indictment hath been fully proved.

Peters. I desire that witness may be admitted which I spoke of, his name is Cornelius Glover.

Cornelius Glover not sworn.*

L. C. Baron. Where do you dwell?

Glover. In Paul's Churchyard. I belong to the Post-house.

L. C. Baron. What would you have him asked?

Peters. Whether I was out of my chamber that day the King suffered?

Glover. I was come to Mr. Peters a little before that time, to live with him as his servant; it fell out that day he was ill in his chamber all the morning; the soldiers in St. James's House were all gone away; I had a desire to go see the meet-

¹ Till the Act of 1st Anne, c. 9., the witnesses for prisoners were not examined on oath.

ing, where they were at Whitehall: saith he,
" Thou seemest to have a great desire to go and
look about thee; it is very sad, but if you will go
you may." I did go over the Park; and I came
back again, and Mr. Peters was in his chamber
then.

Counsel. Was Mr. Peters sick?

Glover. Yes, he was melancholy sick as he
used to be.

L. C. Baron. Mr. Peters, have you any more
to ask him?

Peters. I brought him to testify that I was
not out of my chamber that day, and that I was
sick.

L. C. Baron. This gentleman is examined
only to one particular, nothing at all to the main
proofs.

Peters. I bring him only to vindicate myself
from that aspersion of my being upon the scaffold.

L. C. Baron. They do not lay the weight of
their evidence upon that: the King's Counsel
have done with their evidence; if you have any
thing to say, you have your liberty.

Peters. May it please your Lordships, I will
give you an account of the business. I lived fourteen years out of England; when I came over I
found the wars begun; I began no war, my Lord,
nor have been the trumpeter. When I came out
of the West Indies, I fled from the war into Ireland, to the Western part there; and it was after
the rebellion, when some of the Irish had been
stirring there, I went and spent my time there.
I was neither at Edge-hill, nor Naseby; but, my
Lord, after I came over there was war that the

people were engaged in; I was not here in the
beginning of it, but was a stranger to the carriage of it. When I came into the nation I
looked after three things: one was, that there
might be sound religion; the second was, that
learning and laws might be maintained; the
third, that the poor might be cared for; and I
must confess I have spent most of my time in
these things to this end and purpose. There was
a noise in all parts of some miscarriages in matters of religion; after it was settled I lived in Ireland. I must profess for my own part, solemnly,
that my carriage hath been upon these heads.
For religion, I have, through God's mercies, spake
of the truths of the Protestant Church; upon this
account I did stay to see what God might do: I
was sent over to his Majesty, that we might have
a little help in point of excise and customs, and
encouragement in learning. I had neither malice nor mischief in my heart against the King;
upon this I did engage so far, being invited. I
went into the wars, and there I found very strange
and several kinds of providences, as this day hath
been seen. I do not deny but that I was active,
but not to stir in a way that was not honourable.
I challenge a great part of the nation to manifest
my carriage among them: I shall make it good
divers ways; I had so much respect to his Majesty, particularly at Windsor, that I propounded
to his Majesty my thoughts three ways to preserve himself from danger, which were good, as
he was pleased to think, though they did not suc-
ceed, and the work died; as for malice, I had
none in me. It is true, there was a difference

amongst us, an army, and an army. I never had a groat or penny from Oliver Cromwell since I knew this place. I profess I have had no ends for honour or gain since I set foot upon this shore. I challenge any man that belonged to that party whether they had not the same respect from me as my own party. I have not persecuted any with malice; I will only take off malice.

L. C. Baron. Your business is matter of fact.

Peters. I am unskilful in law, this that I offer is to show that I had no malice in me; I was so far from malice, that I have a certificate, if worth the reading, from one of the most eminent persons in the nation, to show I had no malice. It is concerning the Marquis of Worcester, under his lady's hand, beginning with these words: " I do hereby testify, that in all the sufferings of my husband, Mr. Peters was my great friend," &c.

L. C. Baron. I am not willing at all to interrupt you, or hinder you; that which you speak is not at all to the point. You hear the matter alleged against you; pray come to the matter.

Peters. My Lord, I cannot remember them.

Lord Chief Baron. Then I will remember [1] you: you are charged by this indictment for compassing and imagining the death of the King, and there is set forth sundry particulars to prove the overt act, that you, with other persons named in that indictment, did consult and meet together

---

[1] This sort of recapitulation, by the Judge, of the main points proved, in order to assist the prisoner in his defence, was at this period not unfrequent. The practice has now been long disused. The summing up is now made after the prisoner's defence.

how to bring about the King's death.   Then
you are charged with several acts of contriving
and endeavouring the King's death.

The Chief Baron then minutely summed up the
evidence.   Peters said nothing, except making
an occasional protestation that the witnesses spoke
false.   When the Chief Baron ended.

Peters. My Lord, if I had time and opportunity, I could take off many of the witnesses,
but because their testimony is without control
I cannot satisfy myself; I have no skill in the
law, else I might have spoke for myself; I do not
know what to say more, unless I had more time
and counsel.

The Solicitor-General then, according to one
of those irregular practices frequent at the time,
made some observations on the evidence.

The Jury went together, and after a little consultation settled in their places, and pronounced
a verdict of Guilty.   Cook, the republican Counsel, who had been before found guilty, was then
placed by the side of Harrison at the bar; and the
Lord Chief Baron, after a solemn address, passed
on them the sentence of death, which the law
awarded to traitors.

Two days after his trial, on the 13th of October, 1660, Harrison underwent, at Charing
Cross, the awful and certainly barbarous sentence which the law at that time inflicted on
traitors.   In Newgate, and on the scaffold, he
was, as usual, cheerful, fearless, and even exult-

ing. Some friends asked him how he did. He answered, " Very well; and cannot be in a better condition if I had the desires of my heart: we must be willing to receive hard things from the hands of our Father, as well as easy things." When he came to Newgate there were chains put upon his feet; and he said, " Welcome, welcome; oh, this is nothing to what Christ hath undergone for me; this is out of his great loving-kindness and faithfulness, and my God is all-sufficient in all conditions." Soon after his coming into the dungeon, a woman belonging to the gaol, who was sent to make clean the room, and to make a fire for him, was asked, when she came out, how the Major-General behaved himself, and what he said; to which she answered, she knew not what he had done to deserve to be there, but sure he was a good man, and never such a man was there before, for he was full of God; there was nothing but God in his mouth; and his discourse and frame of heart would melt the hardest of their hearts.

On the day of his execution he told the sheriff that his support was, that his sufferings were upon the account of Jehovah, the Lord of Hosts. He said, he looked upon this as a clear answer of his prayers; " for many a time," said he, " have I begged of the Lord, that, if he had any hard thing, any reproachful work, or contemptible service to be done by his people, that I should be employed in it; and now blessed be the name of God, who accounteth me worthy to be put upon this service for my Lord Christ."

He parted with his wife and friends with

great joy and cheerfulness. He told his wife he had nothing to leave her but his Bible; but that he was assured that God would make up all her losses in due time; and desired, that those that did love him, should manifest their love in being loving and tender to his dear wife.

Then he was carried away in the sledge, having (according to the account of a cotemporary) a sweet smiling countenance, with his eyes and hands lifted up to heaven, his countenance never changing in all the way as he went to the place of execution, but was mighty cheerful, to the astonishment of many. He called several times in the way, and spoke aloud, " I go to suffer upon the account of the most glorious cause that ever was in the world." As he was going to suffer, one, in derision, called to him, and said, " Where is your Good Old Cause?" He, with a cheerful smile, clapt his hand on his breast, and said, " Here it is, and I am going to seal it with my blood." And when he came to the sight of the gallows, he was transported with joy, and his servant asked him how he did; he answered, " Never better in my life." His servant told him, " Sir, there is a crown of glory ready prepared for you."—" Oh, yes," said he, " I see it." When he was taken off the sledge, the hangman desired him to forgive him. " I do forgive thee," said he, " with all my heart, as it is a sin against me;" and told him he wished him all happiness. And further said, " Alas, poor man, thou dost it ignorantly; the Lord grant that this sin may not be laid to thy charge!" And putting his hand into his pocket, gave him all the

money he had; and so parting with his servant,
embracing him in his arms, he went up the ladder
with an undaunted countenance; from whence
he spake to the multitude:—

"Gentlemen,—I did not expect to have spoken
a word to you at this time; but seeing there is a
silence commanded, I will speak something of the
work God had in hand in our days. Many of
you have been witnesses of the finger of God,
that hath been seen amongst us of late years, in
the deliverance of his people from their oppres-
sors, and in bringing to judgment those that
were guilty of the precious blood of the dear servants of the Lord. And how God did witness
thereto by many wonderful and evident testimonies, as it were immediately from Heaven,
insomuch that many of our enemies, who were
persons of no mean quality, were forced to confess, that God was with us; and if God did but
stand neuter, they should not value us: and
therefore, seeing the finger of God hath been
pleading this cause, I shall not need to speak
much to it; in which work I, with others, were
engaged; for the which, I do from my soul bless
the name of God, who, out of the exceeding
riches of his grace, accounted me worthy to be
instrumental in so glorious a work; and though I
am wrongfully charged with murder and bloodshed, yet I must tell you, I have kept a good
conscience both towards God, and towards man.
I bless God I have no guilt upon my conscience;
in this I have comfort and consolation, that I
have peace with God, and do see all my sins
washed away in the blood of my dear Saviour.

" I have again and again besought the Lord with tears to make known his will and mind unto me concerning it, and to this day he hath rather confirmed me in the justice of it, and therefore I leave it to him, and to him I commit my ways; but some that were eminent in the work, did wickedly turn aside themselves, and to set up their nests on high, which caused great dishonour to the name of God, and the profession they had made. And the Lord knows I could have suffered more than this, rather than have fallen in with them in that iniquity, though I was offered what I would if I would have joined with them; my aim, in all my proceedings, was the glory of God, and the good of his people, and the welfare of the whole Commonwealth."

The people observing him to tremble in his hands and legs, he, taking notice of it, said—

" Gentlemen,— By reason of some scoffing that I do hear, I judge that some do think I am afraid to die, by the shaking I have in my hands and knees; I tell you, no; but it is by reason of much blood I have lost in the wars, and many wounds I have received in my body, which causeth this shaking and weakness in my nerves; I have had it these twelve years; I speak this to the praise and glory of God; he hath carried me above the fear of death: and I value not my life, because I go to my Father, and am assured I shall take it up again."

" Oh, the greatness of the love of God to such a poor, vile, and nothing-creature as I am! What am I, that Jesus Christ should shed his heart's blood for me, that I might be happy to all eternity, that I might be made a Son of God, and an heir of heaven! Oh, that Christ should undergo so great sufferings and reproaches for me! And should not I be willing to lay down my life, and suffer reproaches for him that hath so loved me? Blessed be the name of God, that I have a life to lose upon so glorious, and so honourable an account. [Then praying to himself, with tears; and having ended, the hangman pulled down his cap; but he thrust it up again saying,] I have one word more to the Lord's people. Let them not think hardly of any of the good ways of God for all this; for I have been near these seven years a suffering person, and have found the way of God to be a perfect way, his word a tried word, a buckler to them that trust in him, and will make known his glorious arm in the sight of all nations.

"And as for me, oh! who am I, poor, base, vile worm, that God should deal thus by me? for this will make me come the sooner into his glory, and to inherit the kingdom, and that crown prepared for me? Oh, I have served a good Lord and master, which hath helped me from my beginning to this day, and hath carried me through many difficulties, trials, straits, and temptations, and hath always been a very present help in time of trouble; he hath covered my head many times in the day of battle. By God I have leaped over a wall, by God I have run through a troop, and by my God I will go through this death, and he will make it easy to me. Now into thy hands, O Lord Jesus, I commit my spirit."

He was then hanged, and was cut down alive, and quartered, according to the sentence.[1]

Hugh Peters, together with Cook the republican Counsel, was executed at Charing Cross on the 16th of October, 1660. During his trial he had exhibited neither courage nor capacity, and in his last moments, Burnet says, " he was the man of all of them that was the most sunk in his spirit, and could not in any sort bear his punishment. He had neither the honesty to repent of it, nor the strength of mind to suffer for it as the rest did. He was observed all the while to be drinking some cordial liquors to keep him from fainting." According to Burnet, he had been " a very vicious man," and an incoherent sermon[2], which he preached in Newgate the day after his trial, on the text, " Why art thou cast down, oh my soul, and why art thou disquieted within me? Hope thou in God, for I shall yet praise him, who is the light of my countenance and my God," sufficiently shows his desponding spirits, and the reproaches of conscience which

---

[1] Pepys, in his Diary of 13th October, 1660, says, — " I went out to Charing Cross to see Major General Harrison hanged, drawn, and quartered, which was done there ; he looking as cheerful as any man could do in that condition. He was presently cut down, and his head and heart shown to the people, at which there were great shouts of joy. It is said, that he said he was sure to come shortly, at the right hand of Christ, to judge them that now judged him, and that his wife do expect his coming again. Thus it was my chance to see the King beheaded at Whitehall, and to see the first blood shed in revenge for the King at Charing Cross."

[2] See State Trials, vol. v. 1279.

he endured. The popular indignation, which set strongly against the regicides, showed itself towards Peters as well as the others in insulting expressions and shouts.

Being carried upon the sledge to execution, and made to sit therein within the rails at Charing Cross, to behold the execution of Mr. Cook, one came to him and upbraided him with the death of the King, bidding him (with opprobrious language) to repent; he replied, " Friend, you do not well to trample upon a dying man; you are greatly mistaken; I had nothing to do in the death of the King."

When he was going to his execution, he looked about and espied a man, to whom he gave a piece of gold (having bowed it first), and desired him to go to the place where his daughter lodged, and to carry that to her as a token from him, and to let her know, that his heart was as full of comfort as it could be; and that before that piece should come to her hands, he should be with God in glory.

When he was going to die, he said, " What, flesh, art thou unwilling to go to God through the fire and jaws of death? Oh!" said he, " this is a good day; He is come that I have long looked for; and I shall be with him in glory:" and so smiled when he went away.

Much of what he said at his execution was inaudible, as his voice was very low, and the people interrupted him by their shouts.

Besides Harrison and Peters, eight others of the Regicides were convicted and executed in October, 1660, viz. Carew, Scot, Jones, Clement,

Scroop, Cook, Axtell, and Hacker. Colonel Okey, Colonel Barkstead, and Miles Corbet, were tried and executed in April, 1662. The trials of Harrison and Hugh Peters have been selected as being the most remarkable, on account of the conspicuous parts acted by these two singular men, and the curious details disclosed in the proceedings. The Regicides who were convicted, but whose lives were spared, were imprisoned during their lives; many in the Tower, and some in other places. The witty, profligate, and impious Henry Marten, who, according to Burnet, " moved every thing upon Greek and Roman principles," died of apoplexy in Chepstow Castle, in 1681. His defence on his trial was subtle rather than forcible. The popular and extravagant Alderman Pennington died in the Tower, in December, 1661. Owen Rowe also died in the Tower, in the same month, and was buried at Hackney. William Heveningham, of Heveningham in Suffolk, had the same fate: Charles II., out of regard to the loyalty and antiquity of his family, restored his estates to his son. Robert Lilburne was imprisoned at St. Nicholas, near Plymouth, where he died in August, 1665. Fleetwood, one of the Lords of Cromwell's " other House," and brother of Cromwell's son-in-law, appears, soon after his sentence, to have been permitted to go at large, through the interest of his venerable father, Sir W. Fleetwood, Cupbearer and Comptroller both to James I. and Charles I. Colonel Hutchinson ended his days at Sandowne Castle, in Kent, in September, 1664. Though he had attended the trial, and

z

signed the warrant for executing the King, he was included in the act of oblivion through the interest of Sir Allen Apsley, his wife's father. His estates were thus saved to his son and heir. He was arrested at Owthorpe, in October, 1663, and confined till his death.

*** As an authority is not always referred to for the statements in the text, it is proper to mention, that the materials of this volume have been derived from the following sources: — Cobbett's State Trials; Godwin's History of the Commonwealth; D'Israeli's Commentaries on the Life and Reign of Charles the First; the Diary of Thomas Burton; the Diaries of Samuel Pepys and John Evelyn; Clarendon's History of the Rebellion; Hume's History of England; Burnet's History of his own Times; Noble's Memoirs of the House of Cromwell; Noble's Lives of the Regicides; Ludlow's Memoirs; Sir Thomas Herbert's Memoirs; Denzil Hollis's Memoirs; Sir John Berkley's Memoirs; Ashburnham's Narrative, published by Lord Ashburnham; Whitlock's Memorials; Rushworth's Collections; Mrs. Hutchinson's Life of Colonel Hutchinson; Ormerod's History of Cheshire; Ellis's Letters on English History; Baron Maseres's Tracts; Clarendon's State Papers; The Parliamentary History.

THE END.

LaVergne, TN USA
17 February 2011
216930LV00004B/86/P